Marketing and Communication in Higher Education

Series Editor
Anthony Lowrie
Emerson College
Boston, MA, USA

This series seeks to critically address marketing and communication related issues in higher education. The series aims to be broad in scope (any aspect of higher education that broadly connects with markets, marketization, marketing and communication) and specific in its rationale to provide critical perspectives on higher education with the aim of improving higher education's emancipatory potential.

The concept of emancipation and higher education's contribution to it is one of the important themes in this book series. Yet, it is difficult to think of being emancipated without being emancipated from something that denies or oppresses that emancipation. In exploring higher education's emancipatory potential, I would also encourage authors to explore the darker side of higher education. Consider, for example, the failure of diversity in many institutions of higher education in many countries, the 'McDonald' rates of pay for adjuncts, and brand inequality, i.e., the name matters.

Innovation and globalization are impacting higher education in immense and often unpredictable ways. Some argue, including Carey (2015) in Education Policy at the New America Foundation, that there is a long overdue and welcome shakeup coming from the new technology platforms based, if only metaphorically, in 'Silicon Valley' and its equivalents across many countries. Opinions such as these along with public concern about the increasing costs and questionable outcomes, now evident in many countries, occupy the thoughts of higher education administrators, politicians and citizens. Whether you agree or disagree with the theories and perspectives driving such notions, concepts of innovation and globalization form part of what shapes the debate around higher education. Such debates and communication position higher education in the public mind, but how much of this debate and communication is an accurate representation is a matter of conjecture. The editor would like to encourage a plurality of approaches to understanding higher education marketing and communication dynamics including, but not limited to, anarchist, critical theory, feminist, labor process, Marxist and post-Marxist, post-structuralist, postmodern, postcolonial, and psychoanalytic perspectives. Quantitative approaches are welcome if the intent has a critical theory perspective.

I believe that there is a critical market of readers who want a more nuanced and intellectual understanding of higher education's role in society. Authors are encouraged to consider how the idea of higher education is marketed and communicated, how the above plays out in institutions and why and how institutions of higher education are marketed as they are and how institutions of higher education may improve their position in society. If the main social and economic function of higher education is to 1) higher educate the general population on a just and equitable basis, not some of the population and not some provided with a better higher education than others, and 2) develop and distribute knowledge/power on an equitable basis, then how can this be achieved? From a policy perspective at the local, national and international level, readers will be interested in how to expand the higher education offer to more people and improve the quality of that offer for a plurality of constituencies. I encourage authors to submit manuscripts that address these issues from a critical perspective.

Authors are invited to submit manuscripts that provide critical insight into the marketing of higher education and communication in relation to the social, economic and political functions of higher education, what it means to be higher educated and how higher education fulfills an emancipatory role while (re)producing and distributing power/knowledge within and across diverse and plural communities.

Single or multiple authored or edited books are welcome. Contact the Series Editor, Anthony Lowrie, at a.lowrie.02@cantab.net.

More information about this series at
http://www.springer.com/series/15431

Anthony Lowrie

Understanding Branding in Higher Education

Marketing Identities

Anthony Lowrie
Emerson College
Boston, Massachusetts, USA

Marketing and Communication in Higher Education
ISBN 978-1-137-56070-4   ISBN 978-1-137-56071-1   (eBook)
DOI 10.1057/978-1-137-56071-1

Library of Congress Control Number: 2017951636

This Palgrave Macmillan imprint is published by Springer Nature
The registered company is Nature America Inc.
The registered company address is: 1 New York Plaza, New York, NY 10004, U.S.A.

For Sinéad, Eugene, and Cleo

PREFACE

The main issue addressed in this book is the formation of identity through naming. My approach and motivation comes from a long-standing dissatisfaction with positive theories of identity creation and analysis, especially in the creation and management of brand meaning. A secondary motivation draws on the criticism voiced by critical theorists interested in the marketing of higher education, which is that marketing academics when researching and writing about higher education import methods used in a business context. Taking account of Adorno's critical thinking, the method used to investigate an object configures the object, I have sought to avoid the criticism of configuring higher education as a commercial enterprise and provide a more innovative approach congruent with the idea that higher education is a social good and not a commercial practice. We do not need to make it more profitable; we need to make it more socially viable. I recall in 1998, when tuition fees were first enacted into law in the UK and charges introduced in the academic year 1999–2000; the worry was that the introduction of fees was the thin end of a very large capitalist wedge. Oh, no, no, no, came the replies from the then government, and besides government ministers said, fees are capped at £1000 per year, *circa* $1600 at the then exchange rate. In 2017–18, the cost of university tuition fees in England is capped at £9250.00 per year plus inflationary increases, and students face similar levels of debt as US students. The lesson for all of us in every country is that if we treat our higher education systems as commercial enterprises, then that is precisely what we will get, a commercial enterprise and not an enterprise for the education of citizens for their own good and the good of the community.

If we fail to look after our higher education in the USA, fight for all to be educated to the highest degree, and resist commercial intrusion, then it is a safe bet that the intrusion will not stop until there is nothing left but a shabby replica incapable of supporting the American democratic dream. We will have a form of higher education that further divides those with economic and cultural capital from those who do not have economic and cultural capital rather than creating self-reliant and united communities whose survival is inter-dependent and seen to be inter-dependent.

Boston, Massachusetts, USA   Anthony Lowrie
September 2017

CONTENTS

LIST OF BOXES

LIST OF CHARTS

LIST OF FIGURES

LIST OF TABLES

.

Introduction

When writing a book about branding higher education, there is a presumption that there is the existence of something called higher education that you are branding. While education is a name drilled into our psyche from a young age, few if any of us would have a problem with its importance to our well-being, the qualifier 'higher' in higher education brings with it the baggage of much debate if not controversy. The comparative form implies that higher education is higher, above or indeed superior to other forms of education which are therefore by necessity lower. I am not convinced that this is an insightful way of conceptualizing education. It is a reasonable assumption that one form or aspect of education must come before the other, but this does not mean that one is superior. They are certainly different. In my childhood in Ireland, we attended primary school, and my daughter attended elementary school in the USA. It seems to me that a strong case can be made for elementary carrying a more primary or crucial meaning than higher. This book is about how we name, brand, and therefore think about higher education. More than anything else it is an exploration into the naming process. It is not a book on how to brand colleges and universities. If you are a reader looking for a book on how to brand the college, then this is probably not the book for you. No doubt there will be those readers who will attempt to decode and distill its theory into the dos and don'ts of branding colleges and universities.

© The Author(s) 2018
A. Lowrie, *Understanding Branding in Higher Education*,
Marketing and Communication in Higher Education,
DOI 10.1057/978-1-137-56071-1_1

The risk of writing a book on resistance to branding in higher education is the unpicking of the theoretical content for resistance by those who will build marketing promotions antithetical to the core purpose of higher education, which is to educate as many citizens as possible to the highest level. No doubt there will be those who will use the content of this book for the perfidious practice of getting the most selective bums on the most expensive seats. I acknowledge that administrators of colleges and universities, especially private not-for-profits, are in a difficult position, and it would seem they must go to market and set out their stall with their wares. But necessity, a concept I explore in the naming process in Chap. 4, is not necessarily the same as claims of necessity, and the latter is no excuse for either poor performance, lack of transparency, or downright unethical behavior when it comes to practice in higher education. I have always thought that doing the right thing is easy when it doesn't cost you anything. The test of ethical behavior comes when there is a cost attached. Of course, this is not to say that ethical behavior must always have a cost. That is to say something quite different but choices in the administration of higher education are often not easy and there are dilemmas to be faced, including how and who are selected to receive what form of higher education. Selection ought not to form part of the purpose of higher education, and this is an ethical position worthy of fighting for because it strengthens our democratic institutions by demonstrating that education, higher or otherwise, is not simply a question of money or merit. Moreover, it makes economic sense to educate as many citizens as possible to the highest level possible in a modern, democratic, knowledge economy. Democracy is strengthened by arming people with the cognitive ability to both shape and claim their rights and to help others do the same. While some may claim to love the uneducated, I have no love for ignorance or poverty, and often, though not always, they keep close company. There is a social and economic need to eradicate both ignorance and poverty, and higher education is a major contributor to that social and economic goal.

No doubt there are those who would argue that there is no point in allowing students into higher education who do not have the cognitive ability to complete the work. To those, I would say (a) that the normal range of human cognitive ability provides more than sufficient ability to complete a first degree albeit with the provision of some remedial work for those lesser academically qualified (see discussion of the Open University in Chap. 3); (b) a little higher education is better than none, and more is better than a little. If we are to break the endless cycle of generation after generation of family members not attending college, then despite the educational attainment not being as good as it might be, the benefit will accrue to their sons and daughters, who would be more likely to attend college (see Chap. 3 and Table 6.1); and (c) the benefits of a higher education are not limited to the individual but are social (see Fig. 4.1).

Today, I read the cover story in *The Chronicle of Higher Education:* 'Where the journey to college is no fairy tale for seniors at one low-income high school, spring is marked by hope, frustration, and limited choices' (Hoover, p. A14). Most if not all readers will be sympathetic to the plight of these potential students, but far too few are willing to do anything about it. There is hope from some directions such as the call by Senator Sanders to make college free, the free tuition policy in New York State and the call for college transparency by the latest cross-party committee on the Transparency Act for higher education in Washington. I discuss the notion of transparency in Chaps. 7 and 8 and make some suggestion about what needs to be made transparent and how it may be done. It is important to note that all the transparency in the world will not improve higher education for all where we still insist on supporting selection, as illustrated in *The Chronicle* article mentioned earlier. Offers of places are meaningless and are sometimes even a cruel use of marketing to enhance the notion of a non-existent diversity in a college, something I discuss in Chap. 6.

The removal of selection will encourage critical action as opposed to what is much referred to as critical thinking. At the bottom of individual performance lies selectivity, which by necessity is based on the few at the expense of the many. Individuals may well learn to think critically for themselves, but where selection is continuously discharged in an educational environment, students also learn to think of themselves and not others. We cannot complain about student behavior or attitude under current administrative and pedagogic circumstances in which we teach them that their academic survival is based on individual performance and not the performance of the community. They learn to game the system in favor of themselves and learn to use whatever economic and cultural assets are available to them. Group and teamwork under such circumstances will only engender performative compliance as community learning has no basis for meeting their need to do well; students continually learn that their interests are served by individual selection and competition. We know that in a modern democracy and knowledge-based economy, progress is made through collaboration and yet we play down the importance of community in favor of the individual innovator and name the entrepreneur as a social and economic messiah (see Chap. 4). It is the fantasy of the name that supports the illusion that we depend upon the entrepreneur when in fact it is the work and contribution of ordinary people multiplied by hundreds of millions who generate the wealth and knowledge of the country.

The point of a brand name is to promote something, to attract buyers, to somehow encapsulate a meaning that will communicate what buyers recognize as satisfying what they need and therefore want. Under normal commercial circumstances, it does not matter that everyone does not have the capability to turn this need and want into a demand so long as there are sufficient people who have the resources to make the demand and complete an exchange, usually in the form of money, for the product. But as outlined in *The Chronicle* article, far too many students do not have the economic or cultural resources to make the demand and enable the exchange. Chapter 2 explores the concepts of needs, wants, and demands and their applicability in the marketing of higher education. The chapter offers the basis for an alternative model for the marketing of higher education in the form of desire as the primary concept of concern. In this chapter, I further consider the major marketing literature that addresses the subject of desire and find this marketing literature as theoretically and conceptually confused. In my exploration of the concept of desire, I specify desire by way of Freudian and neo-Freudian theory and set out the foundations for a more radical conceptualization of desire which is developed in Chaps. 3 and 4, culminating in a set of theoretical propositions in Chap. 5.

I explore the concept of relevance in Chap. 3 in terms of desire as a split concept. I take the Freudian concept of *wunsch*, and Lacan's concept of desire, and develop desire as an analytical concept split between the unconscious and the conscious. While we cannot easily get to our unconscious minds, I argue that the meaning of the unconscious is in the form, which is to say that what occupies our unconscious mind can only have meaning for us through interpretation of form, which must always be our conscious naming of the form of the *wunsch*/desire. What gets named, I argue, is what is relevant to us. Because higher education is of enormous importance to our own and our children's well-being, indeed survival, I connect relevance and desire to higher education and use the concept of split desire to explore higher education, the desire for emancipation, and the pursuit of conscious self-interest. Split desire is a position where the form of unconscious desire meets the naming of desire articulated in logics of equivalence and difference.

It is in the naming process that brands are formed. I explain the process in Chap. 4 and draw on the descriptive and anti-descriptive literature to develop the concept of the name as a political process. I illustrate how the name attaches to the rather problematic American idea and definition of a liberal arts education and introduce the notion that higher education at the liberal arts college is a bit of a gamble, encapsulated and expressed in my use of the generic name Roulette College. Currently, learning in liberal arts higher education has the potential to follow many random paths as curriculum and choice expand with no sure sight of educational outputs guiding the choice for the undergraduate. The gamble is the roll of the educational die across the board of choice that seems determined by marketing practice rather than educational logic and pedagogy.

Chapter 4 makes use of mathemes, a type of discourse function, to illustrate the process of naming in the development of *point de capiton,* also referred to as a quilting point, node of meaning, brand node, and empty signifier. I make use of some topical political discussions of President Trump and the naming of excellence and diversity in current higher education debates to illustrate the process of naming. Chapter 5 is the last core theoretical chapter. In this chapter I set out seven theoretical propositions, which have been developed from Chaps. 2, 3, and 4. Chapter 6 is a critical reading of the liberal arts idea that draws upon the previous theoretical chapters and points to an ethnographical account and a critical discourse analysis (CDA), in Chap. 7, of the names excellence and diversity. I make some suggestions for delivering teaching and learning 'excellence' in the form of transparency. Pedagogic and administrative practice can never be named excellent without radical transparency. In order to achieve a radical form of excellence, we need to remove the structural gaming of administrators, faculty, and students, all of whom follow their self-serving interests. The latter is particularly problematic with administrators as they are in a position to take advantage of information others do not have. Others do not have information because administrators refuse to share it, collect it, or are blinded to its import by their self-interests. For diversity to be entirely inclusive, I argue that selective practices based on affordability and merit must end and that the meaning of the name diversity must be extended to all otherwise it is not diverse at all. However, such a form of diversity does not suit the interests of administrators.

I recommend that chapters are read in the order they appear, as the book develops interlocking concepts to advance the argument for a higher education open to all regardless of gender orientation, ethnicity, religion, and income. Some readers may see this book as having a rather gloomy outlook for the prospects of higher education. I do not see it that way. I hope this book encourages the reader to think about what type of higher education they would like to see for themselves, their families, and their community, and then work to move it in that direction. The insistence on transparency is the first step. With transparency, we will be able to see what our higher education looks like rather than depend upon those with too much self-interest telling us what it is and is not and who name what it is in their own interest. When we get transparency, then we can figure out as a community what we want our higher education to be.

CHAPTER 2

The Desire for Relevance

DEMANDS, NEEDS, WANTS AND DESIRES

In the discipline of marketing, the conceptual framing of needs, wants and demands are considered central to understanding both customers and consumers, and developing strategies for satisfying needs. This has been the intellectual position for decades: 'But it should be remembered that the need leads to the drive, and therefore needs are what must be satisfied … Regardless of how the needs develop, consumers want them satisfied. Their motive (drive) leads to what we call consumer behavior' (McCarthy 1964, pp. 239–240). Similar framing is evident in Kotler along with many marketing textbooks that include classical explanations of consumer behavior and decision-making based on habitual decision-process behavior (H-D-P-B) models such as Engel et al. (1968). Emphasis and resource is focused on determining the need for brands that range from detergent to chocolate ice-cream and then building resources around satisfiers of that need. The driving force, or motivator, for the process and the demand for these satisfiers is thought to be consumer need, as per McCarthy, as need leads to the drive. A demand in marketing is a resource-backed want that enables exchange. The concept of companies determining what the customer need is and developing delivery mechanisms to satisfy that need has been with us so long that we hardly question it, until that is, something grates the ethical teeth of the consumer. What is acceptable for many in one context, detergent and ice-cream for example, can become disconcerting in another context such as the marketing of higher education.

© The Author(s) 2018
A. Lowrie, *Understanding Branding in Higher Education*,
Marketing and Communication in Higher Education,
DOI 10.1057/978-1-137-56071-1_2

Longstanding consumer models based on concepts of need and want assume (a) that what people want is derived from a need; (b) that people, that is, customers and people working in companies to satisfy customer needs, can know what this need is and (c) that wants may be considered equivalent to choice objects that satisfy that need. That is to say that the need is the marketing priority and 'must be satisfied … regardless of how the needs develop' (McCarthy 1964, pp. 239/240). I connect point (a) above in this literature with two further important points for the premise of this book: (i) the concept of need is vague, has not been intellectually specified in any convincing way and, with the exception of biological need, the derivation of need remains unknown as implied by the phrase 'regardless of how the need develops', and (ii) that in marketing literature it is considered not relevant to know the derivation of the need, just that it exists, for the operationalization of either marketing or satisfaction. Such an intellectual position raises many difficulties, particularly when it comes to marketing services such as higher education. This lack of understanding regarding the need in terms of marketing higher education in part explains why it is sold by some like branded Vodka or a Rolex (Carey 2015, pp. 63–64).

I want to take issue with the 'regardless' aspect of this intellectual position found in the marketing literature. Taking point (a) further, the want is a choice object determined by the need. The need, however, remains indeterminate. As a concept, need is a black box and remains an unspecified given in marketing literature. For such an important concept in marketing to remain black boxed is a source of intellectual ambiguity that is itself a source of intellectual dissatisfaction and I contend that fewer academics are 'buying' into it as a concept than the literature would lead you to expect. Moreover, it is this black-box concept that 'leads to the driver'. It is unclear in McCarthy, Kotler and other authors of the same marketing tradition what need, motivation, and drive mean. McCarthy states that the need, in terms of what is to be satisfied, leads to the drive/motivation, that is, mental processes that set in motion how we go about satisfying our need, and that drive and motivation are interchangeable terms. It is further unclear what function drive/motivation has in terms of why the choice object is wanted in the first instance, especially as it is the need, according to McCarthy and other marketing management texts, that gives rise to the drive/motivation. Need, as conceptualized in McCarthy and Kotler, points us to the realm of the unconscious as the seat of motivation/drive. Need drives the search for satisfying objects that can be specified and operationalized (through the multitude of marketing Ps) and used to build brands and products that will satisfy the need and subsequently remove the drive for satisfaction by removing the initial need. The theory fails to specify the concept of need and therefore the concept of satisfaction is also unsatisfactory. There is something unspecified that motivates people over and above biology. There is a generator of psychological need. I argue in this book that this generator is desire. To a considerable extent this book is about exploring and specifying desire as much as it is about branding higher education. It is only through having a clear focus on why we desire to be educated to a higher level that we can market the service of higher education to communities we wish to serve in a way that ethically engages that generator of need.

Regarding points (b) and (c) above, the reader is taken for a swim into further murky waters on four counts. First, it may prove impossible or at least very difficult to know what the need is because the concept of want becomes the focus of operationalizing satisfaction. The problem arising from operationalizing want as a need-satisfying object is that the two distinct concepts are confounded. This may result in satisfying wants but then giving rise to dissatisfaction because the needs of people are neither understood nor met. For example, students want grades that come early in the alphabet, and for very good reason as often future income, careers and so living well are attached to grades, but it is questionable that this is what people need when it comes to the higher education that they consume either as a learner or a member of the community depending on the learner who has been educated to a higher level. Secondly, there is the ethical ambiguity concerning satisfying needs that are not understood, that is, 'regardless of how the needs develop' (McCarthy 1964, p. 240). Thirdly, it is perfectly feasible, besides the impropriety in satisfying all needs, that consumers may not want their needs satisfied despite the outward appearance of the behavior toward the choice object of want suggesting that they do want the need satisfied. This argument leads to the notion, and fourth point, that the relationship between needs, wants and satisfaction is neither straight forward, directional nor linear (Kano et al. 1984) and this lack of directionality and linearity is evident in higher education (Gruber et al. 2012). Furthermore, I propose that attempting to deliver satisfaction is not ethical in all circumstances. Satisfying the need may result in dissatisfaction because the need may be masked by desire. You may want and buy kitchen gadgets or a book, but the gadgets end up at the back of the cupboard and the book never read. In such cases, trivial as these are, the need and want are connected through the choice object driven by an unspecified desire. Desire, need, want and demand are quite distinct and yet inseparable concepts. Marketing texts tend to ignore desire, which in many respects is the more important concept but the more difficult to specify. The language used to explicate what motivates people is inadequate to the task. We need language and concepts more suited to exploring not just what people need and want but what motivates them to need and want it. In other words, what is the *desire*.

EXPRESSIONS OF DESIRE

Many products are thought of as functional, that is, motivation is generated by an external need to get the job done, such as household cleaners (Park et al. 1986). However, academic opinion on the concept of functionality is not straight forward and even Park et al suggest that their typology of functional, symbolic and experiential brands allows for the possibility of positioning any brand within any of the categories within their typology. In other words, the functional brand may be just as symbolic and experiential as the more overtly symbolic brand, such as a car, or experiential brand, such as ice-cream. What people want may be more to do with their unconscious than most marketing practices and marketing literature suggests.

The shifting perspective of how we may consider products and brands when it comes to what we want and why we want them has been written about for quite some time. Earnest Dichter (1964) talks about the 'tyranny of things' and the role of objects in our lives: "The objects which surround us do not simply have utilitarian value..." (Dichter 1964, p. 6). An early Freudian application in consumer behavior, Dichter's work is remarkably thin on the explication of methodology. Indeed, he did not see himself as a card-carrying Freudian (Tadajewski 2013, p. 195). However, it is clear that he is fully committed to the unconscious as the decider of purchase behavior. His works are interesting and enlightening narratives which draw on the Freudian perspective with practical application, written for producers rather than academics or consumers. He draws on psychoanalysis for directing his method: "Whatever your attitude toward the modern psychology of psychoanalysis, it has been proved beyond any doubt that many of our daily decisions are governed by motivations over which we have no control and of which we are often quite unaware" (Dichter 2008, p. 14).

Whether for commercial reasons or to keep the reporting of his findings on a faster and more entertaining pace, he does not provide the reader with much insight into how he reached his findings or indeed what would make these stand up to closer scrutiny.

> I decided to talk to people about such things as daily baths and showers, rather than to ask people various questions about why they used or did not use Ivory Soap. I personally conducted a hundred non-directive interviews where people were permitted to talk at great length about their most recent experiences with toilet soap. (Dichter 2008, p. 33)

In addition to the early reference to understanding branding, there is the vague reference to the non-directive interview plus expansive interviewing with presumably a large amount of language data. What is missing is any account of analytical concepts that were used to explore the data. He is unclear on how his findings were (a) obtained and (b) providing sufficiently robust methodological arguments to persuade the reader of their validity. We simply do not know how he analyzed his language data sets. We know the interpretations, but we do not know the analytical concepts guiding his thinking other than vague references to psychoanalysis. While it may be a mistake to assume that his findings are not based on sound methodological principles, the reader is justified in making that assumption if they have not been provided with methodological arguments. His account of methodology is distributive and underwritten while underpinned by psychoanalytical theory. When reading each of his studies the reader finds additional insight into how he works. But the reader never finds a robust methodological account of any single study. The emphasis is on the 'talking cure', listening to people talk followed by analysis and interpretation. However, in Dichter's work there is no patient only customers of a company seeking commercial advice and so issues of transference are unlikely to arise. Where the object of interest is likely to be of little unconscious importance to the interviewee it is difficult to see how there would be any significant insight into unconscious motivation. Nevertheless, the focus is on language and its interpretation as a way of understanding the unconscious.

> We suffer from illusions of rationality in our motivations rather than accept as a superior form of rationality the existence of emotions. We often replace theological, authoritative goal-setting for realistic, humanistic clinical strategy.

> We have been prematurely concerned in the social sciences with techniques rather than with interpretation and understanding because we are blocked by our beliefs that techniques alone can provide the answer. (Dichter 2008, p. 55)

His analysis works on a case by case basis with interpretation based on a long and dedicated commitment to his career and discipline. He is reminiscent of Freud himself who dedicates a life's work promoting psychoanalytical principles and their application in the individual case. Unlike Freud, Dichter does not provide methodological insight, such as those we get from reading *Interpreting Dreams* (Freud 2006) and case studies of individuals such as *Dora* (Freud 1997). Like those who follow consumer culture theory perspectives with an interest in desire (Belk et al. 1996, 2000, 2003; Belk and Xin 2007; Belk et al. 1993), Dichter constructs a duality between rationality and emotions thereby adding to the notion that reason and emotion are opposed mental processes rather than perhaps being part of the same thinking process, albeit that the 'existence of emotions' is a superior form of rationality. The phrasing is curious. He does not say that emotions are superior, but rather that the existence of emotions is a superior form of rationality. Dichter maintains the emotion/rational duality by going out of his way to avoid the direct comparison.

Dichter resisted the wholesale importation of positivistic perspectives in consumer behavior and applied the theories of psychoanalysis, which are based on the study of an individual from a clinical perspective in a social context, to the behavior of the individual in the context of consumption. Yet, despite the contribution of psychoanalytical theory to consumer behavior, there is a yawning methodological gap in the accounts of how the unconscious gets us as consumers to the results we can observe but not quite understand in terms of unconscious desire. I pick up on Freudian and neo-Freudian theory throughout this book, for rarely has there been so much inappropriate business and marketing theory applied to the marketing of institutes of higher education without understanding what people desire from their higher education.

In many respects, Zaltman's Metaphor Elicitation Technique (ZMET), (Zaltman 1997, 2003; Zaltman and Coulter 1994, 1995; Zaltman and Zaltman 2008) owes much to Dichter, and both Dichter and Zaltman owe much to the work of Freud. It is difficult to envisage from whence 'deep' metaphors, transformations, journeys and control are derived if not from Freud's theory of the unconscious. If 'deep' means anything in Zaltman (1997, 2003), Zaltman and Zaltman (2008) it means journeying into the unconscious. Freud and Dichter are significantly present in Zaltman's body of work by their absence, or more precisely, lack of referencing and acknowledgement to the derivation of ZMET. For example, Freud's explication of dream-work makes use of analytical concepts that are not intellectually far removed from 'deep' metaphors found in Zaltman but without the conceptual depth underpinning Freud's dream-work and analytical concepts such as 'compression' 'displacement', and 'modes of representation' used to explore the unconscious and wish fulfillment. What Zaltman provides is lots of technique, method without the 'ology', that is to say the 'technique' that so bothered Dichter.

Like Dichter, Zaltman (1997, 2003) and Zaltman and Zaltman (2008) provide little in the way of (method)ology—perhaps for similar monetary reasons. Such methodological gaps undermine the intellectual contribution. Rather like deep metaphor, methodology is buried in obscurantism. The typology of three levels of metaphor is more of a rhetorical device than it is founded in any language theory and analysis explicated in the Zaltman books, despite the back-cover blurb quoting Steven Pinker in praise of the content—another rhetorical devise. Such books on helping us get to the motivations of consumers leave the reader wondering about just how did the author(s) get to these findings and where is the (method) ology. The method(ology) may well be there in the studies, but we as the reader are not privileged to such proof of intellectual rigor and validity.

Ambiguous as the methodologies of Dichter and Zaltman are, the connection to Freud's analytical concepts is more certain. Although not referenced, the importance of our unconscious desires in motivating human behavior is conceptually Freudian. Not to reference Freud's work is a neglect of the debt to the literature on the unconscious. Countless references to and discussions of 'deep' metaphors are an illustration of language avoidance technique for the unconscious in Zaltman; that is to say an avoidance of the use of the word unconscious in terms of his method. Numerous illustrations of how psychology has demonstrated that there are permanent distorting factors which interfere with the objective observations of the motivational field lend support to the view that the authors are drawing on Freud's conceptualization of the unconscious. Our desire to appear rational to ourselves and to others (in Dichter) is 'deeply' Freudian in intellectual derivation.

The question arises, why is Freud so 'obviously' written out? The answer to that question may lie in the desire to avoid the charge of 'hokus-pokus' (McLeod 2009) rather than any conscious form of intellectual neglect to acknowledge the debt. To a considerable degree, Freud has had some bad press (Dufresne 2003). Similar reasons may also explain why Zaltman goes to considerable length to contradict the main premise in his work. That is to say that he emphasizes the role of the unconscious in decision making and choice but formulates empirical steps as a form of reliability and validity, which if followed will get to solid conclusions concerning unconscious choices of subjects that are generalizable to a population of interest. In other words, the reader and would-be ZMET researcher are provided with a set of empirical steps, which if followed, result in the truth of the 'deep' unconscious decisions of not just one person but the group.

That you can get to a generalizable unconscious seems implausible given the nature of the unconscious set out by Freud, neo-Freudians and those who adhere to psychoanalytical theory. The advocates of psychoanalysis and the theory of the unconscious insist on the complexity of the unconscious and the time involved in any exploration of the unconscious (Elliott 1999). Indeed, Dufresne (2003) attacks the notion that the unconscious exists and that the complexity giving rise to lengthy explorations of psychological problems is a cloak to mask fraud, deliberately punning on Freud, which may be more of a slip that he cares to recognize. However, despite Dufresne's vigorous and indeed vicious protestations, clinical trials support the case for the effectiveness of long-term psychoanalysis (Fonagy et al. 2015; Leichsenring and Rabung 2008; Milrod et al. 2007). Either way, it seems very unlikely that any 'quick and easy method' will get the researcher to any valid or reliable understanding of the unconscious workings of desire.

Like Dichter's reliance on language analysis and interpretation, Zaltman and Zaltman (2008) quote Kövecses to help make the case for the role of language in getting into the 'deep':

> Emotion (sic) language is largely metaphorical in English and in all probability other languages as well. [Metaphor is necessary] to capture the variety of diverse and intangible emotional experiences. Methodologically, then, this language is important in finding out about these experiences. The language, however, is not only a reflection of the experiences but it also creates them. Simply put, we say what we feel and we feel what we say. (Kövecses 2000 cited in Zaltman and Zaltman 2008, p. 14)

This is as near as we get in Zaltman and Zaltman (2008) to a radical and innovative concept, which goes unexplored and indeed unexploited as an analytical concept: Language creates experiences. This concept will be explored further for here we have a door to the creative unconscious. In other words, language is not simply a means to communicate but creates what is to be communicated. This goes further than 'deep' metaphors which, for Zaltman, provide access to the depth of the unconscious, indeed, 'deep' in Zaltman is a metaphor for the unconscious. To state that language creates experience is to say that people are created by their language, as our experiences shape who we are. We could extend this notion to 'people are written by their language'. This theoretical position is not new. The idea that people are spoken or written into being through language, while not unknown, is controversial and much debated in the post structural psychoanalytical literature. This concept is further explored in Chaps. 4 and 5.

Marketing academics identify needs, wants and demands as central to marketing, yet fail to address what these concepts may be or consist of; these are givens and taken without question. Marketing motivational literature attempts to address these issues but there is a yawning theoretical gap in the literature in terms of what these concepts are and how we might explore them. There is a failure to put forward any compelling argument for how we may define and get to our unconscious desire in marketing literature. The broad body of popular and influential literature in marketing and loosely-termed motivation theory or motivation research skirts around Freudian notions of the unconscious without specifying the method*ology* for exploring the depth of the unconscious desire in the role of decision making and behavior. There is an attempt in this literature to specify methods in terms of steps for getting to unconscious desire but none of this literature specifies what desire is or what analytical concepts marketing academics may have to get to an understanding of unconscious desire other than vague notions of language as a gateway to the unconscious.

SPECIFYING DESIRE

Unlike Dichter, Zaltman, and Zaltman and Zaltman (discussed above), who do not attempt to specify the concept of desire, Belk et al. (2003, p. 326), position desire as "the motivating force behind much of contemporary consumption". For these authors, there is no 'explicit development of the construct' in 'consumer behavior literature' (Belk et al. 2003, p. 326) and they set about trying to define the construct but unfortunately very quickly come unstuck by confounding the concept of desire with that of passion in what is reminiscent of mediaeval romantic literature:

> A sharp distinction between consumer desire versus needs or wants is evident in the way that we refer to these concepts in everyday language. In a conceptual paper, we observed that: 'We burn and are aflame with desire; we are pierced by or riddled with desire; we are sick or ache with desire; we are seized, ravished, and overcome by desire; we are mad, crazy, insane, giddy, blinded, or delirious with desire; we are enraptured, enchanted, suffused, and enveloped by desire; our desire is fierce, hot, intense, passionate, incandescent, and irresistible; and we pine, languish, waste away, or die of unfulfilled desire.'

In Belk et al. (2003) I think two points are important: (a) the author(s) identify the failing of marketing literature to analyze and specify the distinct elements of desire, need and want; (b) the author(s) confound desire with emotions, specifically passion. Such conceptual development of desire belongs more in romantic fiction than it does in academic literature. The authors continue in their discussion of desire in terms of passion in a way that confounds distinct concepts: 'Consumer desire is a passion born between consumption fantasies and social situational contexts' (p. 327). In this sentence desire equals passion; desire arises from fantasy (consumption) and desire arises from social context. As the authors attempt to explicate the concept of desire they in fact show the difficulty and their ultimate failure in defining the concept of desire. Here, for example, the authors position the concept of desire as a passion, a strong felt emotion. However, the use of emotion to define desire infers a dualism that constitutes meaning in terms of a counterpart. The meaning behind passion and emotion requires reason and rationality as a negative counterpart to define emotion and passion. In other words, passion cannot have a conceptual definition without having a negative constitution. This misdirects the understanding of desire and positions desire as emotionally and negatively charged. However, such a position cannot hold as desire *can* be rational. For example, we may desire to be free from pain and suffering, we may desire to be happy, we may desire to earn a good living and we may desire to be educated to a higher degree. All of these desires are rational expressions, not emotional, while sustained by and so forming part of the unconscious desire. People rationally and consciously know they cannot be free from pain and suffering, cannot be happy all the time or spend all their time educating themselves but all the rationality available to us does not dismiss the desire. Moreover, the desire for freedom from pain, unhappiness and ignorance prevail, despite its impossibility of being, while the desire for pain, unhappiness and ignorance does not prevail despite the all too often existence of these conditions. We are quite capable of wasting our time on attempting the impossible and sustaining the attempt through expressions of conscious desire that are rational forms of unconscious desire. Higher education, in part, is rooted in that duality of desire. That conscious thought cannot strike out that which is impossible and does not (a) necessarily make that thought of the impossible (conscious desire) emotional and/or irrational and (b) suggests that this thought of the impossible (conscious desire) does not solely depend on conscious rationality but another form of rationality that operates elsewhere in the mind as hinted at but unspecified in Dichter above.

While happiness may be an emotional state the desire for it is perfectly reasonable and logical. It is evident that much of the literature that considers desire, particularly consumer desire, is poorly conceptualized. In itself, desire is neither good nor bad, it is neither rational nor emotional. In other words, expressions of desire connect to wanting something but with a recognition that the meaning of the desires is not necessarily or irrationally connected to the pursuit of the object. Objects of desire such as emancipation or freedom from pain are impossible to obtain, and that there is a conscious awareness of the impossibility of attaining such objects of desire suggests the desire is rational or at least bounded by rationality. Desire most certainly is not a passion of any sort or description. Where desire is to be discovered is much of what it is. That is to say, desire operates as part of the unconscious. Expressions of desire, that is, conscious desire because it has been expressed, are connected to the unconscious desire but are not the unconscious desire *per se*. Desire would only be irrational if the desire had no sense of reason pertaining to the desire. There is the conscious expression of desire and there is the unconscious desire. Often when we say we desire something we mean we want something. Often when we say we need something we mean that we want something. But confounding desire with wants and needs or emotions or passions only narrows the potential contribution of the concept of desire to the understanding of consumer behavior in general and brand identity in particular. In short, what customers or consumers say they desire is inconsequential in terms of intellectual grounding: what people say they desire is not desire but rather the conscious expression of desire; however, expressions of desire are intimately connected with desire which lies elsewhere, namely the unconscious. Analyzing expressions of desire, that is, the language of desire, is a psychological bridge to unconscious desire. Note that the analysis of the language of desire is far removed from what people say they desire. Certainly, building quantification around conscious expressions of desire is limited.

Belk et al. (2003) place the genesis of desire between consumption fantasy and social context. Taking consumption fantasy first, it is not made clear at all (a) how consumption fantasy differs from fantasy, (b) what fantasy is and (c) if fantasy generates desire or desire generates fantasy. More often than not in literature dealing with fantasy, fantasy is connected with dreams and wishes. For Freud, dreams and dream-work are nothing more than wish fulfillment. This is true, according to Freud, for all dreams even those dreams that cause the greatest of anxiety for the dreamer. Consumption, on the other hand, is an activity occurring in the waking world where rationality is never far from the behavior regardless as to how the behavior may be situated in wish or fantasy fulfillment. The point is that consumption is not fantasy, but the actualizing of choice based on an object of choice and this necessitates conscious desire, which may be supported by unconscious desire in some cases. Like the dream, that is wish fulfillment, the fantasy has little if anything to do with the consumption of the object but rather more to do with the desire that lies elsewhere in the mind. Attempts to understand the fantasy of consumption is a stepping away from an understanding of desire. Desire generates the fantasy. Fantasy is a conscious support for the unconscious desire. Fantasy, like the dream, is the outward appearance of narratives that clothe desire in order to disguise it in conscious rationality. Fantasy necessitates conscious awareness of the choice object. You cannot fantasize without first choosing an object and this choice selection necessitates conscious awareness and so, in part, a rational thought process. To conceptualize desire as emotion or passion or fantasy or indeed 'deep' fails to explain how our expressions of desire can be rational as well as not rational. Desire will be interpreted as good or bad, emotional or reasonable depending on the contingency of the social context. We name our desires according to our self-interested perspectives.

Without the 'ology' in method(ology) and interpretation there is no conception of desire. To ask consumers what passions they have or to ask what their fantasies and desires are is to mis-conceptualize what desire is. Consumers can only tell you what they need or want, which is the rationalized object of choice. Knowing what consumers want is not unimportant in terms of analyzing desire. However, it is rather like the dream, a place to start analysis and interpretation through methodology to understand (un)conscious desire. The 'un' has been put into brackets because desire *per se* cannot be analyzed, only the objects of desire and/or the manifestation or expression of desire, which must be a conscious representation of desire whether in the form of fantasy or dream or even choice. Fantasies, dreams and choices are expressed forms of desire. It seems reasonable to assume that the form is important.

DESIRE AND THE UNCONSCIOUS

As need is 'degraded to a secondary role' (Belk et al. 2000, p. 105), a further explication of desire as a primary force in consumer and customer motivation is set out below. Zaltman (1997, 2003). Zaltman and Zaltman (2008) draw on but fail to specify and acknowledge the writings of Freud. Dicther too fails to specify the extent of his theoretical debt to Freud other than references to terms such as pyscho-psychology/psychoanalysis. Belk et al. (1993, 1996, 2000, 2003), Belk, and Xin (2007), Eckhardt et al. (2015) similarly 'forget' Freud when analyzing and interpreting desire. Yet Freud is central to the literature concerning the importance of desire and so identity and choice. The conceptualization of desire has a basis in Freudian and Neo-Freudian contributions to our understanding of desire as being core to our identity and the choices that reflect and contribute to what makes us who we are.

Freud's term *wunsch* is translated in English as wish by Strachey in the standard edition and other translators follow. However, the English term wish does not have the same sense of force as Freud's use of the German 'wunsch'. The French translations and Lacan elected to use the term desire, which is close to the English term desire and is used for all English translations of Lacan's work. Thus, the term wish in the English translations of Freud are not to be read as mere wishful thinking but rather with the force of the unconscious desire.

> An essential component of that experience is the appearance of a certain perception (in our example: being fed), recollection of which henceforth remains associated with the memory-trace of arousal of the need. As soon as that need reappears, thanks to the association a psychical stirring will arise that seeks to recharge the memory of that perception and recall the perception itself – in fact, to put it another way, it aims to restore the situation of the first satisfaction. Such a stirring we call a wish; reappearance of

the perception is the fulfilment of that wish, and when arousal of the need invests such a perception with a full charge, that is the shortest way to such wish-fulfilment. There is nothing to prevent us from positing a primitive state of the psychical apparatus in which this path is actually followed – in other words, wishing turns into hallucination. So this initial psychical activity aims at an *identity of perception*, namely at repeating the perception associated with satisfaction of the need. (Freud 2006, p. 582)

Regardless of dream content, all dreams for Freud are wish fulfillment (Freud 2006) where desire and its satisfaction are coterminous. No distinction between unconscious desire and satisfaction exists. A dream is an unconscious desire or fulfilled wish. But it is the wish that is satisfied, not the person who has the wish (Wollheim 1973, p. 68). This is an important distinction and it connects with our desire for all sorts of consumer goods, including higher education. If the assumption is accepted that Freud got it right when it comes to dreams and that fantasy is a conscious form, like dreams, of the unconscious desire then the American Dream, including the opportunity for higher education, may offer a form of fantasy that connects to wish fulfillment but does not translate necessarily into satisfied people on the fulfillment of the fantasy. That the American Dream, and higher education as part of that American Dream, is a form of fantasy does not make it a form of irrationality, on the contrary it makes it a form of rationality that is a disguised aspect of the unconscious desire which makes it persistent and important to the subject in pursuit of that desire. So, higher education is not like a tin of beans, a bottle of branded vodka or a Rolex watch, as these branded items are unlikely to play a significant role in occupying the unconscious desire that is centered on both (a) the well-being of our children and (b) our inner most desire to survive, prosper, love and be loved that are more closely aligned with biological need. This is not to say that the branded Rolex cannot be connected with unconscious desire, but it is to say that there is a qualitative and substantive difference between that which materially and economically impacts our lives in a way that alters life chances, and consumer goods that have little or no impact on survivability and quality of life. To clarify further, I am not arguing in favor of economic fundamentalism but rather that higher education, at this point in time and in most current cultures, is privileged as a driver of economies and major contributor to wellbeing and personal income. Indeed, such a privileging is part of higher education identity formation and central to its marketing as an institution. For example, the anxiety surrounding debt as widely discussed in the press and the willingness of many to take on that debt to consume the higher education offering is testament to the preoccupation of higher education in the minds of many consumers.

At the theoretical level, the objection may stand that Freud was wrong. The standard objection is that if all dreams are disguised wish fulfillment then how is it known that there is wish fulfillment if this wish is so disguised, that is, the wish is removed from awareness of it. In part, the objection is refuted by Freud's conceptualization of dream-work. Two forms of content in the dream are proposed: manifest and latent content. Manifest content is what is experienced/remembered. Latent content is the meaning. Only analysis and interpretation uncovers meaning. But then we get into considerable theoretical difficulty as it cannot be assumed that interpreters/analysts are void of meaning, or rather more precisely they contribute to the construction of dream meaning as analysis and interpretation of the dream meaning is conducted. Dufresne (2003, p. 23) took the criticism much further, even to the extent of claiming that Freud was a fraud. For Freud and Neo-Freudians, the resolution to the problem on the veracity of meaning in the interpretation of dreams is found in the clinical perspective and cure. That is to say that Freud was concerned with dreams from the clinical perspective, which affords the opportunity of presenting patients with diagnosis and treatment and so evidence for the validity of the analysis and interpretation. However, within Freud's writings there is little in the way of documented evidence, indeed evidence of any kind, that proves that patients were cured and so providing reasonable evidence that his theories on psychoanalysis worked. And here too Dufresne presents a compelling case for dismissing Freud's claim to cure. However, it may be somewhat unfair to dredge so far back in medical studies in order to dismiss the claim of modern medical science. Recent studies support the 'talking cure'. There is compelling evidence that supports the 'talking cure' (Fonagy et al. 2015; Leichsenring and Rabung 2008; Milrod et al. 2007).

While there is criticism based on the lack of actual clinical evidence in Freud's writings alongside some of his theories such as the proposed id, ego and superego structure (Dufresne 2003) there is also much support for his contribution to the understanding of the unconscious in the thinking process. That it is possible to get to the unconscious process, at least to a considerable extent, is one of Freud's great contributions to the theory of the mind. Time after time Freud emphasizes the unconscious as repressed and that what is repressed returns through the disguised configurations of dreams, symptoms, parapraxes (Freudian slips) and jokes. But is it reasonable to assume that all expressed forms in dreams, symptoms, parapraxes and jokes all the time are expressions of the repressed unconscious? Freud would say yes. However, getting caught up on every single incidence of joke, parapraxis or reading meaning into every single dream or fantasy is to miss the more important question: are all unconscious thoughts worthy of conscious investigation in order to unearth 'deep' meaning? In other words, does the fantasy of owning the Rolex watch get as much of our unconscious time and effort as the American Dream (a form of fantasy) of seeing our children aspire to a better life than our own. Though perhaps interesting, life is too short to analyze and/or reflect on all our expressions of desire all the time. That would be a route to madness. In other words, conscious and rational thought is necessary in order to select what is worthy of analysis and interpretation. The half-eaten plate of beans sitting on a kitchen table may be of interest to some cultural theorists (Arnould and Price 2006) and to Heinz and other producers of baked beans, but to my mind it adds little to our understanding of substantive issues that people have to grapple with in the twenty-first century and are subsequently likely to play a lesser role in our expressions of desire that connect to the unconscious desire.

Two questions remain on the table: (a) which forms of communication are repressed configurations in dreams, symptoms, parapraxes and jokes and (b) which are not. My response to this is in two parts: (i) if not all dreams, fantasies, jokes and parapraxes are wish fulfillment, we cannot tell which manifestation of our dreams and so on are disguised expressions of our unconscious desire and (ii) as stated above, this is not the important question. Even if we accept that *all* our dreams, symptoms, parapraxes and jokes are 'Freudian', that is, repressed forms, the more important question to pursue is which are of such significance to merit our closer conscious attention? In other words, what is more relevant to the circumstances of the subject's life?

For the purpose of further exploration, let's say that *all* dreams, parapraxes and jokes are aspects of repressed thoughts. Such a position leaves the individual hopelessly lost in a Salvador Dalian world of distortion emanating from the unconscious mind. This misconceived popular view is sometimes promoted by academics. In marketing, for example, authors like Zaltman (1997, 2003), Zaltman and Coulter (1994, 1995), and Zaltman and Zaltman (2008) make use of the conception 'that the unconscious is a deeply hidden or mysterious place'. However, Elliott (1999) following Mitchell (1974) argue for the unconscious as knowable and normal. Belk et al. (1993, 1996, 2000, 2003) add to the misconception of the analysis of the unconscious by confounding concepts of desire with sets of passions and emotions. For Freud, who was clinical in his perspective, the emphasis is on the talking cure which presupposes mental illness. The primary purpose and efficacy for making judgments concerning intervention and the evaluation of that intervention was and still is clinical.

> Whereas the practical aim of treatment is to remove all possible symptoms and to replace these by conscious thoughts, we may regard it as a second and theoretical aim to repair all the damages to the patient's memory. (Freud 1997, p. 11)

The important point here is that the insight gained from transferring Freudian analysis and interpretation concerning 'deep' motivation and unconscious consumer desire is somewhat exaggerated and for two reasons. (a) Freud was clinical and his interest in patients' social circumstances was a clinical perspective and tended toward the immediate family rather than the broader social setting or culture.

> It follows from the nature of the facts which form the material of psychoanalysis that we are obliged to pay as much attention in our case histories to the purely human and social circumstances of our patients as to the somatic data and the symptoms of the disorder. Above all, our interest will be directed towards their family circumstances.... (Freud 1997, pp. 11/12)

Marketing academics borrowing from him are either consulting oriented or interested in consumer behavior often from a cultural theory perspective and in both cases the analysis and interpretation concerns reasonably well-adjusted human beings talking about trivia (other peoples' 'deep' interest, that is, those trying to sell 'stuff'). (b) Invariably, the marketing analysis is superficial in comparison to the timescales and ongoing analysis that psychoanalysis typically requires. In clinical studies the time necessary for effective analysis and treatment is circa 50 sessions (Fonagy et al. 2015, p. 315). To make the case clear, where the desire is trivial, that is, consumer objects that do not occupy unconscious desire, the interplay between the expression of desire and the unconscious desire is tenuous. Despite Dichter, claims concerning the tyranny of objects are somewhat exaggerated. There may not be a 'deep' connection between expressions of desire for an object and the unconscious desire. It is reasonable to assume that unconscious desire has 'more on its mind' than the choice of beans. In other words, unconscious desire is more likely to be concerned with the objects of desire that greatly impact our lives and these objects are likely to be limited by the case history of the 'patient' and their social circumstances (*a la* Freud). In other words, what is relevant to them.

EXPRESSIONS OF DESIRE AND THE UNCONSCIOUS

When it comes to interpreting dreams, Freud was insistent that hunting for meaning was misguided. While it may be more obviously incorrect to seek meaning in manifest content, Freud also insisted that those analysts who sought meaning in latent content were also misguided. The question arises: If it is not the obvious manifest content or the underlying latent content then what is being interpreted? Freud suggests:

> I used to find it extraordinarily difficult to accustom readers to distinguishing between manifest dream-content and latent dream-thoughts. Repeated arguments and objections were drawn from uninterpreted dream, as preserved in memory, while my demand for dream to be interpreted was ignored. Now since analysts at least have got used to substituting for the manifest dream its meaning as discovered by analysis, many of them are guilty of making a different mistake, to which they cling to just as obstinately. They seek the essence of dream in that latent content, overlooking the fact that latent dream-thoughts and dream-work are different. Dream, basically, is nothing but a special *form* of thinking made possible for us by the conditions of the sleeping state. It is *dream-work* that creates that form, the dream-work alone constitutes the essence of dream, accounting for what makes it special. I say this to do justice to the notorious 'prospective tendency' of dream. That dream should concern itself with seeking solutions for tasks facing our mental lives is no more remarkable than that our conscious waking life should so concern itself; the only thing dream adds is that this task can also proceed in the preconscious, which we knew already. (Freud 2006, p. 524, note 14)

The unit of analysis is the dream *per se*, that is, the form because the form is the product of dream-work. To take the point further, meaning is the form and is concerned with what is of importance in our mental lives. It is never the tin of beans but the tin of beans may connect with a pronounced concern that you have at the unconscious level, the precise interpretation of which will never be the choice of beans in a supermarket. What it means depends on the form of the dream, which is the direct output of dream-work. The crucial interpretative question is why is the content in this form? Answering this question gets the analyst closer to the unconscious (repressed) desire.

The unit of sense is the form and so the chain of logic equals the form. Forms are expressions of desire that are embedded in the unconscious desire. As forms are the shape, style and format in which content is delivered, form is the rhetorical part of identity, that is to say the shape of what and how content is identified. If further evidence were needed as to the paucity of metaphorical analysis as a method for getting to 'deep' meaning, then this is it. Metaphors are only one aspect of form or chain of logic that holds content together. While metaphors are important, any analysis limited to them alone is bound to be inadequate.

Metaphors come in all 'shapes and sizes'. Nor are metaphors necessarily creative in the innovative sense of the word but can be, and often are, a cliché through use that has established a pathway to thought patterns, for example, 'all hands on deck'. Moreover, much of the literature on metaphor within the consumption literature (see Coulter and Zaltman 2000) takes the view that metaphors are comparisons between two objects or representations of one thing in terms of another. This is positive identity formation, that is, something signifies or equals something else and fails to grasp (i) that identify formation involves a negative dialectic and (ii) power as an aspect of grammar and language choice and use. Given points i and ii, consideration of metaphor as positive identity formations is wholly inadequate as an analysis of a well-known and used (clichéd) metaphor illustrates (Fig. 2.1).

What is vital to grasp here is that the meanings of this metaphor could be missed if you were hearing it for the first time or had no conceptualization of the perils of the sea. It is only through the form of the cliché that the metaphor works. The form is one of danger transferred by way of substitution and association occurring as quickly as it takes to say or read. But the applied situation reads backwards to the premise of danger, implied or fictionalized, to undermine the premise: we are not really at sea and the situation is not really dangerous. The form by necessity incorporates the negation of the premise: this is not that. The expression of the desire is not the desire. The form rather than the manifest or latent content gets closer to the desire. The form is without human subjects; that is to say that there is no 'I' demanding and there are no people commanded to do. This has the rhetorical advantage of allowing the form to be applied to new situations but the disadvantage for the user of the form

All hands	on deck
Hands = entire person: substitution of part for the whole.	Deck = ship: substitution of part for the whole.
Ship and all hands associated with sailors.	Ship associated with sea.
Hands associated with work. Everyone required on deck associated with emergency given imperative mood.	Sea associated with possible life-threatening emergency given imperative mood and associated knowledge of the sea as dangerous.
Life-threating situation demands action by everyone applied to non-life threating situation	

Fig. 2.1   Metaphor with multiple substitutions and associations
Source: Author

is non-sustainable logic and the advantage for those who disagree with the command to challenge the logic of comparability. For the analyst, form provides two aspects of analysis not open to other forms of qualitative research that purports to plum the 'depths' of unconscious desire. (a) It provides an opportunity to ask why this form and what is being disguised by the form that connects to the unconscious desire of the user of the form regardless of whether or not the user is aware of the unconscious desire. It is also vital to note that the form is not a conscious process of representation, although it is a conscious form or representation of the prior unconscious process, and so asking the respondent to gather information that purports to reflect how someone may 'really' feel about an object is useless in terms of analysis. (b) It is also important to note, unlike metaphor analysis, that the interview or conversation about objects 'should concern itself with seeking solutions for tasks facing our mental lives [and that this] is no more remarkable than that our conscious waking life should so concern itself; the only thing dream adds [as does fantasy, parapraxes and jokes] is that this task can also proceed in the preconscious, which we knew already'. The caveat is that analysts should not assume that the gathering of a few choice forms of dreams, fantasy, parapraxes or jokes will lead to any reasonable conclusion about the unconscious desires of subjects pertaining to the expression of desire formed by the subject in the form of their language choices, including the choice of metaphor. Overtime, there should be repetition of form, not the manifest or latent content, as that form is likely shaped by the subject's unconscious desire connected 'with seeking solutions for tasks facing our mental lives' (Freud 2006, p. 524, note 14). Whether a parent, student or prospective student, whatever form of higher education you end up with occupies substantial time of mind and as such provides suitable subjects for neo-Freudian analyses. What is relevant to us shapes just how much mental time we give to any subject, object or topic and so repetition of thoughts through form occurs.

BIBLIOGRAPHY

Arnould, E. J., & Price, L. L. (2006). Market-Oriented Ethnography Revisited. *Journal of Advertising Research, 46*(3), 251–262.

Belk, R. W., & Xin, Z. (2007). Live from Shopping Malls: Blogs and Chinese Consumer Desire. *Advances in Consumer Research, 34*, 131–137.

Belk, R. W., Ger, G., & Lascu, D.-N. (1993). The Development of Consumer Desire in Marketizing and Developing Economies. *Advances in Consumer Research, 20*, 102–107.

Belk, R. W., Ger, G., & Askegaard, S. (1996). Metaphors of Consumer Desire. *Advances in Consumer Research, 23*, 368–373.

Belk, R. W., Ger, G., & Askegaard, S. (2000). The Missing Streetcar Named Desire. In S. Ratneshwar, D. G. Mick, & C. Huffman (Eds.), *The Why of Consumption: Contemporary Perspectives on Consumer Motives, Goals, and Desires* (pp. 98–119). New York: Routledge.

Belk, R. W., Ger, G., & Askegaard, S. (2003). The Fire of Desire: A Multisited Inquiry into Consumer Passion. *Journal of Consumer Research, 45*(December), 326–351.

Carey, K. (2015). *The End of College: Creating the Future of Learning and the University of Everywhere*. New York: Riverhead Books.

Coulter, R. H., & Zaltman, G. (2000). The Power of Metaphor. In S. Ratneshwar, D. G. Mick, & C. Huffman (Eds.), *The Why of Consumption: Contemporary Perspectives on Consumer Motives, Goals, and Desires* (pp. 259–281). New York: Routledge.

Dichter, E. (1964). *Handbook of Consumer Motivations: They Psychology of the World of Objects*. New York: McGraw-Hill Book Company.

Dichter, E. (2008). *The Strategy of Desire*. New Brunswick: Transaction Publishers.

Dufresne, T. (2003). *Killing Freud: Twentieth Century Culture and the Death of Psychoanalysis*. London: Continuum.

Eckhardt, G. M., Belk, R. W., & Wilson, J. A. J. (2015). The Rise of Inconspicuous Consumption. *Journal of Marketing Management, 31*(7–8), 807–826.

Elliott, A. (1999). *Social Theory and Psychoanalysis in Transition: Self and Society from Freud to Kristeva.* London: Free Association Books.

Engel, J. F., Kollat, D. T., & Blackwell, R. D. (1968). *Consumer Behavior.* New York: Holt, Rhinehart, and Winston.

Fonagy, P., Rost, F., Carlyle, J.-A., McPherson, S., & Thomas, R. (2015). Pragmatic Randomized Controlled Trial of Long-Term Psychoanalytic Psychotherapy for Treatment-Resistant Depression: The Tavistock Adult Depression Study (TADS). *World Psychiatry, 14*(3), 312–321.

Freud, S. (1997). *Dora: An Analysis of a Case of Hysteria.* New York: Touchstone.

Freud, S. (2006). *Interpreting Dreams.* London: Penguin Books.

Gruber, T., Lowrie, A., Brodowsky, G., Reppel, A., & Voss, R. (2012). Investigating the Influence of Professor Characteristics on Learner Satisfaction and Dissatisfaction. *Journal of Marketing Education, 34*(8), 165–178.

Kano, N., Seraku, N., Takahashi, F., & Tsuji, S. (1984, April). Attractive Quality and Must-Be Quality. *Journal of the Japanese Society for Quality Control, 14*(2), 39–48 (in Japanese).

Kövecses, Z. (2000). *Metaphor and Emotion: Language, Culture, and Body in Human Feeling.* Cambridge: Cambridge University Press.

Leichsenring, F., & Rabung, S. (2008). Effectiveness of Long-Term Psychodynamic Psychotherapy: A Meta-analysis. *Journal of the American Medical Association, 300*(13), 1551–1565.

McCarthy, E. J. (1964). *Basic Marketing: A Managerial Approach.* Homewood: Richard D. Irwin.

McLeod, A. (2009). "Pseudo-Scientific Hokus Pokus": Motivational Research's Australian Application. *Journal of Historical Research in Marketing, 1*(2), 224–245.

Milrod, B., Leon, A. C., Busch, F., Rudden, M., Schwalberg, M., Clarkin, J., Aronson, A., Singer, M., Turchin, W., Klass, E. T., Graf, E., Teres, J. J., & Shear, M. K. (2007). A Randomized Controlled Clinical Trial of Psychoanalytic Psychotherapy for Panic Disorder. *American Journal of Psychiatry, 164*(2), 265–272.

Mitchell, J. (1974). *Psychoanalysis and Feminism.* London: Penguin.

Park, C. W., Jaworski, B. J., & MacInnis, D. J. (1986). Strategic Brand Concept-Image Management. *Journal of Marketing, 50,* 135–145.

Tadajewski, M. (2013). Promoting the Consumer Society: Ernest Dichter, the Cold War and FBI. *Journal of Historical Research in Marketing, 5*(2), 192–211.

Wollheim, R. (1973). *Freud.* London: Fontana Press.

Zaltman, G. (1997). Rethinking Market Research: Putting People Back In. *Journal of Marketing Research, 34*(November), 424–437.

Zaltman, G. (2003). *How Customers Think: Essential Insights into the Mind of the Market*. Boston: Harvard Business School Press.

Zaltman, G., & Coulter, R. H. (1994). Using the Zaltman Metaphor Elicitation Technique to Understand Brand Images. *Advances in Consumer Research, 21*, 501–507.

Zaltman, G., & Coulter, R. H. (1995). Seeing the Voice of the Customer: Metaphor-Based Advertising Research. *Journal of Advertising Research, 35*(4), 35–51.

Zaltman, G., & Zaltman, L. (2008). *Marketing Metaphoria: What Deep Metaphors Reveal About the Minds of Consumers*. Boston: Harvard Business Press.

CHAPTER 3

The Conceptualization of Relevance

The aim of this chapter is to develop the conceptualization of relevance. As argued in Chap. 2, what is relevant to the individual takes up mental time, and this in turn makes for a suitable topic for the analysis of unconscious desire through the form of expressed desire over time. Repetition of form is therefore a substantive aspect of analysis. The person worried about college debt or college choice is likely to process the concern consciously and unconsciously more than the purchase of their next tin of beans, although in fairness to beans if you do not know where your next plate of beans is coming from, then they might get a little more of your thought time. It rather depends. In other words, what gets hold of your mental time has relevance for you, and what is relevant to you gets your time.

Pursuing Relevance

Cardinal Newman's concerns in 1857 may not seem entirely relevant to higher education in 2017; however, there are some surprising parallels, not least that Cardinal Newman was concerned with the lack of higher education for a minority who suffered at the hands of a colonial power and whose lives did not seem to matter as much as other lives.

© The Author(s) 2018
A. Lowrie, *Understanding Branding in Higher Education,*
Marketing and Communication in Higher Education,
DOI 10.1057/978-1-137-56071-1_3

I had to encounter the serious objection of wise and good men, who said to me, "There is no class of persons in Ireland who *need* a University;" and again, "Whom will you get to belong to it? who will fill its lecture-rooms?" This was said to me, and then, without denying their knowledge of the state of Ireland, or their sagacity, I made answer, "We will give lectures in the evening, we will fill our classes with the young men of Dublin."(Newman 1905/2012, p. 480)

Setting aside the obvious gender bias, the parallel I trust is an obvious one: the idea of a university education for all is still controversial, with sections of the population in most countries effectively barred from higher education mostly through the political mechanisms of (a) affordability (price) and (b) adequate entry-level qualifications (merit/selection). Points (a) and (b) are not unrelated. In America, the percentage of young people (18–24 years) in higher education is *circa* 40%. If you are a young black male, the percentage falls to 25.6% (Digest of Education Statistics, 1970–2014: table 302.60). While the USA may lay claim to being one of the most highly educated countries in the world defined by the percentage of people who have a tertiary degree (42% of all 25–64-year-olds have tertiary (higher education) attainment), it is not the 'greatest country in the world' from this perspective. Other countries perform better on this statistic: Canada (51%), Israel (46%), Japan (45%), and the Russian Federation (54%) have higher tertiary attainment levels among this age group (OECD 2012a). Another telling statistic in terms of attainment is the percentage of younger adults with a tertiary attainment. In 2010, the USA ranked 14th among 37 OECD and G20 countries in the percentage of 25–34-year age group with higher education attainment. There has been some improvement in the tertiary attainment percentage. In 2015, the USA moved up the rank to 11th place (see Chart 3.1) for the percentage of 25–34-year-olds with a tertiary education (46.5%). A comparable country like Canada has an attainment rate of 59.2%. The policies of the Obama administration appear to have made progress on this metric, but policy changes and cuts in the Department of Education may threaten this progress. Growth rates in higher education attainment in the USA are slowing down compared to other countries: 'between 2000 and 2010, tertiary attainment in the U.S. grew an average of 1.3 percentage points a year, compared to 3.7 percentage points annually for OECD countries overall' (OECD, United States Country Note, Education at a Glance 2012b, p. 2).

Moreover, these statistics do not tell you anything about the quality of the higher education attained; these statistics simply show how many attain

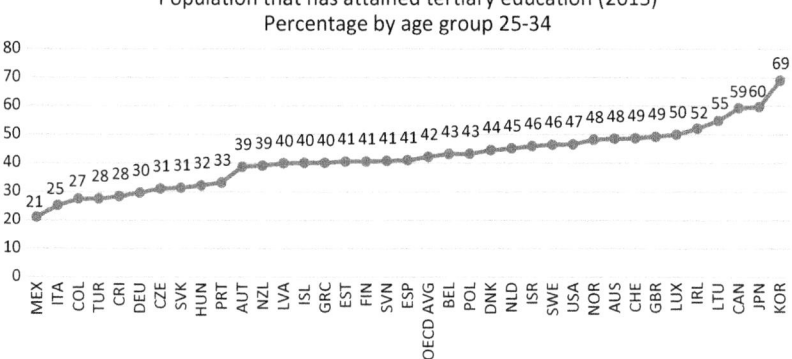

Chart 3.1   Higher education attainment rate by country
Source: OECD (2015a); Note: figures rounded

tertiary education, but nothing of the quality of that higher education. Arum and Roksa (2011, 2014) and Arum et al. (2016) tell a very bleak story of the level of attainment in terms of the quality of this higher education. Bok (2013, pp. 408/9) sees the urgent twin priorities of American higher education as raising 'the percentage of young Americans who earn a college degree' and 'the amount they learn while they are there', by which he also means the quality of what they learn. The higher education of US citizens in terms of STEM (science, technology, engineering and mathematics) is not optimistic. According to the Organization for Economic Co-operation and Development (OECD): 'In 2030, if the proportions of STEM graduates continue at these levels, China and India will account for more than 60% of the OECD and G20 STEM graduates. Considering the BRIICS countries' … [Brazil, Russian Federation, India, Indonesia, China and South Africa] …'it is estimated that they will produce three-quarters of the global STEM graduates. Europe and the United States will be lagging well behind with 8% and 4% of STEM graduates by 2030 respectively' (OECD 2015b, p. 4).

The former entry barrier, affordability (price), is well publicized, while the more obviously unfair barrier it is not without a level of support: "How Clinton's Free College Could Cause a Cascade of Problems" in *The Chronicle of Higher Education* reveals (Carlson and Supiano 2016). Making higher education affordable is named as a bad thing, depending on your vested interest in the matter. But it is the latter, entry-level qualifications (merit/selection), which is the more pernicious and indeed pressing problem facing higher education for all. Those who lack entry-level education often 'just' happen to be poor, and so a justifiable exclusion mechanism operates with impunity. Rather like the denial of higher education in Ireland in the early twentieth century, the form of denial is one of fitness for purpose,[1] that is, many people are deemed unfit to sit in a university classroom. Instead of throwing out the service design as unfit for people, we discard people as unfit for the service. Is it any wonder that so many young people 'felt the Bern'[2] for a free higher education?

Harold Wilson, a UK Labour Party prime minister, founded the Open University, which opened its doors in 1969. UK citizens can study for their undergraduate degree without first having attained entry-level qualifications or scores on a test. Entry is on a first come, first served basis. Massive open on-line courses (MOOCs) and other platforms offer the same possibility if expanded to include degree granting status. However, it is not higher education for all that gets the attention of administrators but rather how this might be monetized and/or used to recruit the best-and-brightest students. In other words, MOOCs are only likely to perpetuate higher education inequality.

With the will and a little imagination, there are ways to open up higher education to those who want to be educated to a higher level regardless of prior formal educational attainment so long as the learner has a desire to undertake the work necessary to attain the required level of education that meets the standards for the award of the degree. This can take many years of part-time study, but as the history of the Open University and number of students enrolled testifies, many people are willing to undertake such study. In 2014–15, the total enrolment in the Open University was 173,889, of which 126,215 were undergraduates, and this is in a country with *circa* 65 million people compared to *circa* 320 million (2015) in the USA. Since 1969, 1.94 million students have achieved their learning goals through the Open University. According to the Open University, 40% of enrolled students had one A-level[3] or less and 76% of students work full-time or part-time while studying (Open University Facts and Figures 2014–15). Based on country population, if deemed sufficiently relevant to implement, proportionately an American Open University would enrol *circa* 620,000 undergraduates. The social strategy approach to and management of attainment level in higher education in the USA is not keeping up with other countries. There is too narrow a view of higher education relevance and what policy makers should do in order to educate the American population to degree level.

Going 'Deep' on Relevance: Who and What Is Relevant?

The bracketing of relevance from knowledge is difficult to justify post-Schutz (1970, 1973), Habermas (1987), and Foucault (1989a, b, 1991a, b), where the production of knowledge is bound up with relevance, human interests, and power. Given the views of these authors, it is difficult to conceive knowledge without an intrinsic relevance to human interests. People with less social and economic capital have different interests from those who are better invested with social and economic capital.

The debate on the relevance of knowledge produced by higher education heated up in the 1990s and continues. Despite the fact that the literature on the relevance of higher education has been with us for quite some time and goes back at least as far as Plato's Republic, books III and VIII, the debate was reinvigorated in the 1990s. The idea of relevance as posited by advocates such as Gibbons et al. (1994), and Starkey and Madan (2001) is not to say that some universities produce non-relevant knowledge but rather that the knowledge produced is not relevant to the organization of some other interests in higher education (Olssen et al. 2004). The debate continues and can be seen in the work of Carey in advocating for the University of Everywhere, meaning digital/on-line delivery of content, and 'educational identities [that] will become deep, discoverable, mobile, and secure' (Carey 2015, p. 219). He means delivering higher education via the internet, which he argues will bring to an end the 'traditional meritocracy' of the current college system and 'emancipate hundreds of millions of people' (Carey 2015: inside cover). He provides a scathing attack on the current relevance of higher education and its failure to reach many who could benefit but are barred from access. He refers to the PhD method of educating those who teach in higher education as 'a sham, a bauble, a dodge' (Carey 2015, pp. 13–36), while at the same time singing the praises of the new technology platforms such as edX. He conveniently forgets that the content delivered via these platforms is developed and often delivered by no less than PhD-trained faculty. He inadvertently provides evidence contrary to his argument: 'Only a few hundred people out of tens of thousands got a perfect score. He and the edX designers were eager to learn who they were' (Carey 2015, p. 214). It is evident that the long tail of non-perfect scorers, unconsciously or otherwise, get filtered out of the desires that senior academics and administrators have for the use of MOOCs. Without the desire for the emancipatory purpose of higher education, I do not hold out much hope for the contribution of MOOCs, or any other platform for that matter, when forming a higher education for all regardless of (a) affordability (price) and (b) entry-level qualification (merit/selection). Both are some other person's constructed relevance that disadvantages many millions of American citizens.[4] Unlike Cardinal Newman's diplomacy (and irony) in not directly confronting those who would deny a higher education to citizens 'without denying their knowledge of the state of Ireland, or their sagacity' (Newman 1905/2012, p. 480), a more radical opposition is necessary. For too long the way into higher education has been blocked and justified by the crossed batons of affordability and qualification, both of which affect the already disadvantaged.

There is some merit in what Carey (2015) says in terms of criticism, but his answer to higher educating the millions who could benefit but are denied a higher education is seriously flawed on two counts. The first is how we learn. To envisage large populations across the world studying for their degrees while sitting in their 'virtual underpants' fails to take into account how human beings have developed and think as social animals and have a desire for social interaction. Our intelligence and our desire for social life are intertwined and built for survival; this will not change just because it is cheaper to reach more people via the internet. Higher education on virtual platforms will not provide the human interaction that is so important to our well-being and how we develop as human beings. Learning was and still is crucial to survival. We survived as a species because we learned from people who had a vested interest in our learning as their survival also depended on it. As a species, we have a cognitive niche that gave us an advantage against those who would have us for lunch. The extended childhood of *homo sapiens* provides the opportunity of extended learning within the group. See Tooby and DeVore (1987) for an account of the cognitive niche theory and Pinker, who argues that survival advantage is in large part derived from the 'coevolution of intelligence, sociality, and language' (Pinker 2010, p. 8993). As people, we still desire the company of others, learn from them and evaluate our learning in comparison to others and derive a sense of self and value from others. This concept is evident in Dewey (1916–97), Mead (1934), Cooley (1922), Marx (1990), and even latter-day marketing professors such as Vargo and Lusch (2004).

The substantial problem of contemporary higher education, like other commodities, is that distance between producers and consumers introduces a lack of care as relevance is shifted to vested interests as fragmentation between multiple producers increases. The survival of producers, colleges, and their administrators has become disconnected from those whose higher education they administer. Moreover, while faculty in the classroom are the only direct connection with learners, the joint-interest of faculty and students has become not merely disconnected but placed in direct opposition through the administrative imposition of policies such as student evaluations of teaching (SET). See Chap. 7 for a further exploration of SET. Neither administrators nor faculty have a vested interest in ensuring the development of the cognitive ability in the individual student. Students, administrators, and faculty are vested in different outputs. Students want grades. Administrators want income. Faculty need good SET scores if they are to survive in their work environment. I am suspicious of any faculty or administrative contrivance, including technology, that breaks the social bond between learner and teacher thereby making it easy to shed social responsibility and manipulate learning outcomes. The obvious, scandalous, and most pernicious of such manipulation of learning outcomes is a number on a scale, usually 1–5, that is taken as good, bad, or indifferent teaching and learning.

The second flaw in Carey's argument is the failure to count for vested interest. Does he imagine for one moment that *Les Grandes Ecoles*, the Oxbridges, the Russell Groups, and the Ivy Leagues of this world will open their doors to all because it would be the morally right thing to do? Vested interests will not be removed by simply introducing virtual platforms. What is considered relevant rather depends on vested interests. Power and money, unfortunately, are never far removed from what our universities are: it is part of their ontological DNA. Despite the college brochures of smiling presidents and senior administrators promoting happy families, colleges are not families (happy or otherwise). The college president earning $700,000 to $3m (Bauman 2016a) has limited interests in common with the faculty member earning $65,000 to $100,000 per year (see the chronicle data) and students who are anxious about how they can afford their education. The college president hires and fires administrators to suit the college strategy, which is configured according to what s/he sees as relevant. The latter sense of what is relevant is evident, despite college presidential promotional messages of caring for students and being student centered, in the above inflationary increases, especially private non-profits, in college fees and room and board (see Chart 3.2 below). Who would price their family out of a higher education? And how can such extraordinary increases in fees for non-profits be viewed as student centered?

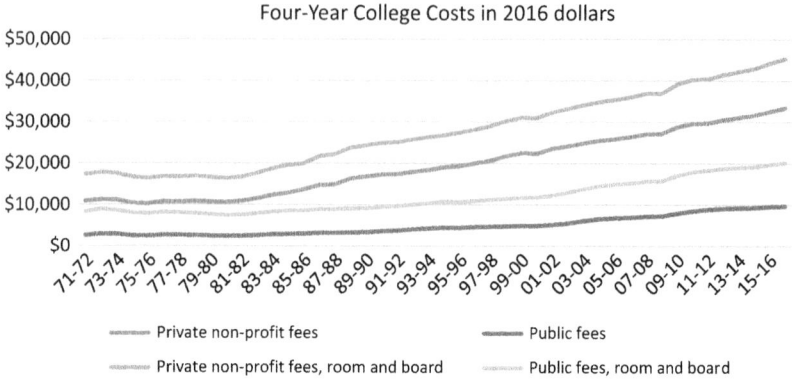

Chart 3.2   Rising costs of college tuition fees and room and board from 1971–72 to 2015–16
Sources: College Board, Annual Survey of Colleges; NCES, IPEDS data

In seeking emancipation through higher educating people, we would do well not to forget the vested interests of higher education institutions. As Dewey (1916–97) pointed out, 'And it is well to remind ourselves that education as such has no aims. Only persons, parents, and teachers, etc., have aims, not an abstract ideal like education.' Only people (and administrators) have interests they wish to pursue. Two related questions then arise: (a) What are the vested interests in higher education? (b) How do we deal with such interests? To answer these questions, the reader can take the Gerry McGuire approach and ask 'show me the money', then follow it. Who gets paid most in higher education? And who pays them? See O'Leary and Hatch (2015), 'Executive compensation at private and public colleges'. Such presidents as that at Wilmington University, Delaware, in 2014 earned *circa* 47 times that of the average full professor in the private university/college sector, 70 times that of the average associate professor, and 85 times that of the average assistant professor in 2013–14. There were '39 private-college leaders [who] earn[ed] more than $1 million,' and 'leaders who served full years in both 2013 and 2014 saw a pay increase of 8.6 percent' (Bauman 2016b). While extreme, such extremities set the bar for compensation and salary negotiation for presidents and senior administrators. There is little in the name of service to the community in such examples. At the other extreme, there are colleges and universities where presidents and senior administers take very little, sometimes nothing, in the way of additional compensation. For faculty salaries at individual institutions and sector comparisons see *The Chronicle* data (2016). With such obvious rapaciousness, leadership and commitment to the community fail. No faculty or staff member is going to take seriously presidential or administrative calls for more service or greater commitment to the community when they themselves draw such obviously disproportion rewards for their work. The only commitment demonstrated here is to self-service which leads faculty and staff to the necessity of looking after their own interests, after all, it is what the senior administrators are doing. Leadership by example is part of the brand naming process.

Administrators continue to push up prices for students and their families while increasing their own salaries. The increase in published tuition and fees at public four-year colleges and universities between 2006–07 and 2016–17 represents an average annual increase of 3.5% in inflation-adjusted dollars. In 2016–17, the maximum Pell Grant covers 17% of the average published tuition and fees of $33,480 at private non-profit, four-year colleges and universities and only 13% of the average tuition, fees and room and board ($45,370). Between 2006–07 and 2016–17, the rate of increase at private non-profit four-year institutions was 2.4% per year (from a higher base than public). Moreover, the average hides annual increases of 4 and 5% at some colleges. Between 2006–07 and 2016–17, the maximum Pell Grant increased by an average annual rate of 2% per year over the decade after adjusting for inflation (College Board 2016, p. 27). The strategy of administrators is to increase prices every year, build dorms to increase room and board fees, and hire adjuncts and clinical faculty to cut salary costs. I remain unconvinced that such uninspiring strategies that lack innovation deserve administrative salaries in the current range. And, of course, this is all happening at a time when current average wages are stagnant and the American Dream, in part a desire fuelled by higher education, is rapidly fading for many Americans. See Chart 3.1 above for the disappointing rates of higher education attainment by the largest economy in the world, Arum and Roksa (2014, 2011) for the poor level of higher education quality, and Chart 3.3 for stagnant incomes for the higher educated. None of these perspectives on higher education paint a pretty picture.

Board members who hire and set presidential salaries, who in turn hire and set the salaries for other administrators is a process with too narrow a set of vested interests. Colleges, especially private not-for-profit colleges, need a broader set of stakeholders to oversee 'corporate governance' and vote on remuneration for administrators in line with appropriate performance

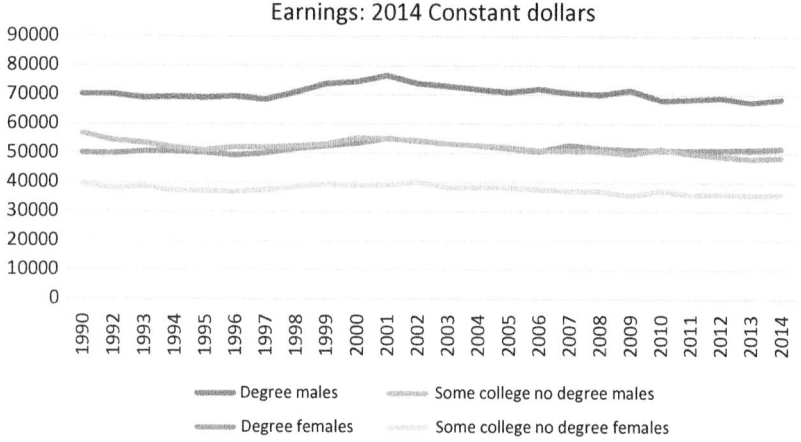

Chart 3.3   Median annual earnings in constant dollars for full-time, year-round workers 25 years old and over, by bachelor's degree, and some college no degree 1990 through 2014
Source: NCES table 502.20 (2015)

measures. Included in these presidential performance measures should be learning outcomes independently determined by external audits. In addition to external, independent measures of learning outcomes, perhaps along similar lines as proposed by Arum and Roksa (2011), income returns for graduates, fees, and room and board charges in line with real wage increases should be included. Simply putting up fees, building dorms, and increasing room and board rates is hardly innovative and is not delivering social value and benefit to the broader community.

The broader financing of higher education needs closer scrutiny and regulation. According to Moody's, two-thirds of the total wealth in higher education is in the hands of 40 universities (Selingo 2016). The top ten universities control nearly one-third of the overall wealth. And yet, student debt cannot be escaped, not even in bankruptcy because the standards are so difficult to meet. The median cash and investments of the wealthiest universities was $6.3 billion compared with $273 million for the rest (Selingo 2016). To put this into current political discourse and the historical imbalance of wealth, less than 1% of higher education institutions have 67% of the wealth. According to the Integrated Postsecondary Education Data System (IPEDS), there are 7112 Title IV (receiving student federal funding) colleges in the USA, 2321 of which are four-year public/private not-for-profit colleges (accessed 2016). This is not a family or indeed even a community teaching the next generation how to survive, thrive, and pass on the knowledge to secure the well-being of the entire community for future generations. This is a contemporary and virulent form of what Slaughter and Leslie (1997) referred to as academic capitalism. This is a small proportion of the population looking after its own vested interests at the expense of the rest and funded mostly by the rest in federal aid over many generations. This is not 'higher' education but the lowest level of unchecked human instinct leading to the abuse and exploitation of the already educationally disadvantaged. As it stands, the higher education system is more relevant to the few than it is to the many and even within that few, a smaller proportion benefit considerably more than others. This is not a system fit for supporting a modern democracy, social engagement, and justice. The community of higher educators needs to re-think what is relevant to our community.

THINKING ABOUT RELEVANCE: ALL KNOWLEDGE IS RELEVANT

I make some small references to the work of Schutz, Relevance Theory (RT), Habermas and Foucault, not to privilege any particular position of their work but to show the need to get beyond 'relevance', for every Thomas, Richard or Harrold will have their interest and will follow what is relevant for them. While writing this chapter, I received an email promoting the American Marketing Association Summer Conference, previously called the Summer Educators' Conference: "This year's theme is 'Regaining Relevance: Doing Research that Reshapes the Practice of Marketing'." The erasing of 'educators' is relevant because it is not relevant to someone. I propose that it is foolhardy to claim that knowledge ought to be relevant: all knowledge necessarily has relevance. The implication of this proposition is that there is something quite disturbing about the current dialogic restriction of relevance that more often than not polarizes around the campfire shadows of tradition or market relevance. It is a restriction on the possibilities of other forms of relevance: a suppression of the relevance of emancipation and pluralism. For those of us interested in emancipation, to take sides in this debate is a distraction.

For some considerable time, the debate concerning relevance in higher education is a contested one with academic arguments favoring market relevance (Gibbons et al. 1994; Greenaway and Haynes 2000; Starkey and Madan 2001; de Weert 2011; Carey 2015) that are both confronting and confronted by opposing arguments (Newman 1905/2012; Dewey 1916/1997; Willmott 1995, 2003; Delanty 1998, 2002; Trowler 1998, 2002; Prichard 2000; Grey 2001; Prichard and Trowler 2003; Marginson 1997, 2012). There is little encouragement for resistance to government higher education policies that construct relevance as 'an imagined line of causation from competition to consumer sovereignty to better efficiency and quality that is the virtuous ideal glowing at the core of micro-economic reform in higher education' (Marginson 1997, p. 5 cited in Olssen et al. 2004, p. 187). In this discourse, relevance constitutes traditional higher education as a 'more-or-less ivory tower, detached from external criticism' (Grey 2001), while the defense of traditional higher education is expressed with the counter claim that traditional higher education is more relevant to knowledge development by being free from the immediacy of market. In this way, relevance (re)constitutes discourses of relevance such that it becomes impossible to know who and what is legitimately relevant. What is relevant rather depends on the position of the vested interest.

Concern for the importance of relevance is not a recent phenomenon and much consideration has been given to its significance for meaning and communication. The debate on the relevance of higher education tends to ignore any consideration of the meaning of relevance itself. What does it mean to say that something is relevant? For the phenomenologist Schutz, all our actions, thoughts, and deeds are guided by and founded on relevance. Topical, interpretational, and motivational relevance form a system of relevance that leads to the structuring of knowledge. Without relevance knowledge would not exist. For Schutz, it is nonsense to speak of relevant and non-relevant knowledge.

> Motivational relevances lead to the constitution of the "interest" situation, which in turn determines the system of topical relevance. The latter bring material which was horizontal or marginal into the thematic field, thus determining the problems for thought and action for further investigation, selected from the background which is, ultimately, the world which is beyond question and taken for granted. These topical relevances also determine the level or limits for such investigation required for producing knowledge and familiarity sufficient for the problem at hand. Thus, the system of interpretational relevances becomes established, and this leads to the determination of the typicality structure of our knowledge. (Schutz 1970, p. 66)

This suggests that relevance predates knowledge. Relevance becomes a constitutive and organizing phenomenon that constructs and organizes the contents of our minds by bracketing, a phenomenological reduction, such that from a stream of undifferentiated experiences we construct knowledge. All knowledge is trapped in relevance. For knowledge to be brought about, pragmatic human interest must be aroused. 'To carry out my plans and projects, I must act on it, change it, and experience its resistance to my efforts; thus, in my paramount reality my interest is pre-eminently pragmatic' (Schutz 1973, p. 230) in a world not merely an 'object for thought nor primarily for knowledge, but a field of action and domination' (xix).

Although there are significant differences between the positions of Schutz, relevance theory (RT), Habermas and Foucault, here I discern some commonality of thinking about knowledge where relevance is conjoined with knowledge and linked to human interest and domination. For Schutz, the world is articulated into multiple realities and it is 'the meaning of our experience and not the ontological character of the objects that constitute reality' (Schutz 1973, p. 280). Schutz remains steadfastly a phenomenologist 'by the attempt to work on certain aspects of knowledge exclusively relating to the individual mind' (Schutz 1970, p. 134). This is akin to Husserl's (1964, p. 210) private or internal sphere of experience where the mind can have knowledge and meaning outside and prior to language. However, it is difficult to see how Husserl's private sphere of experience or Schutz's relevance can construct and order our minds and knowledge without first being constructed in some sense.

Relevance theorists (Sperber and Wilson 1986/1995; Sperber 1996) argue that verbal communication involves coding and decoding with contextual assumptions playing a communicative role in shaping meaning. Sperber and Wilson (1986–95) assert that people typically pay attention to the most relevant phenomena available, construct the most relevant possible representations of these phenomena, and process these representations in a context that maximizes their relevance.

Two principles are central to RT: (a) cognition tends to be geared to the maximization of relevance and (b) communication communicates a presumption of its own optimal relevance (Sperber and Wilson 1986–95). The principles are problematic. With regard to the first, the causal direction of cognition-maximizing relevance may well be reversed such that relevance maximizes cognition. The latter would be more in line with a Habermasian and Foucauldian view of the world where human interests give rise to knowledge/power (Habermas 1987; Foucault 1989a, b, 1991a, b). After all, you may be more interested in beans and for very good reasons. The agricultural land-grant university grew out of an interest in beans, that is to say feeding the nation.

With regard to the second principle, this too is difficult to substantiate, as whatever is communicated is taken to be the optimal relevance but this may or may not be the case as the communication necessarily excludes other relevance. While environmental scientists consider burning fossil fuel relevant to climate change, the Koch brothers may not. It rather depends on the self-interest driving your relevance. RT does not address the significance of relevance manipulation and selection, that is to say, where does relevant cognition come from. RT gives considerable weight to context in the formation of meaning but is not concerned about how this context may be constituted. Those in charge of the American Marketing Association winter and summer conferences may erase the word 'educator's' from the name of the conference as they re-brand in favor of practitioners, as the energy lobby erases climate change, but the relevance of such changes is only known from a knowledge of the vested interest which may or may not be discernible from the context. Indeed, the vested interest may constitute the context. Context becomes part of the naming process.

For Schutz and RT, relevance is wrapped in context and interpretation but in shaping the context, we also shape the meaning and interpretation of what is chosen by the individual as relevant. Higher education policy such as that privileged by government and its agencies can contextualize relevance in a way that triggers selected meanings of relevance. Relevance becomes, unlike the abstract concept in Schutz and RT, equivalent to economic pragmatism that suppresses other possible interpretations of what may be chosen in a context as relevant to the academic and/or student out of all the possible meanings of relevance. In higher education literature and reports, relevance is rarely conceived of as a conceptual means of analysis for human interpretation but a descriptor of a type, an object privileged by agents promoting interests with a preference for the practical implementation of their own interests.

In context, the degree of freedom for interpreting the idea of a relevant higher education is restricted to such an extent that the relevance debate in terms of market use, 'accountability' and 'users' (Rappert 1999), highlights the 'delusion of relevance' (Smith 1996) given to the term by those who favor market implementations rather than an acknowledgment of relevance as endemic to all knowledge production. It is difficult to envisage any form of knowledge production occurring that does not have relevance in the Schutzian and RT conceptual sense. Concepts of relevance are helpful in that they 'shake' the narrow view promoted by higher education policy and the debate found in authors like Carey (2015), Arum and Roksa (2011, 2014), and Arum et al. (2016), the former concerned with meritocracy and access, the latter with learning and quality. However, concepts of relevance are severely restricted if they do not provide an understanding as to how relevance and context themselves are constituted.

Despite the suppression of the broader concept of relevance by the current debate, promoters of the concepts of market relevance and traditional concepts of relevance have failed to promote a clear division between the positions. The discourse of relevance is not closed but open and fluid in its meanings and interpretations, even when a constructed policy context seeks to suppress other possibilities in favor of *a* relevance that is to provide technical solutions to economic growth; a theme that took up much space in the writings of Habermas.

The increase in state intervention in order to grow the economy and the development of a mutual inter-dependence of research and technology that has turned knowledge into a leading force of production are twin themes taken up by Habermas. These themes and Habermas' treatment of them no longer locate surplus value in traditional labor power but in knowledge, particularly scientific, technological knowledge. My point here is not to delve into an exploration of Habermasian arguments but to demonstrate that relevance in higher education in a sense replaces the old labor value arguments and base-superstructure as a position of antagonism, relevance is a frontier for political resistance. I also take from Habermas the notion that serious conflict and indeed resistance is unlikely to break out where these have dangerous consequences for the system.

> State-regulated capitalism, which emerged from a reaction against the dangers to the system produced by open class antagonism, suspends class conflict. The system of advanced capitalism is so defined by a policy of securing the loyalty of the wage earning masses through rewards, that is, by avoiding conflict, that the conflict still built into the structure of society in virtue of the private mode of capital utilization is the very area of conflict which has the greatest probability of remaining latent. (Habermas 1970, p. 107)

In a Habermasian' ontology there is a latent structure just existing below or beyond the discursive. The notion of an ideal communicative situation that proffers hope of a better way of being and living through a 'genuine' consensus is as difficult to envision as a Garden of Eden. There cannot be an ideal speech situation because speech is human interest shot through with relevance. Nevertheless, the desire for such an ideal is emancipatory. To be able to desire it is a beginning in cultivation. The desire is rational in the acknowledgment of its current impossibility and emotional in its pursuit for freedom despite the impossibility.

It is fruitful to see relevance in a much broader conceptual and significant sense that may offer the potential as a political frontier and site for resistance. This is not to claim that it is *the* site but one site of resistance. As Foucault has argued in his consideration of the enlightenment, and which I think is applicable to relevance in higher education, as it is part of the 'historical ontology of ourselves' that has determined who we are, it makes no sense to be for it or against it (Foucault 1991b, p. 45). Rather like George Orwell's farm animals, we are all relevant but some are more relevant than others: it depends on who is deciding the basis for relevance. Black Lives Matter, but fewer African Americans are in higher education and more are in prison relative to the general population, and this situation is not merely accidental. It is a historical outcome that depends on generations of policy that has produced different economic and cultural capital depending on ethnicity. We may not be able to do a lot about the history, but we can rewrite and rename the future.

THE RELEVANCE AND DESIRE FOR EMANCIPATION

Laclau and Mouffe's (1985) post-structuralism is a development of Marxist theory and critical discourse analysis. Laclau and Mouffe build on the structural linguistic conception of language as negatively constituted, in that the meaning of a sign is defined by its difference from other signs rather than some essential, internal meaning. Language is 'absolutely' and 'relatively' arbitrary 'for the entire linguistic system is founded upon the irrational principle that the sign is arbitrary. Applied without restriction, this principle would lead to utter chaos' (Saussure 1983, p. 131).

Arbitrariness is limited by associative and syntagmatic inter-dependences. Associative refers to associations between words made unconsciously 'to evoke in the mind whatever is capable of being associated with it' (*ibid.*, p. 124). Syntagmatic refers to linear 'combinations based on sequentiality' (*ibid.*, p. 121). What precedes and follows gives rise to the meaning of the discursive unit. Moreover, patterns of syntagmatic relationships are constituted in 'sufficiently numerous examples' (*ibid.*, p. 123) and in this way language usage reshapes the discursive formation. Accordingly, language is to be understood in terms of relations of both combination (the syntagmatic) and associative substitutions (the paradigmatic). The pole of substitution is governed by the principle of analogy (associations of the mind), which introduces rhetorical form within the structure of language functioning and language cannot be controlled by the syntagmatic limit but rather by the inter-play of both poles, syntagmatic and paradigmatic. In other words, how we combine words and their association (all the potential meanings of words) is the rhetorical form.

Forms of substitution and combination are not only complementary logics, but are also subversive of each other. A term can be seen as having, in the paradigmatic pole, an 'analogic irradiation' (Laclau 2004, p. 302), which is limited by the dominant syntagmatic differentiations. But these limits are not stable. We can see the components of the associative pole as encroaching upon established syntagmatic combinations—as psychoanalysis has shown, new associations can constantly displace the established parameters of discourse. As with the forms within dreams, that is to say the distortion through dream-work (Freud 2006), language slips and slides in and out of the unconscious and reveals our desires in new forms of associations and word combinations despite our conscious efforts to remain in control of our thoughts. We have in language an essential unevenness: each term, as an analogical center, will have a higher or lower degree of irradiation. Or, to say the same thing with other words, it will be more or less overdetermined (Laclau 2004, p. 302). Our language is flooded with our unconscious desires and as it is a communal and public resource the desire of others is instilled in its use.

Laclau and Mouffe turn to Gramsci and his concept of hegemony to demonstrate that the different identities and social forces can be linked together in a common project. Hegemonic projects or formations stabilize systems of meaning (Laclau and Mouffe 1985, p. 142). However, Laclau and Mouffe (1985) argue that Gramsci retains an essentialist core in that even though the meaning of social relations depends on hegemonic articulations whose success is not guaranteed by any laws of history, Gramsci insisted that class is always a single unifying principle. One of their conclusions is that the direction of the workers struggle and of all other social movements is not uniformly progressive and that there are no privileged positions (Laclau and Mouffe 1985). In terms of higher education, we cannot assume that it is necessarily progressive and/or emancipatory. Higher education relevance will be determined by vested interests.

Another key influence is Althusser, who developed a Marxist structural conception of ideological systems that obfuscate uneven distributions of power and resources in the capitalist economic system. Laclau and Mouffe appropriate Althusser's, following Freud, concept of overdetermination (Althusser 2005) which conceives identity as a fusion of a multiplicity of identities that prevents its closure. Laclau and Mouffe argue that Althusser also fails to develop a theory free from a reductionist form of Marxism by his insistence that it is economic processes that ultimately determine the functioning and reproduction of society.

REJECTION OF ESSENTIALISM AND A DISCURSIVE SHIFT FOR DESIRE

For Laclau and Mouffe (1985), the retention of essentialist and reduction-ist assumptions is the unsustainable argument that is the source of the crisis in Marxism. Laclau and Mouffe argue that 'every object is constituted as an object of discourse' (1985, p. 108). Their notion of discourse assumes and then reworks a Foucauldian distinction between discursive and non-discursive practices (Laclau and Mouffe 1985, pp. 107 and 145 note 13). Every object is constituted as an object of discourse and there is no ontological difference between discursive and social practices. Within this framework there is a strong case for shifting analytic attention to the linguistic. For Laclau and Mouffe, what is denied is not that such objects exist external to thought, but the rather different assertion that they could constitute themselves as objects outside any discursive conditions of emergence (Laclau and Mouffe 1985, p. 108). Like Freud's dream-work, the form is what is important. While the object exists, while relevance may appear obvious, it is how the formation takes shape in our minds through discursive choice. The way we talk about something or someone forms what it is, what they are and what we are in turn. The objects we desire are constituted in our language. But to stress the point, this does not mean that objects and structures do not exist and operate upon us, but rather how these objects and structures operate on us is a question of how we talk about how they operate upon us. Despite existing, we form structure, objects and subjects into existence by how we talk about them and to them.

The post-structuralist thinking that informs Laclau and Mouffe's work emerges from a critique of structuralism but builds on and moves beyond the insight of Saussure that language is arbitrary: the relationship between the signifier and signified is arbitrary. Saussure (1983) conceptualized language as a chain of signs, with each sign made up of a signifier and a signified. The meaning of signs is relational, so that it is derived from its difference to other signs (Saussure 1983). For example, a cat is identified not because of some essential, internal quality, but because it is different from a dog, or a mouse (Best 2000; Eagleton 1983). Saussure sees signs as the products of conventions of a 'speech community', rather like Dewey's conventions of education in the community, so that individuals are subject to a social contract that fixes the arbitrariness of meaning in the signifier (sound pattern) and signified (concept). Derrida (1976, 1978) saw this as a limited dualism.

Like structuralists, Derrida's readings of texts began by identifying the conceptual opposites: speech-writing, body-soul, literal-metaphorical. The post-structuralist bit comes from his next analytical steps: subject these oppositions to internal critique that destabilizes them, then ask the question what makes these oppositions possible. Answers to this last question pushes thought and language to its limit. In doing this you end up with *différance*, a neologism, punning on deferring and differing, a perpetual slippage of meaning from sign to sign or moment to moment in the linguistic chain. This results in the *impossibility* of achieving a theorized account of structures or of the relations between meaning and language as a closed system of differential signs as you cannot reduce or limit the infinite differing-deferral of meaning. Drawing on Derrida's (1976, 1978) notion of *différance*, Laclau and Mouffe run with Derrida's idea of a 'desire for a centre in the constitution of structure, and the process of signification which orders the displacements' that 'is never absolutely present outside a system of differences' (Derrida 1978, p. 280/2001, p. 253 quoted in Laclau and Mouffe 1985, p. 112). With the acceptance of the idea of the impossibility of ultimate fixity, Laclau and Mouffe (1985, p. 112/113) develop the idea of Derrida's 'desire for a centre' to the concept of partial fixity of meaning, a nodal point, a borrowed term from Lacan, to construct the concept of privileged signifiers that fix the meaning of a signifying chain.

All objects are invested with meaning as indeed are structures and subjects. Laclau and Mouffe (1985) progress this argument to all social activity and meaning as discursively mediated. People are invested with meaning like signs. Identity is formed within this discursive context. Laclau and Mouffe's theory of meaning is extended to a theory of the subject in a human sign system overdetermined with shifting and open meanings with some agents trying to fix subject meaning and others trying to break free from assigned places in the system. Identity is thereby partially fixed by the desires and relevant interests of others. The identity of higher education is no exception to such social strategy.

The Promotional Form of Desire in Branding
Higher Education

Discourse is always serving, *inter alia*, a promotional function and this can be examined through critical discourse analysis. The promotional function in a contested area of policy, such as higher education, is particularly open to detailed textual analysis in relation to the blurring of distinctions (Fairclough 2003; Graham 2002; Lury 1996; Wernick 1991). Texts such as university prospectuses, websites and policy reports on higher education purport to be providing information but are performative in that they promote a message often to bring into 'existence' what they purport to be the case but which is contestable (Bourdieu and Wacquant 2001). In this sense, the branding of higher education is bound up with the promotion of relevance that (re)constructs the meaning and position of higher education by people with vested interests. Promotion is not simply the work of marketing practitioners in their attempts to communicate with a target audience, rather it is the articulation of persuasion in the sense that reasons for a belief and the causes of a belief are set forth in an inseparable whole. Branding is a rhetorical investment in form and as such constitutes the relevance of those who make the investment.

> I have argued with Chantal Mouffe in *Hegemony and Socialist Struggle* (sic), there is a name in our political tradition which refers to this peculiar operation called persuasion which is only constituted through its inclusion, within itself, of its violent opposite: this name is 'hegemony'. (Laclau 1996, p. 116)

Structure such as class, gender, and marketization are discursive formulations every bit as much as a written or spoken text: I cannot see that you can have an understanding of social structures other than discursively. In this sense, the practice of (re)articulation (Laclau and Mouffe 1985) has a particular salience for the relevance of higher education. The language of relevance can be used as much for strategies of resistance as it can for strategies of domination and sometimes it is difficult to tell the difference between strategies of resistance and strategies of domination.

The use of diversity and rhetoric building up around microaggressions is a good example of the play of rhetoric and power in competing desires. For some, the discourse makes for a career opportunity, for others it is a fight for justice while for others it is a form of abuse around political correctness that silences them. The discursive terrain is a dangerous one and for some it is best avoided as much as is humanly possible, especially as it may threaten the opportunity for tenure and promotion or even threaten the grades of the student with political views that tend toward, for example, Trumpism within the hostility of 'liberal education'. Within multiple groups concerning diversity and microaggression in higher education, identities are made equivalent within groups and different to other groups and thus draws up positional boundaries that become difficult if not impossible to cross in terms of (a) upsetting others, (b) making yourself vulnerable, and (c) reaching an equivalence that is at the level of organizational functionality. Too much difference between the diversified groups in higher education makes it difficult to get anything done; too much equivalence suppresses difference. Under such circumstances the 'art of diplomacy' is likely to flourish in determining differences. Open debate and communication is likely to be repressed, leaving a vacuum for authoritarian administrations to shut down differences that threaten their own administration but which are essential to democratic institutions. Colleges tend to have many policies in place to promote equivalence in terms of race, gender, and LGBT but then may insist on polices that demean family and worker's rights by actively encouraging and engaging in twenty-four seven communication and insisting upon faculty and staff participation in college events scheduled on family celebratory occasions such as Mother's Day because this is convenient for the administration on other levels. In other countries workers have the right not to have their evenings and weekends interrupted by company emails. The contradiction and rhetorical hypocrisy in college policy is evident but goes unchecked. Any useful analysis must look beyond the promotional rhetoric such as 'it's all about the students' to the desires of those pushing the logic.

A Desire for Equivalence and Difference

The significance of the logic of equivalence and difference resides in its power to form equivalence and differences across 'a vaster discursive context' (Laclau and Mouffe 1985, p. 167) in forming hegemonic relationships and alternative discursive formations. The concept of social classification puts people in boxes and by giving the concept credence lends credibility to the existence of such structural and structuring 'boxes'. For Laclau and Mouffe (1985), social identities are crossing points between the logic of equivalence and difference where neither logic dominates completely and each tends to subvert the other. In this way, subject meaning/identity retains an undecidable relationship between the logics.

The ethos of higher education with respect to educating undergraduates is to provide a sense of an equivalent level of education for all participants. This extends to the degree classification system (UK) or grade-point average (GPA) (USA) which employers use when recruiting. Very few employers look at transcripts (Arum and Roksa 2014). However, to be equivalent in one respect, the provision of higher education has to differ in others, otherwise there would be a simple identity as to what it meant to have a higher education from different institutes. An English degree from Oxford or a major in English from Harvard would be the same as an English degree from the University of Western England (UWE) or a major in English from Emerson College in that the student studied English literature and obtained the same degree classification or grade. However, these institutions connect with other constitutive outside discourses within the vaster discursive context that negate their identities and make them different. The constitutive outside of Oxbridge or Harvard constitutes these as equivalent while the constitutive outside of the UWE or Emerson College are constructed as equivalent but different to Oxbridge,[5] the Ivy League or the Russell Group. They are the same in that the same subject is covered but they are different in identity. To have a great education at a liberal arts college is negatively constituted relative to vested interests. For the sake of discussion, suppose that the education at Emerson College was technically superior to that at Harvard. It is not difficult to imagine that the more desired choice will remain Harvard both for the undergraduate and the employer of that graduate. There is a social investment in the rhetorical form that delivers superior survival returns in terms of social, cultural, and economic capital. In this sense, being the technically superior college is not being the superior college. The identity is in the name.

The theory of the logic of equivalence and difference stresses the growth of the logic of equivalence in the context of an identified common enemy while the logic of difference dominates in the context of the negation of threat (Laclau and Mouffe 1985, p. 127; Torfing 1999, p. 125; Howarth 2000, p. 105). Under conditions of threat it would be expected that the logic of equivalence would be pre-eminent in higher education discourse while the 'withdrawal' of the threat would give rise to the logic of difference. As the threat is not 'universal', the sense of equivalence is also not 'universal' and tends to fracture or create a fissure so that there is a sense of limited and ambiguous difference, thereby giving rise to a restricted pluralism in higher education. An undecidability 'penetrates every relation of equivalence', and 'to be equivalent, must be different' (Laclau and Mouffe 1985, p. 128). The logic of equivalence and difference is a form of power that operates through articulations; and this hegemonic concept of power constitutes the formation of discourses (Laclau and Mouffe 1985, p. 146).

ARTICULATING THE POLITICS OF DESIRE IN LOGICS OF DIFFERENCE AND EQUIVALENCE

The logic of equivalence and difference extends the hegemonic concept of power by extending consent to equivalence so that discursively constituted differences may be subjected to whatever aspects of social structure, including force, considered both necessary and acceptable as discursively constituted. That prisons in the USA have unequal proportions (see Table 3.1) across the population is an example of how the force of rhetorical form of the logic works. A similar, but not so drastic example, is evidenced in higher education where logics of exclusion form around a similar logic challenged by Cardinal Newman in 1857 Ireland. To take the analogy further, the logic of exclusion condemns certain parts of the population to slave labor for survival wages for a lifetime and beyond into generations on the premise of affordability (price) and entry qualification (merit/selection) attainment that lumps them together not merely metaphorically but physically in the same social space and so named differently by comparison to other parts of the population. Having and not having a higher education degree depends on the same brand identity that is higher education. Having a higher education is identity defining. Not having a higher education is identify defining. Both are negatively constituted and depend on the name higher education.

Nevertheless, by equivalence, others in society such as racial minorities or people with little in the way of social and economic capital, can see and demand the same rights and assets as different, 'superior' subject positions to themselves. That is to say, it is transparent to the disadvantaged that what is relevant to the advantaged, such as having a higher education, is also relevant to their lives and their children's and the logics that makes their desires different cannot be squared with the logic of equivalence. Normalization of values for one social group is immanently transferable to and claimable by other social groups: a central social capacity in the formation of active resistance. Where there is power there is resistance. Wherever there is a relationship of subordination the language of equivalence and

Table 3.1 Imprisonment rate of sentenced state and federal prisoners per 100,000 US residents, by sex, race, and Hispanic origin, December 31, 2013

	Total	Total Male	White Male	Black Male	Hispanic Male	Other Male	Total Female	White Female	Black Female	Hispanic Female	Other Female
Per 100,000	478	904	466	2805	1134	963	65	51	113	66	90
Total number of sentenced prisoners	1,516,879	1,412,745	454,100	526,000	314,600	118,100	104,134	51,500	23,100	17,600	11,900

Sources: Carson (2014). Bureau of Justice Statistics

difference can be subjected to critical discursive analysis and re-articulation. Whether it is the case of racism, feminism or higher education for all, a denied right (a right most citizens have but one group does not) is a fissure in the subordinate/superordinate subject position relationship and can give rise to antagonism, resistance, and struggle (Laclau and Mouffe 1985, p. 159). This is particularly pertinent where the denied right is discursively promoted as an extension of equality such as the extension of higher education but within the equivalence of equality there is a recognizable difference in what is delivered and implemented both inter-institutionally and intra-institutionally. So the question of resistance is not why I cannot get a higher education, but why is it that our higher education is not equivalent to yours. If my higher education is thought not as good as yours and it is bought with money that I do not have but you do, a purchase which in turn gives you and your children greater survival opportunities, and indeed the children of your community, then do I not have the right to defend my right and my children's right to survive? Where the cognitive advantage is denied through a lack of access to equivalent higher education, those who see the difference have the right to fight for equivalence.

SUBJECT POSITION EQUALS IDENTITY: THE WRITING IN OF EQUIVALENCE AND DIFFERENCE

Critical Discourse Analysis (CDA) is an intellectual tool which provides an understanding of the (re)formation of subject positions as articulated in an agents' use of language to form equivalence and difference through rhetoric. Moreover, CDA 'exposes' the inherent antagonism in the discursive text produced by the relevance spoken into existence. This offers a revised framework for analyzing discourse in relation to the combinatorial and associated elements of language capable of being articulated in revised ways that suit the desires of vested interests. Discourses of higher education are revised and re-articulated in the conscious and unconscious promotional texts through the mixing up of all possible combinations of words and all their possible associations such that a subject position is formed by the plurality of discourses. The greater the number of subject positions (i.e., identities) discernible in a discourse, the greater the logic of difference and the less the sense of threat to the subject position (identity) held. From new equivalences and differences, new social antagonisms are derived. Where logics of differences are multifarious the more ease exists about identity discourse and people are less anxious about identity. The stronger the logic of equivalence the greater the anxiety about differences. With extreme anxiety comes the formation of discursive camps that form frontiers of resistance to anything different and subject positions coalesce as equivalent. In extreme cases, the logic of equivalence and difference form into two adversarial camps such as relevance and tradition in higher education or diversity bifurcated into Black Lives Matter and all lives matter. While the promotional text 'Black Lives Matter' does not equate with other lives matter less or other lives do not matter, the potential for antagonism and differentiation may be exploited and rendered divisive by others.

Following Laclau and Mouffe (1985) the more predominant the logic of equivalence, the stronger the social antagonism: the expansion of equivalence lessens ambiguity in political frontiers which divide the discursive space into camps (Laclau and Mouffe 1985, p. 131) or subject positions, in the extreme these are often two 'camps'. Laclau and Mouffe (1985, p. 125) argue that social antagonisms are external to the social, that is to say they constitute the limits of the social to the extent that it is impossible for society to constitute itself. Later, Laclau (1990, p. 17) re-defined or refined the concept of social antagonism in terms of the constitutive outside which both constitutes and negates the identity of the inside. This moves the concept of social antagonism away from making society impossible to that of social antagonism constituting the social space that blocks 'full' identity. In this way, social antagonism defines the spaces that are subject positions (identities) articulated by the logic of equivalence and difference. In other words, objects and subjects cannot be the authors of their own identities. Society cannot constitute its own identity because, like Saussure's conception of meaning, the word 'cat' cannot have any meaning without a system of other meanings (antagonisms), such as dog or rabbit, that allows for the difference between all the possible animals we know of or can be imagined from the identity system of cat, dog, or rabbit etc..

Without differentiation and antagonism, subject positions could not be articulated and given identity; without the articulation of subject positions there can be no equivalence between subject positions. Without the logics of equivalence and difference nothing is discernable and therefore no identity is discernable, and no branding of higher education. It is the presence of these two conditions that constitutes a practice as hegemonic, 'without equivalence and without frontiers, it is impossible to speak strictly of hegemony' (Laclau and Mouffe 1985, p. 136). This means that 'equivalence is always hegemonic' but provisional (Laclau and Mouffe 1985, p. 183). Antagonism defines the subject position from which there is sufficient equivalence and difference for the articulation of an identifiable discourse.

Where we find the promotion of the discourses of relevance you have, by necessity, antagonism. Branding is functionally antagonistic. The blurring of tradition/relevance, or indeed the blurring of any form of boundaries in higher education, is the development of a new frontier, a new boundary by a new logic of equivalence that constitutes a new difference.

The concept of split desire (unconscious/conscious) was developed in Chap. 2. The theoretical concepts of the logics of equivalence and logics of differences developed by Laclau and Mouffe were used to show how the concept of relevance is developed in articulations and used to underwrite discourses of vested interest formed through desire. The articulation of these discourses, through the language people use, connects to linguistic mechanisms such as metaphor, including grammatical metaphors, nominalization, collocation and colligations, synonyms and hyponyms—indeed all the language people use to promote equivalence and difference in the formation of desired identities (subject positions). This language, whether written or spoken, consciously and unconsciously, is the articulation of vested interest.

The inscription of power through the articulation of discourses is shown to obscure concrete agency and to (re)form subject positions and identities. Yet these discourses cannot avoid antagonism because without antagonism there is no identity. The basis for struggle and resistance is inherent in the development of a new order of discourse as part of the necessary differentiation required to define the equivalence of its growing hegemonic position. Black Lives Matter but there is no black without white—the one defines the other. This suggests that it is not the discourse of relevance for higher education for one community or the other that we should support or resist. These are discourses of distinct but nonetheless vested interests. Rather, we should support and develop a radical discourse on higher education that delivers emancipation. There is no point in being for or against relevance; it is part of what constitutes being human. The point is to get beyond it and toward an emancipatory relevance for higher education. As Cardinal Newman tried to build a university for all Irish 'men', the pertinent question for all of us working in higher education in the USA is how do we build an Open University for all. Higher education contributes to democracy (Dewey 1916/1997) and because of this quality it should be considered a basic human right that ensures our survival by developing our 'cognitive niche'. Inside and outside the walls of higher education, we are open to attacks from those who would take advantage of those with a lesser level of formal education. By arming all with the tools of the cognitive niche, we protect all. Higher education for all is democracy in action. To deny it to those who desire it on the basis of affordability (price) or entry qualification (merit/selection) is nothing less than the perversion of natural justice and the right to fight for survival; the denial of a developed cognitive ability is the denial of a human right more connected to human survival than the right to bear arms and is worthy of a constitutional amendment to ensure everyone is equipped with a cognitive ability through a higher education to follow their own relevant desires.

NOTES

1. The term is derived from the literature on total quality management stemming from authors such as Deming and Juran and transposed into higher education. See Harvey (undated); Vlăsceanu et al. (2007); Woodhouse (1999); Harvey and Green (1993); Campbell and Rozsnyai (2002); See also Quality Assurance Agency for Higher Education (QAA).
2. The phrase is a reference to the Bernie Sanders' presidential campaign, 2016.
3. Universities in the UK typically require three A-levels. The better the rank of the university the higher the grade of A-level required. See https://www.ucas.com/ucas/tariff-calculator for further details.
4. Nearly 45 million US citizens over the age of 24, that is, one in five adults, 'have some college and no degree' (Selingo 2016, p. 36).
5. Oxbridge is a name for Oxford and Cambridge Universities that equates them but makes them different from other universities. Technically, Oxford and Cambridge are part of the Russell group of universities but their names signify distinctly different identities from other technically similar universities in the Russell Group.

BIBLIOGRAPHY

Althusser, L. (2005). *For Marx*. London: Verso.

Arum, R., & Roksa, J. (2011). *Academically Adrift: Limited Learning on College Campuses*. Chicago: The University of Chicago Press.

Arum, R., & Roksa, J. (2014). *Aspiring Adults Adrift: Tentative Transitions of College Graduates*. Chicago: The University of Chicago Press.

Arum, R., Roksa, J., & Cook, A. (Eds.). (2016). *Improving Quality in American Higher Education: Learning Outcomes and Assessments for the 21st Century*. San Francisco: Jossey-Bass.

Bauman, D. (2016a). Bonuses Push More Public-Colleges Leaders Past $1 Million. *The Chronicle of Higher Education*. Retrieved from http://www.chronicle.com/article/Bonuses-Push-More/237152. Accessed 7 Mar 2017.

Bauman, D. (2016b). 39 Private-College Leaders Earn More Than $1 Million. *The Chronicle of Higher Education*. Retrieved from http://www.chronicle.com/article/39-Private-College-Leaders/238561. Accessed 7 Mar 2017.

Best, B. (2000). Necessarily Contingent, Equally Different and Relatively Universal: The Antinomies of Ernesto Laclau's Social Logic of Hegemony. *Rethinking Marxism, 12*(3), 38–57.

Bok, D. (2013). *Higher Education in America*. Princeton: Princeton University Press.

Bourdieu, P., & Wacquant, L. (2001). NewLiberalSpeak: Notes on the New Planetary Vulgate. *Radical Philosophy, 105*, 2–5.

Campbell, C., & Rozsnyai, C. (2002). *Quality Assurance and the Development of Course Programmes*. Papers on Higher Education Regional University Network on Governance and Management of Higher Education in South East Europe Bucharest, UNESCO, Bucharest.

Carey, K. (2015). *The End of College: Creating the Future of Learning and the University of Everywhere*. New York: Riverhead Books.

Carlson, S., & Supiano, B. (2016, July 27). How Clinton's Free College Could Cause a Cascade of Problems. *The Chronicle of Higher Education*. Retrieved from http://chronicle.com/article/how-clintons-free-college/237266. Accessed 3 Aug 2016.

Carson, E. A. (2014). *Prisoners in 2013*. Washington, DC: The U.S. Department of Justice, Office of Justice Programs, Bureau of Justice Statistics.

College Board. (2016). *Trends in Student Aid 2016*. Retrieved from https://trends.collegeboard.org/sites/default/files/2016-trends-student-aid.pdf. Accessed 5 June 2017.

Cooley, C. H. (1922). *Human Nature and the Social Order*. New York: Charles Scribner's Sons.

de Saussure, F. (1983). *Course in General Linguistics*. London: Duckworth.

de Weert, E. (2011, December). *Perspectives on Higher Education and the Labour Market: Review of International Policy Developments*. The Netherlands: Center for Higher Education Policy Studies, C11EW153.

Delanty, G. (1998). The Idea of the University in the Global Era: From Knowledge as an End to the End of Knowledge? *Social Epistemology, 12*(1), 3–25.

Delanty, G. (2002). The University and Modernity: A History of the Present. In K. Robins & F. Webster (Eds.), *The Virtual University: Knowledge, Markets and Management*. Oxford: Oxford University Press.

Derrida, J. (1976). *Of Grammatology*. Baltimore: John Hopkins University Press.

Derrida, J. (1978/2001). *Writing and Difference*. London: Routledge.

Dewey, J. (1916/1997). *Democracy and Education: An Introduction to the Philosophy of Education*. New York: The Free Press.

Digest of Education Statistics. Table 302.60, 1970 to 2014. http://nces.ed.gov/programs/digest/d15/tables/dt15_302.60.asp?current=yes. Accessed 27 July 2016.

Eagleton, T. (1983). *Literary Theory: An Introduction*. Oxford: Basil Blackwell.

Fairclough, N. (2003). *Analysing Discourse: Textual Analysis for Social Research.* London: Routledge.

Foucault, M. (1989a). *The Archaeology of Knowledge.* London: Routledge.

Foucault, M. (1989b). *The Order of Things.* London: Routledge.

Foucault, M. (1991a). *Discipline and Punish: The Birth of the Prison.* London: Penguin.

Foucault, M. (1991b). What Is Enlightenment. In P. Rabinow (Ed.), *The Foucault Reader: An Introduction to Foucault's Thought* (pp. 3–50). London: Penguin.

Freud, S. (2006). *Interpreting Dreams.* London: Penguin Books.

Gibbons, M., Limoges, C., Nowotny, H., Schwartzman, S., Scott, P., & Trow, M. (1994). *The New Production of Knowledge.* London: Sage.

Graham, P. (2002). Predication and Propagation: A Method for Analysing Evaluative Meanings in Technology Policy. *TEXT, 22*(2), 227–268.

Greenaway, D., & Haynes, M. (2000). *Funding Universities to Meet National and International Challenges.* Nottingham: University of Nottingham.

Grey, C. (2001). Re-imagining Relevance: A Response to Starkey and Madan. *British Journal of Management, 12*(Special Issue), S27–S32.

Habermas, J. (1970). *Towards a Rational Society.* London: Heinemann.

Habermas, J. (1987). *Knowledge and Human Interests.* Cambridge: Polity Press.

Harvey, L. (undated). *Analytic Quality Glossary.* Quality Research International. Retrieved from http://www.qualityresearchinternational.com/glossary/. Accessed 6 Jan 2017.

Harvey, L., & Green, D. (1993). Defining Quality. *Assessment and Evaluation in Higher Education, 18*(1), 9–34. Retrieved from pre-publication draft available here. Accessed 6 Jan 2017.

Howarth, D. (2000). *Discourse.* Buckingham: Open University Press.

Husserl, E. (1964/2010). *The Idea of Phenomenology.* Netherlands: Kluwer Academic Publishers.

Laclau, E. (1990). *New Reflections on the Revolution of Our Time.* London: Verso.

Laclau, E. (1996). *Emancipation(s).* London: Verso.

Laclau, E. (2004). Glimpsing the Future. In S. Critchley & O. Marchart (Eds.), *Laclau: A Critical Reader.* London: Routledge.

Laclau, E., & Mouffe, C. (1985). *Hegemony and Socialist Strategy: Towards a Radical Democratic Politics.* London: Verso.

Lury, C. (1996). *Consumer Culture.* Cambridge: Polity.

Marginson, S. (1997). Competition and Contestability in Australian Higher Education. *Australian Universities Review, 40*(1), 5–14.

Marginson, S. (2012). The Problem of Public Good(s) in Higher Education. In *41st Australian Conference of Economists, Melbourne, 2–12 July.* Retrieved from http://www.ses.unam.mx/curso2014/pdf/Marginson.pdf. Accessed 9 Jan 2017.

Marx, K. (1990). *Capital I.* London: Penguin Classics.

Mead, G. H. (1934). *Mind, Self, and Society: From the Standpoint of a Social Behaviorist.* Chicago: University of Chicago Press.

NCES. re. Chart 3.3. (National Center for Educational Statistics). Earnings. Table 502.20 (2015). Integrated Postsecondary Education Data System (IPEDS), U.S. Department of Education, Institute of Education Sciences.

Newman, J. H. (1905/2012). *The Idea of a University*. New York: Forgotten Books.

O'Leary, B., & Hatch, J. (2015). *Executive Compensation at Private and Public Colleges*. Retrieved from http://chronicle.com/interactives/executive-compe nsation?cid=FEATUREDNAV#id=table_public_2015. Accessed 9 Jan 2017.

OECD (2012a). *Education at a Glance 2012: OECD Indicators*. OECD Publishing. http://dx.doi.org/10.1787/eag-2012-en. p. 26. Retrieved from https://www.oecd.org/edu/EAG%202012_e-book_EN_200912.pdf. Accessed 10 June 2017.

OECD. (2012b). *United States Country Note, Education at a Glance 2012*. Retrieved from https://www.oecd.org/unitedstates/CN%20-%20United%20 States.pdf. Accessed 10 June 2017.

OECD. (2015a). Re. Chart 3.1. Population with Tertiary Education (Indicator). doi: 10.1787/0b8f90e9-en. Retrieved from https://data.oecd.org/eduatt/ population-with-tertiary-education.htm. Accessed 06 June 2017.

OECD. (2015b). *Education Indicators in Focus*. Retrieved from https://www. oecd.org/education/EDIF%2031%20(2015)--ENG--Final.pdf. Accessed 10 June 2017.

Olssen, M., Codd, J., & O'Neill, A.-M. (2004). *Education Policy: Globalization, Citizenship and Democracy*. London: Sage.

OU Facts and Figures. (2014/15). Retrieved from http://www.open.ac.uk/ about/main/sites/www.open.ac.uk.about.main/files/files/fact_ figures_1415_uk.pdf. Accessed 6 Jan 2017.

Pinker, S. (2010). The Cognitive Niche: Coevolution of Intelligence, Sociality, and Language. *PNAS, 107*(Supp. 2), 8993–8999.

Prichard, C. (2000). *Making Managers in Universities and Colleges*. Buckingham: SRHE / Open University.

Prichard, C., & Trowler, P. R. (2003). *Realizing Qualitative Research in Higher Education*. Aldershot: Ashgate.

Rappert, B. (1999). The Uses of Relevance: Thoughts on a Reflexive Sociology. *Sociology, 33*(4), 705–723.

Schutz, A. (1970). *Reflections on the Problem of Relevance*. New Haven: Yale University Press.

Schutz, A. (1973). On Multiple Realities. In M. Natanson (Ed.), *Collected Papers I: The Problem of Social Reality* (pp. 207–259). The Hague: Martinus Nighiff.

Selingo, J. J. (2016). *2026 The Decade Ahead: The Seismic Shifts Transforming the Future of Higher Education*. Washington, DC: The Chronicle of Higher Education.

Slaughter, S., & Leslie, L. L. (1997). *Academic Capitalism: Politics, Policies and the Entrepreneurial University*. Baltimore: The John Hopkins University Press.

Smith, R. (1996). Addressing the Delusion of Relevance. *Education Action Research, 4*, 73–91.

Sperber, D. (1996). *Explaining Culture: A Naturalistic Approach*. Oxford: Blackwell.

Sperber, D., & Wilson, D. (1986/1995). *Relevance: Communication and Cognition*. Oxford: Blackwell.

Starkey, K., & Madan, P. (2001). Bridging the Relevance Gap: Aligning Stakeholders in the Future of Management Research. *British Journal of Management, 12*(Special Issue), S3–S26.

The Chronicle Data. (2016). *The Chronicle of Higher Education*. Retrieved from http://data.chronicle.com/?cid=UCHESIDENAV2. Accessed 13 Jan 2017.

Tooby, J., & DeVore, I. (1987). The Reconstruction of Hominid Evolution Through Strategic Modeling. In W. G. Kinzey (Ed.), *The Evolution of Human Behavior: Primate Models*. Albany: SUNY Press.

Torfing, J. (1999). *New Theories of Discourse: Laclau, Mouffe and Žižek*. Oxford: Blackwell.

Trowler, P. R. (1998). *Academics Responding to Change: New Higher Education Frameworks and Academic Cultures*. Buckingham: The Society for Research into Higher Education and Open University.

Trowler, P. R. (Ed.). (2002). *Higher Education Policy and Institutional Change: Intentions and Outcomes in Turbulent Environments*. Buckingham: The Society for Research into Higher Education and Open University.

Vargo, S. L., & Lusch, R. F. (2004). Evolving to a New Dominant Logic for Marketing. *Journal of Marketing, 68*(January), 1–17.

Vlăsceanu, L., Grünberg, L., & Pârlea, D. (2007). *Quality Assurance and Accreditation: A Glossary of Basic Terms and Definitions* (Revised and updated edition). ISBN 92-9069-186-7. (Bucharest: UNESCO-CEPES). Retrieved from http://unesdoc.unesco.org/images/0013/001346/134621e.pdf. Accessed 6 Jan 2017.

Wernick, A. (1991). *Promotional Culture: Advertising, Ideology and Symbolic Expression*. London: Sage.

Willmott, H. (1995). Managing the Academics: Commodification and Control in the Development of University Education in the UK. *Human Relations, 48*(9), 993–1027.

Willmott, H. (2003). Commercialising Higher Education in the UK: The State, Industry and Peer Review. *Studies in Higher Education, 28*(2), 129–141.

Woodhouse, D. (1999). Quality and Quality Assurance. In Organisation for Economic Co-operation and Development (OECD) (Ed.), *Quality and Internationalisation in Higher Education* (pp. 29–44). Paris: OECD: Programme on Institutional Management in Higher Education (IMHE).

CHAPTER 4

What's in a Brand Name?

Perhaps I am somewhat unfortunate. Maybe I am a little too sensitive if not allergic to strategic brand change. Three of the last five higher education institutions that I worked in have indulged in re-branding. This is not to say that branding higher education is necessarily rash inducing, but it is difficult to understand the rationale for re-branding colleges and universities and the spending of hard-earned tax-payer's dollars and fee income on the baptismal ritual (Kirpke 1981) of re-naming the place of higher education delivery without changing any other aspect of what is delivered, namely a higher education. The use of expensive consultancies is most certainly irritating. I know of no case of re-branding that has made a difference to learning outcomes for students. The practice is self-indulgent, and the motivation for it lies not in improving higher education.

The idea of what a name is, what it does, and, very importantly, for whom it does whatever it does is central to my argument on branding. No reader, I should think, will be surprised to learn that there is a substantial amount written about brands and brand names especially from a managerial perspective, which filters into higher education (see, e.g., *Journal of Business Research* Vol. 69(8) 2016 on branding higher education). Brands and brand names are often used as synonyms. However, it is not always the case that these are the same although to some extent the opinion that the brand and the brand name are the same is reasonable. For example, the reader is unlikely to be a brand, yet some readers could be. While brands have an equivalent name, they must be called some-thing, not all names are equivalent to a brand. Joan Spigglesworth (a name I just made up) is not a brand. Sports and entertainment stars may be brands, but in this case their names mean more than their brand. I am sure their families and friends would testify to this. Even some academics and/or intellectuals may make a claim, or someone may make the claim for them, that they are a brand name even though they certainly are not household names. I argue that it is the name that is of paramount signifi-cance, and I explore names from an ontological perspective (i.e., what they are) and an epistemological perspective (how we know what they are) and so how they work.

One can find advice on building your personal brand in x easy steps—check out Dr. Google. At this point I feel compelled to say that the notion of following the advice of such books or websites to build your personal brand is disconcerting and may be interpreted more of an act of foolish-ness and/or desperation than leadership acumen. There are numerous social media platforms that are all about building a profile, professional, or otherwise. Of course, the vested interests of such entrepreneurial endeav-ors will argue that they are providing the tools for people to build their own brand name, rather like building your own customized house, which would add value. What that value is and what is added to it is a bit of a mystery if not sometimes a misery. If people have the same tool kit, then it is reasonable to expect similar end products. If all the build-your-own-brand book readers, course takers, or platform users are using the same ontological hammers and epistemological saws, then you may end up with different colored little houses but they all look just the same. At least you would hope so. You would hope to have a kitchen and a bathroom regard-less of the difference between kitchens and kitchens and bathrooms and bathrooms.

Despite differences, there is a commonality that stretches across kitch-ens and bathrooms and what goes on in them, often making use of the same ingredients in different forms. From a theoretical perspective, the end-brand result is in the available methodology. Innovation and/or entrepreneurship, whatever your form of brand naming may be, is not so much in how you saw and hammer but rather that you do saw and ham-mer with a given tool kit, which is the major problem facing our presiden-tial re-namers of our colleges and universities: if you keep on using the same consulting took kit, whether a, b, or c consulting, model, or method, the result will be of no significant difference from other colleges and universities. All you will have achieved is reduced cash reserves, wasted resources, and the creation of a distraction from the purpose of a country's education policy, that is, to provide as many people as possible in the general population with a higher education.

If we lived in a world where all we had to communicate to each other was a distinct branded identity, we would inhabit a tower of identity babble. Our commonality is far more important than an illusion of identity grandeur. The same principle is applicable to all our educational institutions, including universities and colleges. All colleges and universities make claims to the appellation of 'excellence', and yet if all are excellent, then none are excellent because the concept necessitates a difference in terms of better than the others. The idea of course is a rather cheap marketing one. If you baptize yourself excellent, meaning name yourself as excellent, and keep calling yourself excellent, others will start calling you excellent too and the name might stick. But universities and colleges should be ordinary; it should be normal and commonplace for citizens to be educated to the highest possible standard.

I recall as a child listening to Pete Seeger singing 'little boxes on the hillside, little boxes made of ticky tacky…little boxes all the same… there's a green one and a pink one …and the people in the houses all go to the university, and they all get put in boxes, little boxes all the same.' Despite being about eight or nine, I understood very well the sarcasm of the lines. But like all language, the authorial intention is no guarantee of meaning (Wittgenstein 2000/1953; Wimsatt and Beardsley 1958). I distinctly remember thinking that I wish I lived in such a house because it sounded so much better than the ordinary house I lived in—as far as being a Catholic in Belfast in the late 1950s, 1960s, and 1970s was ordinary. They might be ticky-tacky but they were bright and vibrant on a hillside and despite being all the same they seemed quite different from the ticky-tacky of a slum or a run-down tenement building. No doubt Pete Seeger is retrospectively guilty of a microaggression against the sensitivities of the poor. Similar to living in ticky-tacky houses, everyone went to university and they were all the same. Maybe that is a worthwhile aspiration. There is a lot to be said in favor of universal housing on a metaphorical hillside a million miles away from the slum or run-down tenement. A higher education for all that looks just the same, that is, the same education that produces equivalently well-educated citizens, is better than a branded uniqueness that educates to divide and distinguishes those who will have an excellent higher education from those who will not have an excellent higher education—if they have a higher education at all. Even today we have neither good housing nor higher education *for all*. From the perspective of higher education for all, brand higher education is not in good shape (see Chart 3.1). One of the reasons that brand USA higher education is not in good shape is because the individual institutions keep wasting resources on trying to be different rather on all trying to do the same thing—educate to a higher level.

It seems to me that branding higher education through the use of the same ontological and epistemological perspectives ensures sameness with the façade of difference and this is qualitatively different from ensuring the provision of the same higher education for all that will provide students with the cognitive ability to think for themselves. As such, the sameness of provision will deliver a praiseworthy identity for individuals in all their differences. The former is the ideological coercion for people to seem different but be the same while the latter is the 'village' community sharing the same benefits by educating individuals equally to ensure the survival and betterment of the community *a la* Dewey (1916/1979). Current concepts of branding do not lend themselves to equivalent higher education. Branding higher education draws on methods and concepts developed for commercial enterprise and equivalently transferred to non-profit institutions charged with educating the population to a higher level. But the point of branding *a la* Keller (2003) and Aaker (1996) and so on is to shape how customers feel and think about your brand in such a way that value is added to the company in terms of superior financial returns. The brand acts as a lens for viewing product offerings available for those in the market (Keller and Lehmann 2006) with a favorable bias. The brand is named and invested in for the interests of those doing the naming and investing. Those who apply such methodological tools to higher education, for example, Chapleo (2015), Williams and Maktoba (2014) among many others, seek to favorably distinguish the institutional brand name from competitors and so earn superior returns for a limited set of people. For companies, the limited set is shareholders/owners who benefit by being able to charge a higher price; for institutes of higher education the limited set is made up of those within the institution, the administrators, faculty, and students, who benefit from higher fees. Faculty benefit from higher fees through improved resources, pay, and conditions. Administrators benefit in the same way but also gain additional resources that make it easier to run the organization. Students in the branded university benefit through the exclusion of potential competitors for the same resources and job opportunities, and are willing to trade off higher short-term costs for perceived long-term advantage. Not all students can afford the short-term cost and are unwilling to take the financial risk given their lack of economic and cultural capital. Many have not accrued sufficient cultural capital to gain entry. So, the long-term benefits accrue disproportionately.

Sternberg (2016) makes a similar point regarding exclusion when he argues in favor of Active Concerned Citizenship and Ethical Leadership (ACCEL) universities, that is, universities in which administrators and faculty promote ACCEL. He points out that it is the exclusion that underwrites cultural and economic capital that favors some but not others. In other words, branding higher education is antithetical to the idea of a higher education for all and so providing equal opportunity of survival for all by dint of providing the tools of cognition advantage (re-named as critical thinking within current pedagogical language) for the entire population and thereby undercutting much of the cultural and economic capital transferred by the brand name alone. In the general market, branding may be considered as anti-competitive (Stigler 1942). Regarding higher education, branding denies access and restricts equality of opportunity and so is antithetical to diversity and competition. The point of branding higher education is to provide an advantage in drawing on scarce resources to benefit one organization and limited set, that is, social group, but in doing so must disadvantage other social groups. In commercial and profit-making organizations branding is deemed as acceptable competitive behavior, though Stigler would disagree, but this is not ethically acceptable when it comes to educating the population and may be deemed discriminatory as some in society are given advantages and others denied access to the benefit of an 'excellent' higher education. Moreover, a poorly educated society is a drag on social and economic life (see Fig. 4.1).

The denial of a higher education, for whatever reason, is entirely unethical, anti-democratic and it robs individuals of the ability to compete and contribute to society and the economy. Those who indulge in current stratagems of branding higher education cannot at the same time claim to be socially responsible and serve the community in educating all no matter what the college brochure or website says. What can be claimed for the branded college is that those who indulge in it, usually administrators, are attempting to give those who enroll in their college an advantage over and above other students not attending their college. To some this is praiseworthy but usually only to those who benefit from such a system of higher

Fig. 4.1 Benefits of a higher education
Source: Department for Business Innovation and Skills, UK

education and who gain more economic and cultural capital at the expense of those with less cultural and economic capital from birth. Such a system is an antagonism to social and educational diversity and is institutionally racist as the cultural and economic fault lines start early and tend to divide along ethnic and social class dimensions (see Chart 4.1). Administrators who follow a branding policy are institutionally antagonistic to diversity, though probably blind to it, in their pursuit of difference from, and better than, those not privileged by participation in their institution's brand identity. One might reasonably argue that branding a college is the mother of all microaggressions in deliberately signaling superiority that often just happens to run along the fault lines of ethnic, cultural, and economic division.

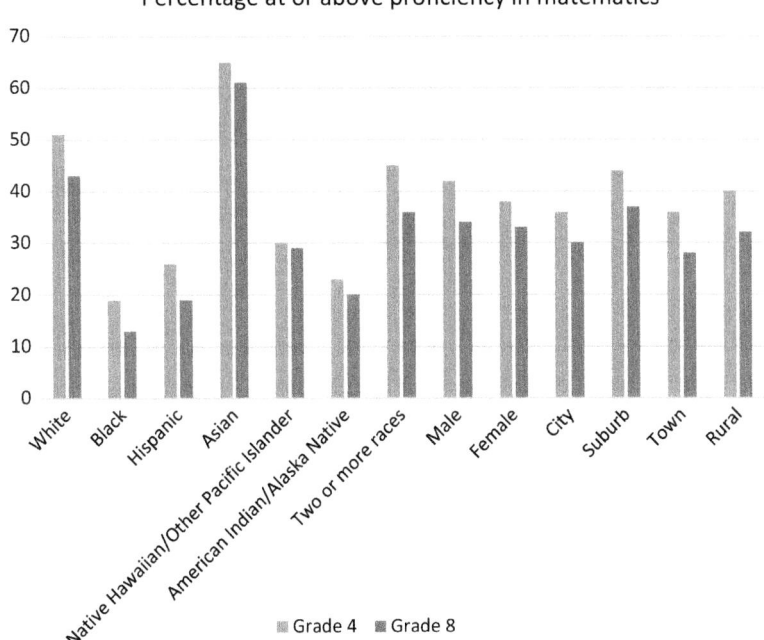

Chart 4.1 Early educational disparities in mathematics
Source: NCES, The nation's report card, NAEP scores (National Assessment of Educational Progress)

So how is it that some higher education brands can charge $40,000–$50,000 per year for four years and some people are willing to pay such fees? Of course, brands cannot and do not charge high fees, people do that. The answer to that question lies in the notion of relevance. For Dewey (1916/1997, p. 3) the idea of higher education was a necessity for the survival of society and an essential element of a democratic state.

> With the growth of civilization, the gap between the original capacities of the immature and the standards and customs of the elders increases. Mere physical growing up, mere mastery of the bare necessities of subsistence will not suffice to reproduce the life of the group. Deliberate effort and the taking of thoughtful pains are required. Beings who are born not only

unaware of, but quite indifferent to, the aims and habits of the social group have to be rendered cognizant of them and actively interested. Education, and education alone, spans the gap.

...Without this communication of ideals, hopes, expectations, standards, opinions, from those members of society who are passing out of the group life to those who are coming into it, social life could not survive.

But these are big words and they bounce around the metaphorical page with a potential for ontological and epistemological slippage in the mind of the reader. Ideas as big as higher education will easily slip and slide around the interests of the authors and parties involved. The Catholic intellectual meritocracy of Newman (1905/2012), the liberal democracy of Dewey (1916/1997), the muddling multiversity of Kerr (1963/2001), the antagonism to academic capitalism of Slaughter and Leslie (1997), the supercomplexity of mental preparation of workers in Barnett (2000), the techno consumerism of Carey (2015), and the leadership of liberal democratic desperation emanating from Sternberg (2016) that will somehow cancel division and conflict are perspectives that will not reconcile. Each see the function of higher education as important, but the relevance of higher education for each is quite distinct. For each what higher education is or ought to be is named differently. There is no fixed idea of higher education. Thus, higher education brands underlying the megalithic structure of relevance slip and slide or are pushed and pulled into contortions of liberating ideals offered in a name that seldom liberates. For those who get to attend the Ivy Leagues and Oxbridges of this world of higher education that is a great outcome for them. Unfortunately, this leaves a rather long tail of people who do not get to the best that society can offer. Indeed, what society is offering is not an excellent higher education system but a divisive form of segmentation or rather segregation along cultural and economic divisions.

FREE LIBERAL-CASH FLOW

The push for entrepreneurship, even within the mission of a liberal education, is quite alarmingly antagonistic to the ethos of liberation through education. This is not so say that entrepreneurship is not important, indeed it is and because of its importance it is named as a subject fit for higher education. But what is good for capitalism and the few is not necessarily good for most individuals. Too often administrators and instructors pushing the messianic message for the glory of entrepreneurship forget to teach basic probability. Enthusiastic administrators and instructors forget their critical role as educators when they fail to inform and advise students of the likelihood of failure in their entrepreneurial endeavors. The six-year survival rate historically runs at or around 50%. Like cigarette packaging or brochures promoting financial investments, these programs should carry a health warning. Indeed, the packaged instructor of entrepreneurship and those generally responsible for promoting such programs should be subject to regulation in their claims. They are, as Taleb (2007) may say, a loaded gun. Consider Roulette College, a fictional name, and the type of promotional claims made. The following quote was taken from a college website on October 28, 2016, and is representative of college communication and marketing:

> More than 150 businesses have been designed through [Roulette's] Entrepreneurial Studies Program since its founding eight years ago, which has about a 30 percent success rate. According to the *Princeton Review*, this rate is 25 percent higher than the majority of similar programs at colleges nationwide.

(Source withheld)

The reason for selecting Roulette College is because, according to the eminent and much quoted *Princeton Review*, Roulette is 'better' than most. Is this misleading promotion? Most people will read this positively because the percentage is named as successful, that is, we have a 30% success rate. But this also means that the failure rate is 70%—not a good bet. But young people think they are fireproof, that is, the risk does not apply to me, that is someone else's risk. It seems to me that we forget our duty of care and the liberal arts mission when we persuade students to play with those odds. Moreover, the reader is not told precisely over what timeline this failure rate covers. It could be a 70% failure rate in year 1 or 70% in year 8 or indeed a 70% failure rate every year. In the latter case, less than 6 startups are left standing after eight years out of an initial 100. Out of 150, less than 9 are still operating if the attrition rate is 70% per year for student startups. And how does this compare to the national average for entrepreneur startups? The eight-year survival rate is around 40/41% so, in fact, Roulette's failure rate is *circa* 10% higher than the national average, which does not make for such good promotional reading. Finally, on Roulette College's promotional text, someone deliberately uses the more emotive descriptor of 'success' compared with the more pertinent term, 'survival rates', used by the US

Bureau of Labor Statistics (see Table 4.1). For good measure, the term 'success' is laden with ambiguity—a useful brand noun for slippery claims. Given that we should expect more from our institutes of higher education, especially when they make claims to pursuing 'Ethical engagement', 'Moral courage', 'Responsible use of resources' (Roulette College's core values), running such programs seems more like 'entrepreneurial opportunism' that takes advantages of naïve students rather than providing them with a serious education. But it should be noted that this is not a criticism of Roulette College, rather an example of what many colleges do. You can round up the usual suspects of promotional appellations from most college websites. Studying the subject of entrepreneurism, rather than learning how to be an entrepreneur, in our society may be a more appropriate curriculum for higher education. Studying such an appropriate curriculum would be a much more ethically and intellectually robust position to take rather than taking money for a how-to course in entrepreneurship with a high likelihood of business failure (Table 4.1). It is notable from reading Table 4.1 that the survival rates are stubbornly persistent despite all the higher education in entrepreneurship. A curriculum that studies and critically evaluates entrepreneurship as a social phenomenon would be more pedagogically ethical and would at least provide graduates with informed choices and the cognitive ability to evaluate decisions.

The great random generator (Taleb 2007) is a destroyer of lives. Those whose entrepreneurial activities fail never make the pages of Forbes, while the tiny numbers of those who become rich are adorned in the financial media with success. Sheer dint of publicity, something you would imagine a critical pedagogy of a university or college would counter balance, gives the notion of financial riches through entrepreneurial behavior as commonplace. Metaphorically, Taleb (2007, pp. 23/24) uses the game of Russian roulette to illustrate the consequences of gambling with entrepreneurial risk:

> The problem is that only one of the histories is observed … and the winner of $10 million would elicit the admiration and praise of some fatuous journalist … Consider the possibility that the Russian roulette winner would be used as a role model by his family, friends, and neighbors … if the roulette-betting fool keeps playing the game, the bad histories will tend to catch up with him. Thus, if a twenty-five-year-old played Russian roulette, say, once a year, there would be a very slim possibility of his surviving until his fiftieth birthday – but, if there are enough players, say thousands of twenty-five-year-old players, we can expect to see a handful of (extremely rich) survivors (and a very large cemetery).

Table 4.1 Survival rates of establishments, by year started and number of years since starting, 1994–2015, in percent

Years since starting	Year																					
	1994	1995	1996	1997	1998	1999	2000	2001	2002	2003	2004	2005	2006	2007	2008	2009	2010	2011	2012	2013	2014	2015
1	100.0	100.0	100.0	100.0	100.0	100.0	100.0	100.0	100.0	100.0	100.0	100.0	100.0	100.0	100.0	100.0	100.0	100.0	100.0	100.0	100.0	100.0
2	79.6	78.8	78.2	78.5	80.1	79.1	78.4	75.7	78.4	79.3	78.9	80.1	78.3	77.3	75.2	76.7	78.6	79.4	79.2	79.6	79.9	–
3	68.1	67.9	66.9	68.3	68.5	67.0	66.0	64.7	67.4	68.4	69.1	68.7	66.3	64.0	63.3	66.4	68.6	69.3	68.7	69.3	–	–
4	60.6	59.8	59.7	60.2	59.6	58.5	58.2	57.6	60.0	61.4	61.2	60.2	56.7	55.5	56.5	59.9	61.6	61.9	61.5	–	–	–
5	54.3	54.1	53.4	53.0	53.0	52.7	52.8	52.3	54.8	55.3	54.5	52.6	49.8	50.2	51.7	54.8	56.0	56.3	–	–	–	–
6	49.6	48.8	48.1	47.6	48.1	48.2	44.7	48.1	48.1	50.0	48.4	46.8	45.4	46.4	47.8	50.1	51.4	–	–	–	–	–
7	45.2	44.4	43.9	43.7	44.4	44.4	44.7	44.2	45.9	44.8	43.7	43.2	42.3	43.1	44.2	46.3	–	–	–	–	–	–
8	41.5	40.7	40.5	40.5	41.2	41.4	41.6	40.9	41.8	40.9	40.5	40.5	39.6	40.1	41.1	–	–	–	–	–	–	–
9	38.3	38.0	37.8	37.7	38.7	38.6	38.6	37.4	38.4	38.1	38.2	38.2	37.1	37.5	–	–	–	–	–	–	–	–
10	35.7	35.7	35.4	35.6	36.2	36.1	35.5	34.5	36.1	36.0	36.1	35.9	34.9	–	–	–	–	–	–	–	–	–
11	33.6	33.4	33.4	33.5	34.0	33.2	32.9	32.4	34.2	34.2	34.0	33.8	–	–	–	–	–	–	–	–	–	–
12	31.8	31.6	31.5	31.5	31.5	31.0	31.2	30.9	32.5	32.3	32.1	–	–	–	–	–	–	–	–	–	–	–
13	30.3	29.9	29.7	29.3	29.5	29.4	29.8	29.5	30.8	30.8	–	–	–	–	–	–	–	–	–	–	–	–
14	28.7	28.4	28.0	27.6	28.1	28.2	28.6	28.1	29.4	–	–	–	–	–	–	–	–	–	–	–	–	–
15	27.2	26.6	26.3	26.2	26.9	27.0	27.3	26.8	–	–	–	–	–	–	–	–	–	–	–	–	–	–
16	25.5	25.1	25.1	25.1	25.7	25.8	26.3	–	–	–	–	–	–	–	–	–	–	–	–	–	–	–
17	24.1	24.1	24.1	24.1	24.7	24.8	–	–	–	–	–	–	–	–	–	–	–	–	–	–	–	–
18	23.0	23.0	23.1	23.2	23.6	–	–	–	–	–	–	–	–	–	–	–	–	–	–	–	–	–
19	22.0	22.2	22.2	22.2	–	–	–	–	–	–	–	–	–	–	–	–	–	–	–	–	–	–
20	21.2	21.3	21.3	–	–	–	–	–	–	–	–	–	–	–	–	–	–	–	–	–	–	–
21	20.3	20.4	–	–	–	–	–	–	–	–	–	–	–	–	–	–	–	–	–	–	–	–
22	19.5	–	–	–	–	–	–	–	–	–	–	–	–	–	–	–	–	–	–	–	–	–

Note: Dashes indicate not applicable

Source: US Bureau of Labor Statistics. https://www.bls.gov/bdm/entrepreneurship/entrepreneurship.htm

We can now add higher education to the list of fawning reference groups that name entrepreneurship as a form of social good and playing on the individual desire for 'success' rather than communitarian values and the cognitive skills that build survival rates for communities. Despite many liberal and critical instructors who fold concepts of social justice into their curricula, and critique the disparity of wealth distribution and the growing gap between the one-percenters and all the rest, university administrators, and mathematically and ethically challenged instructors push, slip, slide, and generally persuade 18–24-year-old students into irrational exuberance, which just happens to suit a given ideology and college cash flows. If college and university administrators recruit enough entrepreneurial players, cannon fodder for capitalism, they will have a few winners as pictorial support for their misleading promotional literature. The brochures will play up the winners and conveniently forget the graveyard debt of those who played and lost. There is something of the night about university and college administrators who prey on the vulnerable through narratives of success that communicate the how-to of entrepreneurship, which often gets interpreted by students as how to get rich in easy steps. University and college administrators who tout how-to entrepreneurship should be named and shamed with their institutions branded with the same level of scorn they usually reserve for the Trump Universities of this world. There does happen to be a limit to the survival of new businesses (Table 4.1). On average and over time most will fail, and it is wrong to encourage students to think otherwise. Moreover, important as new businesses are to the economy and employment they are not the engine of employment they once were (see Chart 4.2). This is not to say that among many of the new enterprises there will not be the new Apple, Google, or Facebook, but it is to say (a) we cannot know which will survive and prosper and (b) that the odds are heavily stacked against any individual entrepreneur surviving. This should be clearly communicated to would-be undergraduate entrepreneurs.

Tuition-driven colleges make a big deal of being student centered. But being totally tuition dependent for revenue streams does not necessarily lead to the welfare of students but the turning of them into revenue fodder, where much is justified not on education arguments but revenue streams. In the roulette of entrepreneurship few students will escape the bullet if encouraged to go into business for themselves. Many will be branded failures and carry the burden of personal failure with them for many years if not the rest of their lives. There are no specific numbers on survival rates for the college-student entrepreneur, that is, those who leave college and

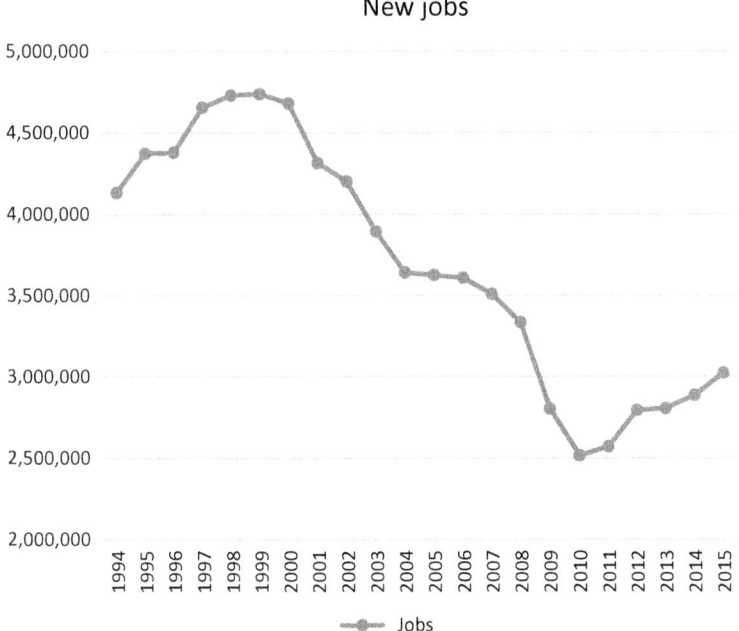

Chart 4.2   Jobs created by establishments less than one-year old, March 1994–March 2015
Source: Bureau of Labor Statistics

set up their own enterprise, but it looks as though it may be higher than the national average and within five years at least half and probably more of our young university entrepreneurs will have failed. And all in the name of entrepreneurship and a misguided desire, which may not necessarily be the student's desire but the desire of administrators for university revenue, driven by self-interest and a willingness to generate revenue regardless of student consequences. Perhaps Peters and Waterman (1982) had a valid point when they argued that organizations should 'stick to the knitting' and not diversify, especially in college education where youthful exuberance may be open to overenthusiastic administrative desires for wealth and success in the interest of college cash flows. Study the social phenomenon of entrepreneurship, yes, most certainly. Given the statistics on survival rates, however, it would be misleading to tell students that you can teach them to be successful entrepreneurs. This is at best ethically dubious and given the statistics more likely to be downright misleading. It rather depends on how we as educators desire to name entrepreneurship as relevant to the education of citizens to a higher level.

DESCRIPTIONS OF LIBERTY

A major contribution to education, which is also applicable to higher education, is Dewey's (1916/1997, p. 84) insight into education's function and contribution to democracy, especially regarding how the very same social conditions can have antagonistic effects.

> In order to have a large number of values in common, all the members of the group must have an equable opportunity to receive and to take from others. There must be a large variety of shared undertakings and experiences. Otherwise, the influences which educate some into masters, educate others into slaves.

Dewey was very aware that the same instruction was different for different people. In effect, what (higher) education is rather depends on perspective. The place of higher education may be the same physical place for all as well as the service delivered to all in the same way, in the same surroundings. Yet the evidence of protesters on campuses across the USA belies the notion that all students are experiencing the same higher education. Under these circumstances, the case can be made for 'the same is different'. Names and descriptions can get us into a confused state of mind regarding what it is that we are talking about when talking about higher educating the population.

For proponents of the descriptive school of thought (Russell 1992/1903; Frege 1949; Searle 1971) we know the identity of what we are talking about by recognizing it. That is to say, the way we describe it. The name Trump, to take an example much in the press at the time of writing, refers to a person and is a family name. The name is a referent to him. We could say Trump is Trump or Donald Trump. It may be obvious to some that this is somewhat circular and so logically problematic. Statements of the type 'it' is what 'it' is do not tell us what 'it' is: Trump = Trump is problematic. Trump is, at least in part, the way we describe Trump, which may change from person to person and over time.

Mill (2012/1843) argued that proper names did not have connotation, only denotation, that is, Trump simply pointed to Trump: Trump = Trump.

Common names have a descriptive content. A table or chair has a set of descriptive content. A table is a flat, rectangular surface mounted on four legs and is used to… A chair might similarly be described but with shorter legs and may be used to… A table might have four legs or six or even three. The list for both objects has potentially no end as different styles and uses may come into being over time. This slipperiness of descriptions was resolved for Aristotle by the idea or essence of a table or chair, tableness or chairness. Although the idea, essence, or universal is in the particular for Aristotle, he does not tell us how we get from the particular chair to the notion of universal chairness. Mill saw tableness or chairness as an attribute of the name. For the descriptivist school (Russell 1992/1903; Frege 1949) the universalness or attribute problem is resolved by a list of essential descriptions. Russell extended the descriptivist theory to proper names such as Trump. For Frege, the proper name is its set of associated (connotation) descriptions. For Russell, the proper name is the set of descriptions by another name (Green 2007): Trump = set of descriptions = Trump. Trump would be an essential description such as the Republican presidential candidate running for office in 2016, a reality TV host, the CEO of Trump enterprises and the person who set up Trump University and became President of the USA in 2017. The difficulty is, just with the descriptions of the table or chair, the descriptions are not stable and open to the vagaries of contingent or random events and occurrences. If Donald Trump did not run for office in 2016, was not elected as president of the USA, or had not been a reality TV host or had not set up Trump University, he would still be Donald Trump.

When it comes to proper nouns, as brands may be considered, there is a difficulty of fixing any sort of referent to the changing descriptors. Names, brands, and identities are dependent upon the vagaries of moments of articulation (Lowrie 2007). Is Trump the name of the man who built a very profitable business empire, as his supporters say, or is Trump the name of the person who failed to pay his suppliers and fails to deliver the promises behind the name Trump University as his opponents say? Searle (1971) argued that a cluster of descriptors (see function/matheme 1) identifies the name and so we know who it is we are talking about when we talk about them, for example, when we talk about Trump. On the other hand, Dummett (1973) argued that there is a fundamental description (see function/matheme 2) and all the other descriptions are subordinated to the fundamental one. You see this notion in company and, indeed, higher education brands, where managers and administrators try and argue, that is, rhetorically persuade, often through some form of communication, in an attempt to get people to see the brand as the essential x without unwanted associations. The contrasting concepts can be summarized symbolically in the functions/mathemes as:

1. Name as cluster (the name is a function of the descriptions)
   $N = f(x)$
   where N = name, x = is a set of descriptors
2. Name as essentialist description
   $N = f(x + y)$
   where N = name, x = essential descriptor and y = subordinate set of descriptors

Organizations, for profit or not-for-profit, tend not to like function/matheme 1 as this allows too much freedom of movement in what a name might mean. Those who manage organizations and have an interest, often economic, in the name of an organization do not want citizens deciding what the name means. Organizations are essentially antidemocratic when it comes to how they wish to self-identify or be identified by name. Matheme 2 is often the preference of those given or made responsible for the organization's name. However, the preference is not to have any negative descriptors (connotation) that distract from the essential x and so we can re-write the function/matheme:

3. $N = f(x + y - z)$
   where N = name, x = essential descriptor, y = subordinate set of descriptors and z = descriptors with unwanted associations.

But there is no limit to the plurality of descriptions that could possibly describe a person or proper name, such as Trump, and no certainty about what he may do or become. Prior to the election result, there was the possibility that he may have won the presidential election, or that he may not have. We now know he did, but he may not have done—it could have turned out otherwise. He may build a wall across the US/Mexican border. He may not. What the name 'is' or means is contingent upon historical outcomes, many of which will be random and so no essential meaning to what his name may mean or come to mean. There is no essential, fundamental or fixed description that will describe Trump or indeed anyone or any object. There is no necessary event or occurrence that will result in a description. Trump may or may not have won the 2016 presidential election and so become different from what currently describes him. In the event, we know he did, but he may not have. The US president who built a wall across the USA/ Mexico border could become the descriptor by which everyone will know Trump and which will act as the essential referent for the man Trump. But he may not build a wall. Some other President could build such a wall. These descriptive statements are contingent, without any necessary condition and without any essentialist descriptor which refers to the man Trump, who is, was, and will still be Trump. Identifying descriptors are therefore contingent. When considering the identity of a person that identity is contingent and similarly the characteristics of that person, say that they are a great leader or are virtuous, is also contingent and non-essential to the identity. People may say that s/he is a great entrepreneur and that this is what we think of when we think of or describe this person, but this is only the contingent outcome. The contingent outcome could have been otherwise. The question arises, if descriptors are contingent and non-essential, what remains the same, that is, what is the x in $f(x)$? What remains the same about Trump or indeed any other name such as Harvard, Cambridge University, Loughborough University, Emerson College, or Trump University?

Some may argue that it is appearance, such as a physical appearance, that allows us to identify with the name. The Ivy of the Ivy League as it were. We may see Trump on TV and so know what he looks like and sounds like: that is Donald Trump. But the appearance of Trump could change owing to plastic surgery or an accident. It does not matter what he does or says or what opinions he holds on Monday or Friday, it would still be Donald Trump. It is the same with his appearance. When he was ten years old he was still Donald Trump. When he is 80, assuming he is alive, he will still be Donald Trump. Even if he were dead you could stand by his grave and say here lies Donald Trump. But in every one of these episodes or situations you are still referencing Donald Trump. It is the name itself that is the unifying element. The name is the common dominator of all the contingent events. Whatever we know about Donald Trump, however we know it, is determined by the name Donald Trump that acts as a rigid designator. If someone asked you who is Donald Trump, you may list a set of descriptors that point to the referent of the name Donald Trump, but this would depend on what is relevant at that time and in that context. The descriptors are contingent. It is the name, the rigid designator Donald Trump, that you are pointing to through the contingent descriptors, that rigidly designates the contingent content: x is a function of N, N is not a function of x. This theory, derived from the anti-descriptivist literature, is a reversal of the previous descriptivist view in matheme 1 where N is a function of x.

4. $x = f(N)$
    where x = contingent descriptors and N = the name as a rigid designator.

In this view, N becomes the organizing element for x, the description or discourse. We can expand this theory further. The contingent event, occurrence or description that is taken as relevant rather depends on the interests and desires of those involved in the discourse and so a determinant of a name is given by the unconscious desire to name in the conscious interests of those doing the naming. While the list of descriptions is historically contingent and available, the name is fixed in the desire to name according to interests that are situationally contingent. The descriptive list is contingent upon what N did, or what happened to N or will happen to N but only those selected to be part of N, that is, named as relevant, will form N and N *per se* will not have control over that selection process, although N does impact what may be available for selection. This raises another element for consideration in the linguistic function/matheme; the referent of N (the named person, object, or indeed person managing the object) does not control the discourse surrounding and contributing to the meaning of N (the name) but will select and invest into the name what is relevant (unconscious desire and conscious self-interest) as will everyone else with an interest in naming N:

5. $x = f(N + r + \text{ce})$
    where x = contingent descriptors, N = the name as a rigid designator, r = relevance (unconscious desire and conscious self-interest) and ce = contingent effect (lack of control of discourse).

It is important to recall from Chap. 3 that discourse is not simply communication but activity interpreted through language, that is, how people talk about behavior, events, and actions. So, the notion of randomness attached to events and occurrences is extended to how people speak about them. Brand managers or managers of names are therefore interested in managing or attempting to control events + discourse about events. This then gives rise to many alternative sample paths or random runs. Note, because the sample paths are initially random does not make the progression of each of these paths equivalent nor equally probable. We may scratch our heads in amazement when Trump does or says something, but as time progresses,

N becomes more fixed in and by the discourse of relevance pertaining to N and our best guesses improve around a possible range of outcomes. There is a narrowing of the field of discourse over time and events which tends toward less randomness. Moreover, discursive reactions from interested parties also become more predictable within the discourse and so while there is always a degree of randomness and lack of control over the discourse surrounding N, it will tend to or point to a more stable and fixed meaning. This partially fixed meaning, for it is always only partial, is a knot or node of meaning that structures future discourse relevant to N.

6. $x = f(N + r + \text{ce}) : n_{t0} \rightarrow n_t$
where x = contingent descriptors, N = the name as a rigid designator, r = relevance (unconscious desire and conscious self-interest), ce = contingent effect (lack of control of discourse), $: n_{t0} \rightarrow n_t$ = such that the initial naming (n_{t0}, i.e., baptism) maps to n_t (a nodal meaning formed over time).

In this way, the name N partially fixes discourse and tends toward a nodal point of meaning that further structures discourse around a new N (N_1). As the process or sequence repeatedly invests meaning in N, repetition of form *a la* Freud, and neo-Freudians, N changes but becomes even more unconsciously fixed as a nodal meaning with conscious interest also raised to further levels of the relevance of the invested meaning. The higher the level of conscious interest, the more likely the arousal of antagonism to those conscious interests that do not favor the relevant interests of others. N_1 replaces x (the contingent descriptors) as N becomes partially fixed. As discourse surrounding the name is modified by the name over time within the contingent field of discourse, the meaning of the name becomes partially fixed and acts as a quilting or nodal point, that is, begins to structure the meaning of the discourse. In talking or speaking about Trump, the name Trump will structure the talk about Trump. The name Trump organizes the discourse.

7. $N_1 = f(N_0 + r + \text{ce}) : n_{t0} \rightarrow n_t$
where N_1 = new nodal meaning through the use of the name, N_0 = the name as a rigid designator, r = relevance (unconscious desire and conscious self-interest), ce = contingent effect (lack of control of discourse), $: n_{t0} \rightarrow n_t$ = such that the initial naming (n_{t0}, i.e., baptism) maps to n_t (a nodal meaning formed over time).

The desire to name is fixed by unconscious desire and self-interest (conscious desire). The interest of the giver(s) of a name, the persons doing the naming, is contingent upon the situation of the giver(s)—those who conduct the baptism of any object or person, that is, talking about the subject or object and/or event in a way that suits the conscious interest and unconscious desire.

To emphasize, baptism is not merely the giving of a name at a family or religious ceremony early on in the life of a person. Rather, it is the continual giving of meaning to a name. The current meaning of the name Donald Trump is not the meaning of the name given to him at or near his birth, although this was the original rigid designator, but rather the composition, writing, and speaking meaning into the name occurred over time. The name is invested with meaning. Creating names is a linguistic investment for dressing the person or object with desire and self-interest. The identity of Donald Trump is not so much of his own making but what others invest in his name by way of a list of descriptions drawing on what he says and does within contingent events for the promotion of self-interest and the fulfillment of unconscious desires. Over time the list of given descriptors that determine the referent, in this case the name Trump, will change. Some may no longer apply while new descriptors are formed. In all this, the name Trump still refers to the same man, although even the gender could change, Trump is still Trump despite the change in x, that is, the descriptors. It would seem the only constant in all this process of change is the act of naming.

For Laclau (2005), the act of naming is not only contingent but the name can become an empty signifier, by which he means that the signifier is emptied of particular meaning. This occurs in function/matheme 7. The name no longer signifies a particular person, Trump in this example, but an entire domain of discourse. We have moved from the particular to the universal. The name is a brand. A signifier is emptied of particular meaning by (a) overdetermination of the signifier: people 'stuffing' in meaning in the form of descriptors. As it is only people who name the act of naming and re-naming is always in favor of the unconscious desire and conscious self-interest of those doing the naming. Laclau points out that overdetermination is only a move toward emptying the signifier, because overdetermining the signifier results in ambiguity of what is named. In other words, there are multiple possible referents that the signifier (or name) can point to: Donald Trump the loving father, Trump the president of the USA, Trump the business leader, besides many other contradictory and competing referents. This is not an empty signifier but a floating signifier.

Following on from (a) above, it is the next step in Laclau's logic which determines an empty signifier: (b) the formation of frontiers of exclusion around floating signifiers. He extends Saussure's theory of language as a system of differences to a signifying system (discourse). All identities are purely relational. If all signifying acts are relational then the entire system of signification is necessary for the act of signification, that is, the totality of discourse is inherent in any single act of signification.

The possibility of a system is the possibility of limits (to the system) and as Laclau points out, following Hegel, to think of a limit is to think of what is beyond the limit and so in this sense a limit is no limit at all. Thus, in thinking about limits of a signifying or discursive system it is impossible to signify the limit. The result is a paradox: what constitutes the signifying system also constitutes what is outside signification, but you can only signify within the system of signification and not outside it. As a signifying totality is a system of differences, difference = identity, thence the signifying system and differences cannot be the limits of the system. The system cannot then have a positive constitutive formation.

All elements of signification exclude. So, while we may have a set of floating descriptors that are formed (by people) to coalesce in the name of Trump, the name is a set of equivalences, a common dominator for all these descriptors, that also acts as a form of exclusion, that is, what is denied access to the set of equivalence in order to form differences from other names that allows the name Trump to form an identity. What is within the name Trump as signifier falls within the discursive brackets and outside the discursive domain brackets are differences that identify Trump as a distinct signifier, that is, name (Fig. 4.2).

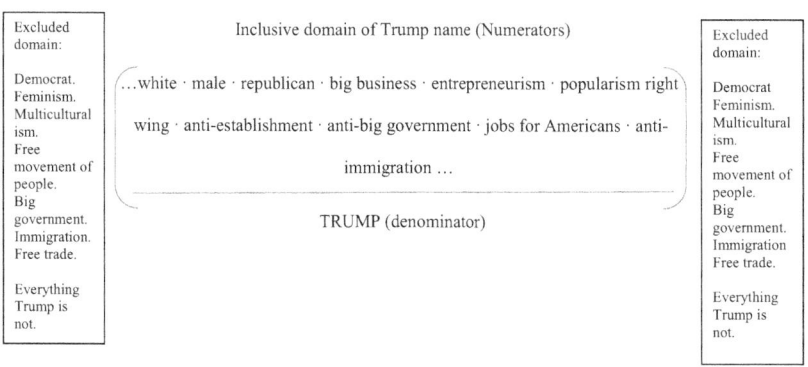

Fig. 4.2 Illustrative inclusive and exclusion domains for Trump name
Source: Author

Thus, differences in naming (everything that is not Trump: $x \neq$ Trump) are equivalent in forming a frontier of exclusion from the name. It is this process of signification, that is, the making of equivalences that exclude and so act as a limit that is formative in the production of empty signifiers. The name Trump is an empty signifier not simply because anything can fit into the numerator but that the denominator, the name itself, sets a limit. But in setting a limit, that is, excluding what is not in the name, all that is excluded is equivalent by being named as that which is excluded.

For Laclau, if the exclusionary dimension of discourse were eliminated or sufficiently weakened, this would eliminate the possibility of a frontier to a signifying chain and so no difference would be apparent and with this no possibility of identification and therefore no meaning. Without the exclusionary dimension, there would be no limit to the signifying system. Exclusion collapses differences within what is excluded thereby making what is excluded equivalent in its exclusion. The exclusion thereby sets limits, delineating what is not excluded and in doing this establishes formative limits to signification and the production of empty signifiers. Exclusion sets limits which produce equivalential dimensions within the exclusion, and this allows for identification not only for what is excluded but for what is included. This is the social production of empty signifiers and may be applied to names such as democracy, justice, diversity, entrepreneur, and excellence. These are not just names floating with ambiguity but linguistic denominators. Brands such as Harvard or Oxford are linguistic denominators, that is, particular names that designate the fantasy form of 'best' in higher education.

The act of discourse in general and naming in particular is both a conscious and unconscious process. The unconscious is not directly representable. Only through such elements as distortions is dream content given form and signification. In dream content, what is signified is made equivalent to other signifiers and so hidden through combinations and associations that are not immediately recognizable and so the referent is 'blurred'. In other words, the equivalence of signifiers is stretched within the discourse of the dream/unconscious. The relationship between signifiers and a particular referent is broken as it is unclear what is signified. The recognized differences are removed and without difference a sign loses identity. In the exclusionary process, whatever is excluded is identified, made different, but what is on the other side of that exclusion and difference is made the same and to the extent of the equivalence, identity is combinatorial and fused with particular identity lost in the equivalence.

We have an emptying of differences and without difference signification becomes void. Where the process is sufficiently well-developed the result is an empty signifier. So the difference between floating signifiers and empty signifiers is, for Laclau, one of radical exclusions resulting in the collapse of an equivalent chain into signification. What is in the radical equivalence chain is empty of content and the chain *per se* is the signifying element, that is, fused combinations. The name Trump becomes a floating signifier as the name as a referent for the man Donald Trump is made ambiguous through the constant reposition of what he stands for. The name only becomes an empty signifier when all that the name signifies is a cluster of contradictory descriptors held together by a radical exclusion, which anchors the identity of the cluster of contradictory signs within the equivalent chain that is the exclusion. The limits set by such radical exclusions are not set by Trump or indeed anyone else but rather by the name acting as a fantasy (a form of fulfillment) for desires. In the case of the name Trump, the desires of those who feel disenfranchised and demand (conscious discursive act of self-interest) an alternative, that is, the alternative as a wish or desire for a better life or way of life made conscious by the act of investing in a name, in this case Trump. As in the naming of Trump, it is also in the naming of the American Dream and the naming of higher education pertaining to the dream. The reason Trump University cannot be a higher education brand is because (as empty signifiers) each has different exclusionary dimensions that provide identity for numerators made equivalent by their respective denominators—Trump and higher education. People have invested differently in each of the names.

In *Hegemony and Socialist Strategy*, Laclau and Mouffe (1985) draw on Rosa Luxemburg's notion of the working class. The unity of the working class is not determined by any positive campaign or movement attempting to build unity but rather by the accumulated effects of internal splits in all demands. A demand is partial because it is perceived not only as a specific demand for an object but also because that object is in opposition to or an antagonism toward that which blocks the demand for the object. For those 'piling' into the name Trump and in doing so effectively re-naming, that is, adding to the overdetermination of the name and thus making it float with ambiguity, it is not merely the desire for a specific demand (in the name Trump) but an antagonism to a broader system (we demand better than x) which is also named. Regarding branding higher education, the theoretical implication is apparent; branding higher education is naming the particular institution as better than others and so making those who attend that particular institution equal in their superiority to those who did not have the opportunity to go to that institution and making those who did not attend equal in their inferiority. Each necessitates the other and depends on that other for its very identity. There is no way of knowing what is better than or superior to x without knowing what is worse than or inferior to x. Naming brings x into being.

All demands are specific and conscious while simultaneously antagonistic and different. Demands are also unconscious in their equivalent confrontation with the perceived repression which gives rise to a sharper identification and so identity of the repression. In this sense, unity and identity is a negative formation—opposite to the common enemy. To fight against something is to name and identify. What is in a name is also what is outside it. Indeed, what is in a name is also what is antagonistic to it. Brands and identities are internally divided, but while toothpaste and detergent do not get much of our mental time, brands pertaining to higher education do. We worry for our own and our children's education because it plays into life chances and survival. The differential demand for brand x of higher education is specific, but the equivalent demand is the desire to survive and be free from the repression that being poorly educated (and so often poor) delivers, and to be 'better than' the previous generation and others in the community.

However, one cannot be free, and so emancipated, from whatever is repressive without having something to be free from. Any act or call for emancipation necessitates the repression from which we desire to be free. The stronger the desire, the stronger the call for action, the stronger the action for emancipation, the more the repression is named into existence. With the growth in the call for diversity, the greater the opposition to diversity comes into stark relief. By forming and expanding the chain of equivalence across diversity, the more it will float as a signifier with additional particular meaning advocated by additional groups with a desire for and interest in diversity. Those pursuing their desire for diversity will align with multifarious groups with a common interest in diversity. African Americans may call for equal pay, equality of opportunity, education, and social justice. Trade unions may call for equal pay, workers' rights, and education. LGBT groups may equally call for similar rights and social justice. Each of these groups can have diversity as a common denominator. Each and all re-name diversity and so the numerator expands to fill the meaning of diversity as the denominator which provides the equivalence for each of the particular demands in the numerator (Fig. 4.3).

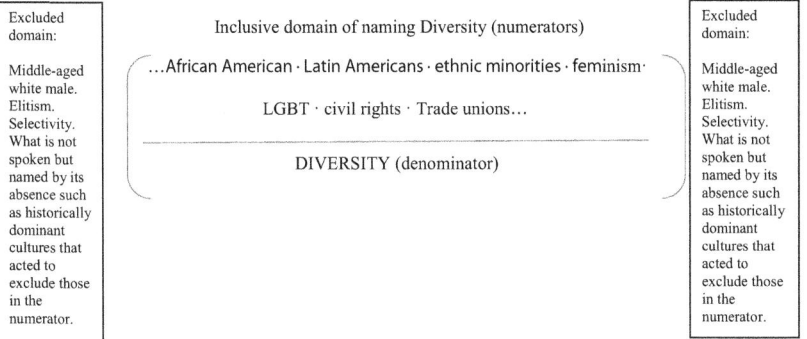

Fig. 4.3   Illustrative inclusive and exclusion domains for diversity
Source: Author

Not all names and descriptors can be dropped into the numerator, even when logic can make a case for it. For example, 'poor-white trash', a particular divisive appellation, will not easily slip and slide through processes of naming in diversity. Despite this group's exclusion from equality of opportunities and higher education, little is done to spread actions of diversity to this group. The reason is because the naming of this group aligns too closely with the naming of a white dominant culture. To have this group included in the numerator of demands through diversity would unpick the nodal meaning or racial discrimination. The numerator is no longer divisible by ethnicity although it still would be by gender, trade unionism, and sexual orientation all of which are currently named into diversity along with ethnicity. The exclusion of this group from diversity in part explains 'Trumpism' by way of jobs for Americans. If diversity is to be emancipatory then it must include all groups. But if all groups are included then what is left outside the equivalent chain of diversity that will give diversity its identity. Presently, diversity ≠ diversity if the numerator is governed by a dominator that is itself discriminatory, that is, it excludes and so negates itself. In this sense diversity is the new opium of the people without a conscious realization. Diversity is a desire for emancipation without a self-conscious logic that encapsulates the self-interest of all groups and so will collapse under the weight of its own contradiction. To a degree this is what is currently playing out in notions of 'Black Lives Matter' and the playing up of the 'value gap' between white people and people of color (Bernstein et al. 2016). Poor people, of which African Americans are a considerable element, are likely to be discriminated against in terms of K–12 education, health care, and a lack of higher education all of which also contribute (Case and Deaton 2015) to mortality rates among white non-Hispanic women.

Frontiers are created as the chain of equivalence expands and cancels differences between groups in their demand to be free from their form of repression. As the equivalential chain expands, a common enemy is formed. With more and more groups 'piling' into the equivalential chain, moderated by the named dominators such as diversity, the following questions arise, who is the common enemy outside the diversity chain of equivalence that gives diversity its identity? Is the white middle-aged male or white 'dominant' culture the agent(s) of repression without whom diversity cannot find identity? I have heard administration spokespersons and students naming the classical literature canon as dead white males. I have heard female clinical (practitioner) faculty complain about white middle-aged men who exclude female entrepreneurs from the 'canon' of entrepreneurship. The entire faculty in my place of work were subjected to chants by students, overlooked by highly paid administrators of the office of diversity standing aloft in the balcony, 'you are racist and you know it'. Are white middle-aged men being corralled into an identity they neither desire nor consciously want? Of course, it would be impossible for the white middle-aged male to know for sure whether he is unconsciously a racist as none can easily get to our unconscious desires on our own. Not that this matters in terms of the diversity discourse, as the individual has little if any say in the determination of the chain of equivalence moderated by the naming and re-naming of diversity. Without a common enemy, a discursive point of difference, the naming of diversity cannot achieve identity. In this sense, the equivalence chain of diversity has a limit beyond which some form of Other must be named and identified as that which is antagonistic to diversity. Under such discursive conditions no one is emancipated. All that results is that you create a new 'enemy' under a different form of exclusion—a new group for persecution. Discriminatory abuse simply shifts to a new domain. New divisions, new components of diversity play into these structural failings. Naming and branding necessarily excludes and those doing the naming and branding need the exclusion for the identification of the name and brand.

BIBLIOGRAPHY

Aaker, D. A. (1996). *Building Strong Brands*. New York: The Free Press.

Barnett, R. (2000). *Realizing the University in an Age of Supercomplexity*. Buckingham: The Society for Research into Higher Education.

Bernstein, L., Hull, A., & Kindy, K. (2016, April 10). A New Divide in American death. *The Washington Post*. Retrieved from http://www.washingtonpost.com/sf/national/2016/04/10/a-new-divide-in-american-death/

Carey, K. (2015). *The End of College: Creating the Future of Learning and the University of Everywhere*. New York: Riverhead Books.

Case, A., & Deaton, A. (2015). Rising Morbidity and Mortality in Midlife Among White Non-Hispanic Americans in the 21st Century. *PNAS, 12*(49), 15078–15083.

Chapleo, C. (2015). Brands in Higher Education. *International Studies of Management & Organization, 45*(2), 150–163.

Dewey, J. (1916/1997). *Democracy and Education: An Introduction to the Philosophy of Education*. New York: The Free Press.

Dummett, M. (1973). *Frege: Philosophy of Language*. London: Duckworth.

Frege, G. (1949). On Sense and Nominatum. Translated by Herbert Feigl in *Readings in Philosophical Analysis*, edited by Herbert Feigl and Wilfrid Sellars. London: Appleton Century Crofts.

Green, K. (2007). *Bertrand Russell, Language and Linguistic Theory*. London: Continuum.

Keller, K. L. (2003). *Strategic Brand Management: Building, Measuring and Managing Brand Equity*. Upper Saddle River: Prentice Hall.

Keller, K. L., & Lehmann, D. R. (2006). Brands and Branding: Research Findings and Future Priorities. *Marketing Science, 25*(6), 740–759.

Kerr, C. (1963/2001). *The Uses of the University*. Cambridge, MA: Harvard University Press.

Kirpke, S. (1981). *Naming and Necessity*. Oxford: Blackwell Publishing.

Laclau, E. (2005). *On Populist Reason*. London: Verso.

Laclau, E., & Mouffe, C. (1985). *Hegemony and Socialist Strategy: Towards a Radical Democratic Politics*. London: Verso.

Lowrie, A. (2007). Branding Higher Education: Equivalence and Difference in Developing University Identity. *Journal of Business Research, 60*(9), 990–999.

Mill, J. S. (2012[1843]). *A System of Logic, Ratiocinative and Inductive: Being a Connective View of the Principles of Evidence, and the Methods of Scientific Investigation*. New York: Cambridge University Press.

Newman, J. H. (1905/2012). *The Idea of a University*. New York: Forgotten Books.

Peters, T., & Waterman, R. H. (1982). *In Search of Excellence: Lessons from America's Best-Run Companies*. New York: Warner Books.

Russell, B. (1992 [1903]). *The Principles of Mathematics*. London: Routledge.

Searle, J. (1971). *Philosophy of Language*. Oxford: Oxford University Press.

Slaughter, S., & Leslie, L. L. (1997). *Academic Capitalism: Politics, Policies and the Entrepreneurial University*. Baltimore: The John Hopkins University Press.

Sternberg, R. J. (2016). *What Universities Can Be: A New Model for Preparing Students for Active Concerned Citizenship and Ethical Leadership*. Ithaca: Cornell University.

Stigler, G. J. (1942). The Extent and Bases of Monopoly. *The American Economic Review, 32*(Supplement), 1–22.

Taleb, N. N. (2007). *Fooled by Randomness: The Hidden Role of Chance in Life and in the Markets*. London: Penguin Books.

Williams, R., & Maktoba, O. (2014). Applying Brand Management to Higher Education Through the Use of Brand Flux Model – The Case of Arcadia University. *Journal of Marketing for Higher Education, 24*(2), 224–242.

Wimsatt, W. K., & Beardsley, M. C. (1958). The Intentional Fallacy. In *The Verbal Icon*. New York: Noonday Press.

Wittgenstein, L. (2000[1953]). *Philosophical Investigations* (3rd ed). Oxford: Blackwell.

CHAPTER 5

The Shattered Brand Fantasy

Desire is *form*ative in the constitution of need, want, and demand. While such a proposition may appear more obvious to those inclined to give credence to psychoanalysis, it is long-standing in the writings of some hard-headed economic fundamentalists.

> The commodity is, first of all, an external object, a thing which through its qualities satisfies human needs of whatever kind. The nature of these needs, whether they arise, for example, from the stomach, or the imagination, makes no difference[2]. [Note 2 reads] Desire implies want; it is the appetite of the mind, and as natural as hunger to the body ... The greatest number (of things) have their value from supplying the wants of the mind.
>
> (Marx 1990, p. 1)

The external object is invested with meaning and so value, often with monetary implications. In other words, the value of the object is written into being. To reiterate, this does not mean that the object does not exist but rather more importantly that what it means and its value is given significance to us as a thing of the mind through a comparative lens.

Trump University has its meaning and value developed in the discourse surrounding and infiltrating the names Trump, University, and Trump University, all of which become organizing and structuring elements for the discourse around the names. The argument here is that brands are commodities with names which we similarly invest with meaning and values

© The Author(s) 2018   91
A. Lowrie, *Understanding Branding in Higher Education*,
Marketing and Communication in Higher Education,
DOI 10.1057/978-1-137-56071-1_5

to a greater or lesser extent just like any other name, and the degree of investment depends on (a) unconscious desire and (b) conscious desire, that is, the conscious form of the unconscious desire. Following this logic, we arrive at the theoretical proposition that brands are expressions of desire.

Theoretical Proposition 1: TP$_1$ = Brands Are Expressions of Desire

What we desire does not come from the ether of brain cells firing off across space that we can study on a picture of the brain, but rather the human mind developed in social relationships where objects are connected with subjects. Value and meaning, and the meaning of value are social, and therefore our cognitive development and survival depends on others. Others are what we are—we take our value(s), learn the meaning of value, whether that is the value of avoiding the saber-toothed tiger or getting a higher education, from others, and value meaning from what others predicate.

> By means of the value-relation, therefore, the natural form of commodity B becomes the value-form of commodity A, in other words the physical body of commodity B becomes a mirror for the value of commodity A[19]. [Note 19 reads] In a certain sense, a man is in the same situation as a commodity. As he neither enters into the world in possession of a mirror, nor as a Fichtean philosopher who can say 'I am I', a man first sees and recognizes himself in another man. Peter only relates to himself as a man through his relation to another man, Paul, in whom he recognizes his likeness. [And again, in note 22]. Determinations of reflection of this kind are altogether very curious. For instance, one man is king only because other men stand in relation of subjects to him. They, on the other hand, imagine that they are subjects because he is king. (Marx 1990, pp. 144 and 149)

Marx prefigures a major socio-psychological conceptualization of desire and identity as a function of human development in the mirror stage *a la* Freud, later Cooley from a sociological perspective, and again Lacan following Freud.

That value and meaning are socially relative is evident in Dewey's (1916/1997) ideas on learning as communitarian and the basis for a democratic society. Cooley's (1922) looking glass self is the identification of human and social justice and order with the reflection of ourselves in others and so the nature of identity is in the other, which facilitates self-reflection.

Why is it, for instance, that such ideas as brotherhood and the sentiment of equal right are now so generally extended to all classes of men? Primarily, I think, because all classes have become imaginable, by acquiring power and means of expression. He whom I imagine without antipathy becomes my brother. If we feel that we must give aid to another, it is because that other lives and strives in our imaginations, and so is a part of ourselves. The shallow separation of self and other in common speech obscures the extreme simplicity and naturalness of such feelings. If I come to imagine a person suffering wrong it is not "altruism" that makes me wish to right that wrong, but simple human impulse. He is my life, as really and immediately as anything else. His symbol arouses a sentiment which is no more his than mine. (Cooley 1922, p. 148)

Our cognitive abilities depend upon the communitarian other (people) without whom no cognitive advantage over other species would develop (Pinker 2010; Tooby and DeVore 1987). Without other people, there would be nothing of the self. As pointed out by Pinker (2010) and Tooby and DeVore (1987), the vulnerability of the human infant and the time taken to reach adulthood gives rise to (a) the child's dependence on others for its survival and (b) a community of carers within and beyond the family who will teach and socialize the child.

Lacan draws on Freud to develop the concept of desire and the Other in framing the object of desire. Lacan argues that the object that people think (conscious desire) will fulfill their desire is a misrecognition of the object; the only object of desire is *objet petit a*, which is the cause of desire. The human subject is born in a state of helplessness and depends on the Other for survival. An infant's cries (demand) calls the Other to administer to his/her needs. But the presence of the Other in seeing to the infant's demands comes to symbolize love. After the need, which was articulated in demand, that is, the infant's cries, is satisfied, the craving for love is left unsatisfied, and this leftover demand that is unsatisfied is desire. As the child develops into an adult s/he continues to seek satisfaction for the initial desire for love and will mis(recognize) other objects that potentially fulfill that desire. This Freudian notion of desire, misconceived by Belk et al. (2003) is develop by Lacan within a broader theoretical framework, which encapsulates his earlier concepts set out in graphical form, see 'The Subversion of the Subject and the Dialectic of Desire in the Freudian Unconscious' in Lacan (2006), but developed over his entire career as a psychoanalyst. The explication of desire, which 'first appears as a lack' (Lacan 1998, S11, p. 236), is not a relation to an object nor simply a relation to a lack, that is, the unsatisfied demand for the love of the Other, but also that 'Man's desire is the desire of the Other' and the 'desire of the Other's desire' (Lacan 1998, S11, p. 235). From Lacan's seminar XX onward, *objet petit a* is not just a cause of desire but a cause of anxiety, that is, anxiety about being/not being desired.

For Lacan, the concept of demand is not simply a demand for satisfaction through the fulfilling of a need but rather demand has a double function. Demand pulls on something other than the motivation for satisfaction—the primordial relationship. As the infant is entirely dependent upon the mother for satisfying its biological need for food through demands (cries) for food, the satisfaction of hunger, it is not only a demand for the satisfaction of hunger but a demand for the proof of love. A strong biological urge is coupled with the psychological one. In this sense, demand constitutes the Other, initially the mothering figure, as having the privilege of satisfying needs and the power to deprive the infant of what alone satisfies the need. While the infant's need for food is satisfied, that is, it is no longer hungry after feeding, desire is the articulation of the demand, and so desire is shaped by the presence of the mothering figure who administers to the infant's need but because of the impossibility of constantly attending to the child, desire is born by the presence or absence of the mothering figure. The desire goes beyond the satisfaction of the need for food by symbolizing the Other's (mother's) love. As the Other/mother cannot provide continuous and unconditional love, which the infant craves, this craving remains unsatisfied and this becomes desire.

> This is why desire is neither the appetite for satisfaction nor the demand for love, but the difference that results from the subtraction of the first from the second, the very phenomenon of their splitting (*Spaltung*). (Lacan 2006, p. 580)

The object of desire can never be obtained because it does not exist as an object. Desire is the remainder after subtracting (the appetite for) satisfaction from demand (for love). Desire is D − S and does not consist in being fulfilled but is the continual reproduction of the demand for love (for the Other) less the appetite for satisfaction. This leads to the second theoretical proposition.

Theoretical Proposition 2: TP$_2$ = The Object of Desire Cannot Be Obtained

In a sense, we are what we demand.

By means of demand, the whole past begins to open up, right down to earliest infancy. The subject has never done anything but demand, he could not have survived otherwise, and we take it from there. (Lacan 2006, p. 516)

We can be understood and analyzed in terms of our demands, which are the (mis)recognized and symbolized forms of a conscious desire born of our unconscious desire, that is, the continual reproductive process of desire minus satisfaction, and so theoretical proposition 3.

Theoretical Proposition 3: TP₃ = Desire Can Never Be Satisfied

TP₃ is, of course, a marketer's dream. For higher education, the desire of life-long learning is a marketing objective constituted as an object of (mis) recognition constituted in desire and anxiety. Accordingly, subjects continually strive to become the object of another's desire and so commodities have no intrinsic worth until desired by another *a la* Marx. The notion of supply and demand co-mingled with looking glass objects reflect our desire to be in demand by and be satisfied by the Other. Initially the mother but later other institutions on which our imagined survival depends. The concept of desire along with anxiety (of not being desired) are central platforms in marketing higher education. For example, see Carey (2015) where increasing the price is a way of reflecting comparative value and easing anxiety about purchase and the merit of learning content and deliverables in terms of future prospects. Without anxiety, and playing on that anxiety in communications with students, there is no basis for accreditation, for example, (see Lowrie 2008; Lowrie and Willmott 2009).

Brands are commodity objects that we demand through a comparative lens. Mostly, and contrary to Dichter, these are not objects of tyranny. This is not to say that commodity objects in demand configured by biological need are not also objects of the mind. But rather more importantly that the 'need of the mind' (Marx 1990) is configured to a greater or lesser level of desire and anxiety given how connected the brand is with our sense of survival. Higher education brands are going to play into our desires and anxieties much more than a brand of diapers, albeit that diapers are important. Brands are symptoms of our desires but some brands are more symptomatic of unconscious desires that others. Contrary to the theory put forward by consumer cultural theorists who make much of the irrational and emotional behavior of many consumers, the consumer is perfectly rational in her or his choices pertaining to the desire that drives those choices. It is perfectly normal and rational to (mis)recognize the object of desire when laboring under the desire (D − S) for the Other's desire. In most cases this is of no interest to the psychoanalyst. Nor is the psychoanalyst likely to be of much use in getting to the 'depths' of soap powder (for example). Higher education, however, plays much heavier on desire and anxiety (of not being desired) because the object (mis)recognition weighs on life chances. Just in case you do not get this in the natural course of daily living, you will get it from your immediate family, your broader family, your school, your friends, and of course all the institutions directly or indirectly associated with education. This gives rise to the fourth theoretical proposition.

Theoretical Proposition 4: TP$_4$ = The Brand Is a Symptom of Our Dis│ease with Our Desire

The barred word dis│ease conveys the Lacanian notion that the human subject split, in varying degrees, in pursuit of their desire is simultaneously (a) at ease with (b) not at ease with, (c) (mis)recognizes the object of desire, and (d) in some cases the desire for the object may be considered unhealthy. For example, life-long learning may be considered healthy when undertaken within moderation, but the pursuit of life-long learning with a high frequency of course-taking which affects other important relationships may be unhealthy on two counts: (a) the behavior may be or become an obsession, (b) individuals may feel that there is little or no choice but to take a course/obtain qualifications in order to earn a living and/or hold onto a living, and this may be considered a form of social or institutional abuse and so constitutes an abusive relationship. Similarly, feeling that you have to check your email at 10 p.m. and answer those student requests is a form of dysfunctional working relationship if not abuse. Because the promotional discourse of learning is constituted as a good thing, this does not mean that it is necessarily good. What is named and invested into the life-long learning is not devoid of the interests of others who do not always have the individual's interests in mind. Roulette College, heavily dependent on student income, is a case in point. To generalize, universities and colleges across the USA, indeed across the world, encourage learning for the sake of learning; an absurdity than can be interpreted as learning for the sake of institutional income. Although it is impossible to avoid in current market structures, once the college indulges in brand naming it is a commodity object chasing the desires of consumers who cannot but (mis)recognize what is on offer. The object of desire that the student buys is not the object of desire that the college sells or the faculty member delivers.

There is no easy solution to the above problem of the (mis)recognition of desires by parties in an exchange process, not least because meaning is not private, something to be owned, but public (Wittgenstein 2000 [1953]; Wimsatt and Beardsley 1958). I have argued elsewhere that the unit of analysis in a textual approach to research is meaning (Lowrie 2016). Words carry meaning but meaning is not equivalent to words. Meanings are slippery and made up by people on an ad hoc basis often with a great deal of post hoc rationalization regarding what is or was meant.

A simple illustration of the slipperiness of meaning is the discourse of entrepreneurship as a route to the recruitment of more consumers (discussed above). The word entrepreneurship in higher education illustrates a very important distinction *between words and meaning*: while the word(s) remain the same, the meaning of the word(s) can be reconfigured through chains of logic and made consistent over time and context, or the meaning can be altered by different chains of logic. Meaning is the chain of logic and so the unit of analysis is the chain of logic. The acceptability of teaching entrepreneurship becomes a metaphor to promote an entirely different agenda by rationalizing the signifier as carrying equivalent yet different meaning: entrepreneurship = success in terms of wealth for students reading the course description, while entrepreneurship = additional fee income for college administrators whereas for course developers/instructors/writers of course descriptions pertaining to entrepreneurship, entrepreneurship = kudos and popularity among the two previous audiences. However, only by knowing the contextual argument and the economic situation of universities can we appreciate the chain of logic knitting together the function of teaching entrepreneurship in colleges and universities.

Thus, the logic: entrepreneurship = success = wealth for one group = increased income = kudos, none of which is subjected to critical debate by college administrators but contextually stated in the discourse, can be put to the test by the analysis of text and context. It seems to me that administrators are not so much interested in entrepreneurship as they are income. Entrepreneurship as a signifier has the potential to incorporate the pursuit of wealth, if not the 'love of money', in a way that is more acceptable to the liberal reader. Instructors, especially if they are not fully aware of the context, are willing to (mis)recognize the object of desire the student is chasing, such as money and status, and fail to offer a critical analysis and a higher intellectual understanding of the phenomenon of entrepreneurship. Instructors are often too willing to become an institutional agent working without reflection on their own desires in relation to the desires of students. There is little in the way of attempting a critical understanding of the meaning of what is taught.

Meaning cannot be controlled because there is no such thing as a repeated meaning. Meanings are always different and as meanings are always different then a frequency distribution of agreed meanings is non-sense. Consider Derrida's (1976, 1978) readings of texts as identifying conceptual opposites: speech-writing, body-soul, literal-metaphorical, signifier-signified, and so on. Derrida subjected these oppositions to an internal critique that 'destabilized' the pairings. He then asked the question, what makes these oppositions possible? His answers to this question pushes the theory of language beyond the binary structure of signifier = signified (word = meaning) or indeed signifier = any signified set. Derrida's deconstruction produces what he called *différance*. Derrida's theory of deconstruction illustrates how the signifier relates to other signifiers and not just the signified. As signifiers trigger other signifiers the possibility of an infinite chain of signifiers undermines the notion of a fixed meaning. There is a continual deferring to other signifiers and differing of meaning; a perpetual slippage of meaning from signifier to signifier or moment to moment in the linguistic chain. Meaning is not fixed by the binary structure word = meaning but rather the meaning of a word is open to endless possible meanings.

Pinker points out the magnitude of meaning that linguistic combinations can generate.

> Like other digital combinatorial systems in biology (RNA, DNA, proteins), language can generate vast numbers of structured combinations. The number of possible sentences (each corresponding to a distinct message) is proportional to the number of words that may appear in a position in a sentence raised to the power of the length of the sentence. With an approximate geometric mean of ten choices available at every position in a sentence, one can estimate that a typical English speaker can easily produce or comprehend at least 10^{20} distinct sentences. (Pinker 2010, p. 8994)

In some ways, it is a wonder we manage to say anything to one another that resembles agreed meaning. However, as Pinker (2007, p. 75) points out, language is not a free for all and 'our ability to stretch a construction to new verbs in the heat of a conversation or text does not mean that the results are accepted as normal sentences. Speakers differ in how easily they stomach the various generalizations that other speakers make, depending perhaps on their age, birthplace, subculture, or even personality.' In other words, despite the endless potential for *différance,* the slippage of language is limited by context, but context also changes and so opens up language to further *différance.* The slippage of meaning is so extensive that it is meaningless to claim that names like entrepreneurship mean the same thing to different people, such as those interested in generating income from consumers (college administrators) and those consumers (students) interested in generating wealth for themselves, whose desires run counter to one another. The slanting of self-interest can be quite nuanced. The choice of a single word to promote our desires by manipulating the desires of others such as the use of success rates as opposed to survival rates when selling a college course on entrepreneurship, as in the case of Roulette College, can make for the difference between ethical and unethical behavior. It may well be argued by administrators and the promoters of how to be an entrepreneur at Roulette College that no harm is meant and no one is deliberately misleading the consumer. But we can see from Chap. 4 that language is never neutral, that it is not private but public, and that you cannot control how people will interpret a name because both the unconscious and conscious desires are to invest in the name in a way that will promote your desires and your self-interest. Therefore, names such as the N word are divisive and the naming of Black Lives Matter is also divisive. The name will come back to bite you and despite the strength of the political correctness discourse, people will not necessarily accept your intention because the meaning of the name is contingent not necessary. This gives rise to the brand concept that you cannot control brand meaning.

Theoretical Proposition 5: TP_5 = You Cannot Control Brand Meaning

How we invest in naming and so branding in higher education, whether for courses or institutional name, there is a greater propensity for connecting to our desires for survival and indeed surviving well, that is, being a success in the eyes of the Other so that the Other will desire us, is of much greater importance and of greater ethical concern than other commodity brands. Our higher education not only plays into our success in the labor market but in our success in mating, that is, finding a similar partner (see Chap. 4 of Arum and Roksa 2014). Colleges and universities are not only institutions of the intellect, they are 'breeding grounds' that match potential type with type, and so act not only as a break in social mobility but as giant social mirrors reflecting social commodity type A to, from and with social commodity B *a la* Marx, Cooley, and Lacan. In a multicollege social context, points A and B are split into multifarious parallax positions (Žižek 2006) by ontological lenses and psychological mirrors in which we see ourselves through others. Named investments such as Ivy Leagues or Community Colleges are scattered seeds of value reflections fed and watered by the desire to be (mis)recognized in the parallax hall of shattered-brand reflections. From the proliferation of liberal arts course offerings to the newly created degree in x, further riven by layers of better and lesser named value, the once perceived transparent idea of higher education lies in shards. The claim to transparency, and it was only ever a claim, is unsustainable. And given higher education's position in connection to desire (see Chap. 2), everyone wants a bit of it in the belief that the shattered fantasy will deliver them to the American Dream that they see, hear, and read in the parallax reflections that others have. This takes us to our sixth theoretical proposition.

Theoretical Proposition 6: TP_6 = Higher Education Brands Are Distribution Mechanisms for Desire

The final theoretical proposition is derived from the argument of Chap. 4 but left to be stated explicitly here because it is the proposition that is likely to be of most interest to those who care about higher education's purpose and its emancipatory potential. Despite its long-abused imaginary for its emancipatory capacity, higher education has been commodified into a fantasy form and this in part is due to its historical purpose, that is, it was defined and built not for everyone but rather a homogeneous group of young, white men. Not in spite of the design, but because of the design, everyone desires a piece of what it can deliver. But there is a logical flaw here. What many saw and aspired to in getting a university education was taken as causal, that is, a higher education resulted in a 'good' life, while in fact it was the other way around. Those who had a good life and came from wealthy backgrounds went to higher education. In other words, a higher education was an effect not a cause. This is not to say that higher education is not without financial benefit, but it is to say that the mechanisms of supply and demand and so wages are likely to be curtailed as plainly visible in Chart 3.3. The more of the population we educate to a higher level, the less financial benefit will accrue to those who have it. Females do not earn as much as males. Again, this must not to be taken to mean that higher education is not a huge benefit (see Fig. 4.1), simply that the financial benefit for the individual will reduce as the supply of graduates increases. The benefit to society will increase the more people in society are higher educated. The cost of higher education could fall per capita as those involved in its production will find that their salaries decrease because there will be a greater supply of doctoral-educated people who desire to pursue a career in higher education. Many will most likely want to pursue a career in higher education because they derive a great deal of pleasure, happiness, and fulfillment from contributing to the well-being and education of others in our society. Counter intuitively, the route to cutting the cost of higher education is to educate more people to doctoral level. For my purpose of developing a theory of branding higher education the above argument has two major implications that can be extracted from the seventh and last proposition.

Theoretical Proposition 7: TP7 = Brand Meaning Is a Retroactive Activity

The first implication, and this is mostly derived from Chap. 4, is that meaning is named into any object or indeed subject. The second and perhaps the most significant is that higher education does not have to be a poorly designed institution based on the notion of education for the elite few and which has ended up feeding the fantasy of entire populations demanding the 'same as them'. While the desire is all too natural, a desire to have a higher education for the few is not a sustainable institution for the many. Legislators with a desire and interest to higher educate entire populations need to be brave enough to tear down higher education and build an institution fit to educate all to a higher level. To do this, we need to work on theoretical proposition 7 and start renaming higher education as an emancipatory institution for all based on first democratic principles: 'We the people ...' It is not 'we with vested interests' or 'we who desire to be wealthier than our neighbor'. It is 'We the people...' regardless of everything. The case for the importance of higher education has been made and won. It is a right that ensures life, liberty, and the pursuit of happiness. Without a higher education, it is highly unlikely that any of these inalienable rights can be fully pursued or achieved. There is a civic obligation for all to demand these rights and to name and shame those who would deny them by any means. Named objects that block the way, such as affordability (price) and entry qualifications (merit/selection), should be named for what they are: the vested desires and interests of those who benefit from others not having a higher education.

BIBLIOGRAPHY

Arum, R., & Roksa, J. (2014). *Aspiring Adults Adrift: Tentative Transitions of College Graduates*. Chicago: The University of Chicago Press.

Belk, R. W., Ger, G., & Askegaard, S. (2003). The Fire of Desire: A Multisited Inquiry into Consumer Passion. *Journal of Consumer Research, 45*(December), 326–351.

Carey, K. (2015). *The End of College: Creating the Future of Learning and the University of Everywhere*. New York: Riverhead Books.

Cooley, C. H. (1922). *Human Nature and the Social Order*. New York: Charles Scribner's Sons.

Derrida, J. (1976). *Of Grammatology*. Baltimore: John Hopkins University Press.

Derrida, J. (1978/2001). *Writing and Difference*. London: Routledge.

Dewey, J. (1916/1997). *Democracy and Education: An Introduction to the Philosophy of Education*. New York: The Free Press.

Lacan, J. (1998). *The Seminar of Jacques Lacan: Book XI the Four Fundamental Concepts of Psychoanalysis*. New York: W.W. Norton.

Lacan, J. (2006). *Écrits* (B. Fink, Trans.). New York: W.W. Norton.

Lowrie, A. (2008). The Relevance of Aggression and the Aggression of Relevance: The Rise of the Accreditation Marketing Machine. *International Journal of Educational Management, 22*(4), 352–364.

Lowrie, A. (2016). Ethnography: Textual Methodology. In P. Hacket (Ed.), *Consumer Ethnography: Qualitative and Cultural Approaches to Consumer Research (Chap. 17)*. New York: Routledge.

Lowrie, A., & Willmott, H. (2009). Accreditation Sickness in the Consumption of Business School Education: The Vacuum in AACSB Standard Setting. *Management Learning, 40*(4), 411–420.

Marx, K. (1990). *Capital I*. London: Penguin Classics.

Pinker, S. (2007). *The Stuff of Thought: Language as a Widow into Human Nature*. New York: Viking.

Pinker, S. (2010). The Cognitive Niche: Coevolution of Intelligence, Sociality, and Language. *PNAS, 107*(Supp. 2), 8993–8999.

Tooby, J., & DeVore, I. (1987). The Reconstruction of Hominid Evolution Through Strategic Modeling. In W. G. Kinzey (Ed.), *The Evolution of Human Behavior: Primate Models*. Albany: SUNY Press.

Wimsatt, W. K., & Beardsley, M. C. (1958). The Intentional Fallacy. In *The Verbal Icon*. New York: Noonday Press.

Wittgenstein, L. (2000[1953]). *Philosophical Investigations* (3rd ed). Oxford: Blackwell.

Žižek, S. (2006). *The Parallax View*. Cambridge, MA: Massachusetts Institute of Technology.

CHAPTER 6

The Death Rattle of the Liberal Arts

The liberal arts as a higher education institution has been around for a long time in the USA; however, because it has been embedded as an ideal not only within the liberal arts college but across the higher education system, it is difficult to be precise about what it is. The liberal arts is more of a commitment to a philosophy of higher educating than it is a name given to a segment of colleges in the market; the liberal arts college and the institution of the liberal arts are not the same thing although the latter is derived from the former. As a way of higher educating students, it is found in research universities, regional public universities, as well as small private not-for-profit colleges with which it is often associated. As an institution, it is derived from US colleges first established in the seventeenth and eighteenth centuries; Harvard was established in 1636 and William and Mary in 1693. The liberal arts college, however, was considerably extended in the nineteenth century (Bonvillian and Murphy 2013).

Distinctive features often claimed for a liberal arts education by liberal arts colleges are their general curriculum and small class sizes. While admired by many, the admirers of the liberal arts tend to be part of the establishment of the liberal arts, and as such self-praise is no recommendation. The liberal arts certainly has many admirable qualities, but is it fit for the purpose of educating all of the people in a constitutional democracy? Indeed, as a national educational institution, the original purpose of a liberal arts education has nothing to do with educating all the people. On

© The Author(s) 2018
A. Lowrie, *Understanding Branding in Higher Education,*
Marketing and Communication in Higher Education,
DOI 10.1057/978-1-137-56071-1_6

the contrary, a liberal arts education and those colleges most closely associated with it are part of the problem of the failure to educate more of the population to a higher level. Liberal arts colleges are a delimiting factor in the dissemination of higher education. In large part, the liberal arts as an institution is a bastion of a constitutional franchise not intended to be shared with or frequented by the great unwashed. Herein lies the problem of the constitutional crisis of educating large numbers of people to a higher level. It is a *constitutional* crisis not a crisis of higher education *per se*. This is a constitutional crisis because it ought, and I use the normative term quite deliberately, to be a right of every citizen to be higher educated: K through 16 should be the norm, the commonplace, the ordinary.

In part, the problem with higher education is K–12. Many citizens of the USA are simply not educated well enough to get into higher education under the current and contingent conditions. But it is not a fault of the elementary, middle, and high school; the fault lies with (a) the vested interests of parents driven by the desires of parents for their children to have the American Dream and (b) the desire of many administrators and faculty for selection. Parents desire their children to aspire to live the American fantasy. And it is a fantasy not simply because most citizens can't have it; although they can't, it is a fantasy because the American Dream does not exist other than wish fulfillment. It is a sublime object of desire (Žižek 1989) that stretches hope into impossible attainment. The attainment is not one of being higher educated but attainment of having the 'Dream' life delivered by education. The more people we inspire to the dream while denying access, the more likely a nightmare ensues. All you achieve is a bunch of people chasing futures of success, which reduces the likelihood of achieving that success. We end up with social roulette, a biased chamber of bullets that protect some and endanger others. Through enabling and disabling practices based on affordability (price) and entry qualifications (merit/selection), some have the right to bare higher education arms and some do not. To be clear, higher education does provide the cognitive ability (critical thinking) to resist transgressions against your liberty, and provide you with the ability to defend and fight for your rights. The best person to defend your rights is a higher educated you and a community with an interest in the same. Many are denied that right. Partial higher education of some of the population is an effective enslavement of the rest to a lesser life because their cognitive abilities have been restricted by a contingent social policy.

There is a social shielding strategy going on within the educational system. Because resources are deliberately kept scarce, vested parents will do the 'right thing' by their children. In most cases you would not expect anything else to happen but for parents to invest in their children. And parents, on average over time, will continue to name and invest into the identity of their children through educating them to the best of their parental ability. A large part of that is the selection of schools and colleges. Well-educated parents know the rules and use, bend, or break them to their child's advantage. Moreover, they will know where to live and can afford it so their children can attend their selected and well-resourced school. Because public schools depend on local taxes, those areas that generate less local tax dollars are immediately disadvantaged. Under the constitution, the responsibility for funding public K–12 is with the state and its localities, although federal government does contribute or inter-fere, depending on how you want to name such funding. In 2012–13, 36.8% of funding came from property taxes (NCES, table 235.10). This percentage has been reasonably consistent since 1989–90. The vested selection process starts here (see Chart 4.1) and continues into higher education (see Table 6.1). On the basis of the twin defenders, affordability (price) and entry qualifications (merit/selection), higher education is shielded from the 'unwashed and unworthy'. Even those colleges who put extensive resources into diversity by way of highly paid administrators who bang the internal and external marketing drum of diversity cannot or will not change the basic intake that may break the cycle of exclusion. For all their claims to a liberal education, liberal arts colleges appear anything but liberal in their practice. Their calls for diversity are ethically dubious public relations tricks that happen to carry big costs in terms of inequality and promote confusion around social diversity. See the comparison of a typical liberal arts college which heavily promotes diversity (I use the fictional name Roulette College for all my references to liberal arts colleges) and a public university not 10 miles away in the same city (Chart 6.1).

As with all Roulette Colleges, at Roulette College in this city it is claimed that diversity gives rise to inclusion as people study and learn together. This is all very well, but you cannot be included if you never get into college in the first place. Mission statements that are informed by liberal arts values of diversity, social engagement, and citizenship are of little use where college doors are closed to those with less cultural and economic capital. Stunning claims for the promotion of diversity by the leading liberal arts colleges is rather like the promises of political party

Table 6.1 Selectivity of first institution (four-year institutions) 2011–12 by parents' highest education level

Selectivity of first institution (4-year institutions) 2011/12	Very selective	Moderately selective	Minimally selective	Open admission	Not public or private not for profit 4-year
	(%)	(%)	(%)	(%)	(%)
Estimates					
Total	14.3	21.5	6.9	9.9	47.5
Parents' highest education level					
Did not complete high school	4.3	9.5	6.2	11.8	68.1
High school diploma or equivalent	4.9	14.1	7.5	13.7	59.8
Vocational/technical training	5.4	15.5	6.4	14.6	58.2
Associate's degree	7.9	21.8	8	9.5	52.9
Some college but no degree	9.7	21.2	6.6	9.9	52.6
Bachelor's degree	20.6	30.4	6.4	7.4	35.1
Master's degree or equivalent	29.6	30.7	7.1	6.3	26.4
Doctoral degree—professional practice	45.1	30.4	5.4	4.3	14.8
Doctoral degree—research/scholarship	43.3	27.8	6.9	2.8	19.3
Do not know either parent's education level	4	9.9	6.2	13.2	66.7

Source: NCES (National Center for Education Statistics), US Department of Education, 2011–12 Beginning Postsecondary Students Longitudinal Study, First Follow-up (BPS:12/14) Computation by NCES QuickStats on March 25, 2017

leaders who know they will not win an election and so never have to implement the policy promise. Given the early selection process in US schools and the lack of cultural capital, there is little danger of ending up with too many African Americans or 'poor-white trash' around campus that may lead to a marketing *faux pas* that would keep away the wealthy and privileged who pay the piper. At *x* Roulette College, according to NCES, 7% are Black/African American, 12% Hispanic, 12% Asian and 54% white. According to the US government census, in 2010 the percentage of Black/African Americans stood at 12.6% and estimated to stand at 13.3%

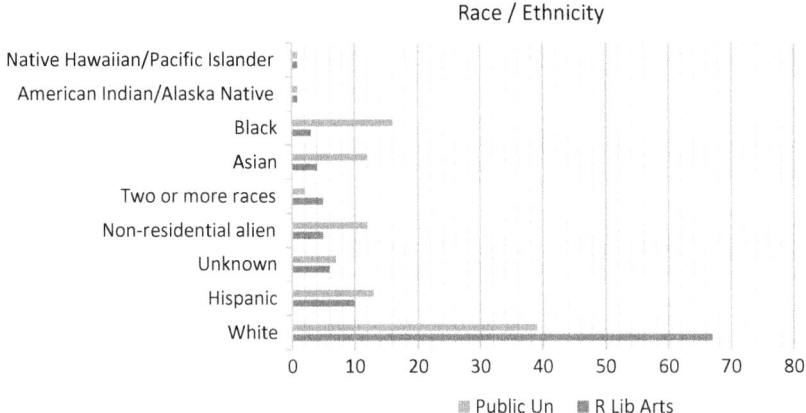

Chart 6.1   Levels of diversity—comparison of public university with a liberal arts college in the same north-eastern city
Source: NCES, IPEDS, The College Navigator, March 2017; Note: Actual numbers are not available for Native Hawaiian/Pacific Islander and American Indian/Alaska Native. These are indicated on the college scorecard as less than 1%. Names of colleges withheld

in 2015 while white alone, non-Hispanic, non-Latino population is estimated to be 61.6% in 2015. Other Roulette Colleges have half that Black/African American proportion and a lot less than local public universities (see Chart 6.1).

The following quote from *x* Roulette College bets on the very low level of 'take-up', somewhat like marketing promotions that assume a low take-up rate, coupon, or prize redemption. In this case, the probability favors Roulette College. There are just insufficient '*exceptionals*' out there, and even if too many applied, the recruitment officer's job is safe because floating signifiers like *exceptional* are ambiguous, safe marketing names that are prudent in retaining flexibility, that is, leave the college lots of wiggle-out room. It would seem that to get an 'excellent' education depends on either having economic capital (price) or having exceptional cultural capital (merit). The rest, that is, most of the ordinary people who make up the bulk of the population, must make do with whatever is available. You are immediately branded as an *unexceptional* human being, that is, assigned a contingent identity, based on being ordinary. Ordinary is just not good enough. Roulette College shorts your worth and bets against you.

Roulette practices need-blind admission ... we seek out *exceptional* students from low-income backgrounds.

(Source withheld, author's italics)

To be clear, the fault does not lie with Roulette Colleges and universities, although it is disappointing not to see more genuine effort to change the system, but rather the fault lies in the institution of liberal arts as an educational-fantasy form—a passport to success. While it is gratifying to see such charity and philanthropy from colleges such as Roulette, it is hardly an effective or democratic way to higher educate the population of a country such as the USA. Try as hard as they may, Roulette Colleges cannot deliver a higher education for all. However, we can see from the latest press release on acceptance rates that the discourse on diversity is challenging these colleges and administrators are responding. Of American applications, 50% are said to be students of color, 195 are Asian American, 195 are Black (*circa* 17% of acceptance offers), 182 are Latino and 246 are first generation college students out of 1159 offers made. This is quite an amazing growth rate in underrepresented groups (*circa* 240%) if those offered places turn out to be enrolled. According to NCES, African Americans represented 7% of students at Roulette in the fall of 2015. Two important points are worth making here: (a) it will be interesting to see how many African Americans and other underrepresented groups turn up at Roulette and (b) if there is not a significant increase in NCES reported figures for 2019 then why not? What is it that has stopped the acceptance rate turning into actual students in classes at Roulette College?

A liberal arts education was never intended for all in the USA, but only the few white-dominant males of seventeenth-century America. Early liberal arts education was a preparation for leadership that lingers into twenty-first-century fantasy enshrined in the mission of Roulette Colleges throughout the country. Roulette College websites are replete with claims such as to prepare students to become leaders. We might consider doing the math. In a diverse and inclusive society, if we are all educated to be leaders who will follow? Who will till the soil and bake the bread? I am given to believe that there are even happy agricultural workers and bakers leading their own lives. Though I must immediately add that it is difficult to see how a happy life can be achieved on slave wages, that is, you can't afford the basics of putting food on the table, paying the rent, and educating your children to their highest potential.

In the USA, most liberal arts universities and colleges are distributed organizations. Like the US constitution, this means that there is a separation of powers across the institution. Rather like the constitution, the college has a president as the executive arm, who appoints administrators, while faculty form a legislative chamber whose members have for generations written the rules and handbooks that guide procedures and committees and who often vote as a body on the rules and procedures. There is often, although not always, a trade union whose members (often the same faculty members) also inform the rules and procedures. Unlike the US constitution, there is no independent judiciary or body of appeal. Even the courts are reluctant to intervene in administrative-faculty disputes regarding tenure (Hendrickson et al. 2013, p. 153). The judicial aspect is held by administrators and faculty who jointly interpret the 'rulebook' and procedures, typically written by faculty but influenced by administrators. In short, US universities and colleges are distributed organizations with an enshrined set of rules of governance established and maintained by vested interests. In private not-for-profit liberal arts colleges, unlike public institutions of higher education, no one is accountable to a public body with a democratic mandate despite being dependent on federal funds through student grants and loans. Herein lies the best and worst of American liberal arts college education.

The liberal arts college is focused on undergraduate education in the liberal arts, often referred to as a general education and covering many subjects with a scattering of graduate courses spliced onto this tree of knowledge for additional income. Its identity is often named into existence in antagonism to vocational and professional education, but with random revenue generating opportunities thrown into the liberal mix as it gets buffeted by the contingent winds of the knowledge economy. In this way, the liberal arts college exhibits a strong and expanding numerator in the process of naming and re-naming what the institution is. While some are wealthy, most are not and are tuition dependent. Considerable virtue is made of that vice of necessity, hence the student-centered naming that often accompanies Roulette Colleges, which administrators slide into governance in their self-interest. Roulette College becomes all about the student and faculty find it increasingly difficult to challenge practices named as student-centered but are in fact damaging to student interests. The most egregious form of re-naming the college as student-centered is student evaluations of teaching (SET). What is promoted as an aspect of governance for the improvement of the quality of teaching in fact damages teaching quality and faculty-student relationships. In the face of mounting evidence regarding the fallacy of SET, administrators insist on using Likert scale SET surveys based on absurd assumptions: (a) students can evaluate good teaching; (b) students are unbiased toward instructors; (c) student responses to the SET survey are independent, that is, not influenced by other student responses; and (d) student SET scores are not affected by foreknowledge or estimates of their final grade given previous feedback and current known grade. Teaching platforms typically allow students to know their grade progression throughout the course and a good thing too. The question arises, why do administrators insist on using SET to make management and organization decisions that negatively affect student learning and faculty careers and therefore the rigor of teaching and grading? The short answer is that it suits the interests of administrators to such an extent that they are willing to overlook the damage caused to student learning and the grade inflation it contributes toward. In other words, administrators could not be further from being student-centered. They are administrator-centered. Few Roulette Colleges are willing to take up the Arum and Roska/AHELO (Assessment of Higher Education Learning Outcomes) challenge of independent student evaluation of learning. If all the Roulette Colleges are truly committed to student learning, they would be committed to finding out what students are in fact learning, but alas such findings are likely to cast a long name of poor learning outcomes over the college that it would be hard to rebuild the name of excellence in teaching and learning. Student numbers and revenue would likely fall. It is the latter driving down the learning and not the learning increasing the former. Typically, Roulette College administrators claim that their college offers excellent teaching without providing transparent, valid, and reliable evidence to support the claim. Students are happy to be silently complicit because they get an 'A' grade and move on further into the fantasy of success reflected in the faculty mirror of a distorted 'A'. To put it bluntly, Roulette College administrators mislead purchasers while trustees, who have a fiduciary duty to the college (see Hendrickson et al. 2013) and so inclined not to ask for the proof to back administrators' claims of teaching and learning excellence to be made transparent and published. It is important to note, by the definition of the name excellence, a claim of excellence implies a much better than average performance outcome. Grade inflation is not just something happening to student grades, but to colleges whose administrators float in the reflected glory of their own policies such as SET, which is a form of fantasy excellence used to name the college in marketing discourse.

As economic pressure bears down on the original design and function of the liberal education for an elite, the liberal arts denominator is re-named by the continuous expansion of the numerator in response to cultural and economic necessity as perceived by the vested interests of those currently capable of affecting the governance of individual colleges. In this way, individual Roulette Colleges formulate social strategy and higher education policy without democratic checks and balances. Those working in these distributive organizations react by making piecemeal changes to the institution to generate funds through student-centered recruitment as deemed necessary. Thus, liberal arts colleges tend to be dominated by a muddling-through strategy (Lindblom 1959) which changes the educational purpose through mission creep (Hendrickson et al. 2013, pp. 12–13). So, as the name still sticks as a denominating node or *point de capiton* (Lacan 2006, p. 681), the spread of the numerating possibilities expands beyond the capacity of the demoninator to unite the numerating discourses and so the demoninator becomes a floating signifier, making it difficult, if not impossible, to know what liberal arts colleges are, what they stand for, what sort of higher education students get for their rather high tuition fees, and what their social purpose is. They are based, in a surprisingly undemocratic way, on a European elitist heritage (Harriman 1935) of enlightenment for the few (Mishra 2017) but Americanized and to a limited extend (re)exported back to Europe and around the world (Redden 2009). Liberal arts colleges can be found, for example, in Europe, Asia, the Middle East, Africa, and Australia. Some recent claims have been made for the importance of the liberal arts in China (Roth 2015). In short, in their scramble for revenue, liberal arts colleges are stretching their meaning beyond the brand nodes capacity to sustain that meaning.

The institution of the liberal arts, not just liberal arts colleges, has gained traction everywhere as fantasies of success are packaged and sold in classrooms in the guise that you will be better off than past generations, you will be better off than your neighbor, you will be superior to your neighbor, you will be successful, and you will be rich. You are not ordinary, you are an 'A' grade student, you are privileged and so better than others. In Roulette Colleges, often the communication of that privilege comes in the form of 'because you are privileged you have a social responsibility', which is (a) an insult to the rest of society in the form of a misplaced paternalism, (b) a form of fantasy superiority, and (c) negatively constitutes all those not in Roulette College as inferior. What was possible for a privileged minority in earlier centuries, and those currently privileged, is such an impossibility for all to have that the fantasy can only crash and burn in the fury of disappointment as the likelihood of the special existence tends toward zero as increasing demands are met for the majority. The institution of liberal arts education claims that it educates leaders, yet can only produce fantasy as more of the population is educated to higher and similar levels. There is no longer the perceived historical inevitability of higher education's contribution to an improved life as the wish fulfillment of the American Dream looks less and less a dream and more a nightmare of pre-purchased slavery into debt and wage labor as a modern take on indentured servitude. And of course, those in debt make for more compliant workers which restricts the critical thinking capabilities higher education wishes to instill in students and considered by many authors as the *raison d'être* of higher education. The branded utility of the Ivy and Little Ivy leagues of liberal arts makes for easy comparison to those under-resourced social groups challenged by economic and cultural capital. Indeed, without naming the difference between institutions of higher education into existence, the superior utility of the branded liberal arts college would have little to communicate about its superiority. Like all commodities, its social and economic exchange value is in its exclusion as a comparative reflector (Marx 1990; Cooley 1922; Lacan 2006). That fewer people have it allows those who do it have to exchange it in the job market for a superior return in the form of wages. In this case, the Freudian form of the American Dream is the fantasy of superior exchange value derived from named excellence that is non-existent. Roulette Colleges and those who attend them bet on the fantasy in a conspiracy of naming numerated by the ideology of excellence and success. After all, who wants to name the college they have just invested four years and hundreds of thousands of dollars in as ordinary; better to accept the party line of named excellence in the brochure and college discourse than name the experience differently to the marketed identity.

The American liberal arts as an educational institution is embedded in the necessity to guard the constitution of the USA. The importance of education in securing democracy is evident in the writings of authors as far ranging as Thomas Jefferson and Dewey. Liberal arts education has a longstanding political function. Thomas Jefferson's view on education is reminiscent of the education set out in Plato's *Republic*. In both cases selection is never far from the purpose. Jefferson embedded racism and gender into selectivity. Although the elements of the curriculum differ, the purpose in both cases is a philosophical and in the end a political one with a final focus on leadership: 'Nor must we omit to mention, among the benefits of education, the incalculable advantage of training up able coun-sellors to administer the affairs of our country in all its departments, legis-lative, executive and judiciary...' (Thomas Jefferson in Lee 1961, p. 120). Plato's higher educated philosophers, in their 50s, 'turn to the wary busi-ness of politics and, for the sake of society, do their duty as Rulers, not for the honour they get by it but as a matter of necessity' (Plato 2007, *Republic*, book VIII, p. 273). It is worth noting that Plato included women in his philosophical and political vision, but like Roulette College the inclusion has quite a get out clause: 'And some of them will be women,' I reminded him. 'All I have said about men applies equally to women, if they have the requisite natural capacities' (Plato 2007, book VIII, 540c, p. 274). Such discourse is another way of naming an exclusionary tactic— exclusion by another name. Name the excellence of merit where it is unlikely to flourish due to deprivation of resources, educating differently and early pre-selection. Such claims and calls for equality and diversity is a form of abuse. Moreover, it is cruel because you provide forms of fantasy and dreams of success and promise while building the assurance of exclu-sion and failure.

Politics is part of what higher education is. It has always been at the core of its shifting and contemporary identity. Table 6.1 shows that selec-tivity tends to run along with the level of educational attainment in par-ents. This is not surprising. People desire the American Dream for their children and see higher education as a way to achieve this. The privileged also know that equality is a mechanism that necessarily lowers the odds of success for some by equalizing the odds for everyone. So, it is convenient for the privileged not to change education in a way that will equalize the odds. However, the fantasy of success is so strong that the less privileged pay for their own enslavement by branding themselves with the lesser col-lege compared to the other privileged brand—lesser Roulette Colleges compared to the sure bet of the Ivy League. This is the new form of inden-ture. Enslave yourself to work in order to pay for the debt that you raised to get a job to pay for the debt... And the job of higher education is to make this form of indenture widely available. But those who are blocked from the fantasy and so cannot have any possibility of achieving it see the same dream and will call it by a different name. The antagonism is baked into the liberal institution that denies most an equal opportunity, thereby branding liberal-college education as illiberal. The purpose of Roulette Colleges across the country is to name a lesser higher education differently so it seems like a higher education equivalent to 'Ivy-Oxbridge' while delivering cultural and economic outputs that are vastly inferior invest-ments. Over time and on average, people educated in the 'Ivy-Oxbridges' of this world will outperform the rest in terms of cultural and economic capital. Injustice is built into a historically exclusionary system that names merit (selection) and price as the architecture of brand success.

In 1824 in a letter to Major John Cartwright, Thomas Jefferson asserts that 'Nothing is unchangeable but the inherent and unalienable rights of man' (Lee 1961, p. 12). The claim is imbedded in the Declaration of Independence: 'We hold these truths to be self-evident, that all men are created equal.' And yet equality in practice was not and is not extended to all. That it is not extended to all in practice does not entirely undermine the political and democratic principle and vision for equality although it does rattle the foundations almost onto death, but not entirely to destruc-tion. Pankaj Mishra (2017, p. 17) has set out a compelling argument for the failings of the enlightenment and modern democracy. He shows that much of our sense of progress and success is illusory and that history is named differently depending on perspective:

> The sanitized histories celebrating how the Enlightenment or Great Briton or the West made the modern world put the two world wars in a separate, quarantined box, and isolated Stalinism, Fascism and Nazism within the mainstream of European history as monstrous aberrations.

Such parallax views (Žižek 2006) are not mere aberrations of perspec-tive, but hard clashes of conscious interests with unconscious desires for emancipation. Once set in motion in forms such as declarations of inde-pendence, emancipation cannot be restricted to the desires of the few. Those who wrote and signed the declaration of independence may not have intended their desires to be extended to all in practice, but once out of the box, the desires of the privileged are no longer theirs but the prop-erty of the public, re-named by all for all, not some of the public but all of the publics. Freedom, independence, justice, life, liberty, and the pursuit of happiness are expanded by the demand of people to have equal access to these benefits. So such named demands become denominating empty signifiers that all can lay a legitimate claim to and use as organizing nodes of naming that structures and forms society. If they can have it, then why can't I? If a man can earn this much then so can women. If their children get a great education, then my children should. Self-interested restrictions may have been intended by those originally pursuing such names, but the restrictions cannot be held. Once voiced, the desires of the privileged are easily translated, colonized, and re-interpreted by and to the desires and interests of the many, regardless of the social and economic resource availability to deliver the demand. This is not mere mimicry (Belk et al. 2003, following Girard 1977) but re-naming the name to suit the desires and interests of those making the new demand and so expanding the form of the fantasy or the dream, American or otherwise. But what is shared between the few cannot be the same as what is shared by the many. The lifestyle and higher education of the one-percenters cannot be the same once redistributed by and to the many. The current necessity of limited resource and the probabilistic outcomes of contingency will alter the content although the form of the desire remains intact. In other words, the desire for emancipation remains the same but the content of that freedom is different when the entire population has an equal share of it. Initially, equal distribution will lower the level of so-called named excellence for some, the privileged, but will over time increase higher education outputs and benefits for all, although the name excellence under such circumstances is inappropriate. Equal higher education for all will improve outputs and benefits because it will be normal and ordinary for all to be educated to the highest degree. More people educated to the highest level makes for a better society and so equal outcomes are improvements for all. Horizontal silos of exclusion based on fantastical desires or conscious self-interest are eradicated by extending numerators that re-name the empty signifying denominators of justice, equality, and emancipation. Higher education's role is one that extends the numerator of higher education for all in order to re-name and defend emancipation for all.

Equality of higher education is the case in point here. Historically, college education has never been equal even for those who were awarded the merit of entry—*exceptionals* selected for inclusion that makes exclusion digestible and read as reasonable. From the get-go, the declaration of education's necessity for the functioning of democracy in the USA was undemocratic and downright discriminatory.

> In this enquiry, they supposed that the governing considerations should be the healthiness of the site, the fertility of the neighboring country, and the centrality to the white population of the whole state ... It was the degree of the centrality to the white population of the State which alone then constituted the important point of comparison between these places .... (Lee 1961, p. 115)

Baked into the concept of a liberal education is gender and racial discrimination and so who can and cannot attend. This is not fit for purpose in a modern, popular, and radical democracy. The current higher education structure named for the education of leaders, derived from how it was spoken into existence, that is, the initial baptism, feeds a culture of social antagonism. Who should attend but white, male elites who had the cultural and economic capital to merit entry 'by a study of the authors of highest degree; and it is at this stage only that they should be received at the University' (Lee 1961, p. 123).

However, like the writings of Freud, Jefferson's work is not free from historical constraints. None of us are free from the conditions of our own existence. While our conditions of existence cannot stand as an excuse for racism and discrimination, the vision and imagination of authors and activists such as Freud and Jefferson offer a vision that can be extended to all but not without consideration for historical conditions nor indeed contemporary interpretation. Once the desire for emancipation is experienced and projected by the privileged, these desires are available to and demanded by the many on the same basis and use of such empty signifying names as equality, justice, and rights such as education for all to the highest degree. The many can place themselves into the same numerator along with the privileged as they too demand justice and equality and so the division of the demands by the few becomes a more inclusive line of differentiation. Regardless of prejudice, Jefferson's enlightenment argument that man is far from fixed 'by the law of his nature' (Lee 1961, p. 119) opens the imagined possibility of emancipation for all and a higher education for all to defend this emancipation. But there is a cautionary note inherent in his comparative analysis between people that underpins his argument and justification for higher education.

> That these are not the vain dreams of sanguine hope, we have before our eyes real and living examples. What, but education, has advanced us beyond the condition of our indigenous neighbors? And what chains them to their present state of barbarism and wretchedness, but a bigoted veneration for the supposed superlative wisdom of their fathers.... (Lee 1961, p. 119)

That we can select what is emancipatory and resist and reject what is prejudice and discriminatory is driven by our desires and self-interest for a better way of living that we can have only if all can have it. It is the vision of an emancipatory life for all, not the desire or vested interest of my interest group, that must govern an institution of higher education if higher education is to achieve its potential for all.

Higher education must be free at the point of entry and open to all on a non-selective basis, otherwise it is a divisive social strategy that names an elite as superior and who will continually name merit (selection) and affordability (price) as just mechanisms of allocating community resources and so divide the community against itself. Without fairness, justice, and equality in the entire system there cannot be a distribution of critical pedagogy that will instill and secure a democratic life for all. Rather than success and leadership, liberal education should have emancipation at the core of its mission. This philosophical principle should set the purpose and course of action to achieve the philosophy. From such principles of justice and emancipation, we can figure out the practicalities of how to get to emancipation. We need to kill off liberal arts education by re-naming it as higher education for all, for emancipation, and for democracy.

BIBLIOGRAPHY

Belk, R. W., Ger, G., & Askegaard, S. (2003). The Fire of Desire: A Multisited Inquiry into Consumer Passion. *Journal of Consumer Research, 45*(December), 326–351.

Bonvillian, G., & Murphy, R. (2013). *The Liberal Arts College Adapting to Change: The Survival of Small Schools.* New York: Routledge.

Cooley, C. H. (1922). *Human Nature and the Social Order.* New York: Charles Scribner's Sons.

Girard, R. (1977). *Violence and the Sacred.* Baltimore: Johns Hopkins University Press.

Harriman, P. (1935). Antecedents of the Liberal Arts College. *The Journal of Higher Education, 6*(2), 63–71.

Hendrickson, R. M., Lane, J. E., Harris, J. T., & Dorman, R. H. (2013). *Academic Leadership and Governance of Higher Education.* Sterling: Stylus.

Lacan, J. (2006). *Écrits* (B. Fink, Trans.). New York: W.W. Norton.

Lee, G. C. (Ed.). (1961). *Crusade Against Ignorance: Thomas Jefferson on Education.* New York: Teachers College, Columbia University.

Lindblom, C. E. (1959). The Science of "Muddling Through". *Public Administration Review, 19*(2), 79–88.

Marx, K. (1990). *Capital I.* London: Penguin Classics.

Mishra, P. (2017). *Age of Anger.* New York: Farrar, Straus and Giroux.

Plato. (2007). *The Republic.* New York: Penguin Classics.

Redden, E. (2009). A Global Liberal Arts Alliance. *Inside Higher Education.* Retrieved from https://www.insidehighered.com/news/2009/04/06/liberalarts. Accessed 10 June 2017.

Roth, M. S. (2015). *Beyond the University: Why Liberal Education Matters.* New Haven: Yale University Press.

Žižek, S. (1989). *The Sublime Object of Ideology.* London: Verso.

Žižek, S. (2006). *The Parallax View.* Cambridge, MA: Massachusetts Institute of Technology.

CHAPTER 7

A Long Day's Journey into Liberal Arts Pedagogy

There are three things important to an academic's career. The first is publications. The second is publications. And the third is publications. Yet, it is the work of pedagogy and service in the liberal arts institution that consumes faculty time. Typically, the teaching load is high, compared to research universities, and service commitments can be exhaustive and exhausting. It is time, I believe, to have a transparent conversation about teaching in American institutions with an emphasis on liberal arts education. They may try and claim a name for research, but really they are student-centered teaching institutions, which is another name for student dependent. The latter is where they make their money. The institution of the liberal arts is not a building called such-and-such a college, but an approach to and a philosophy of higher education. As an institution of higher education, faculty working within institutions with a liberal arts focus are committed, albeit not always willingly, to a general curriculum, and this is regardless of university classification. The notion of the liberal arts is widespread and is to be found in many public universities as well as private not-for-profit colleges, which call themselves liberal arts colleges.

AAC&U is the leading national association concerned with the quality, vitality, and public standing of undergraduate liberal education. Its members are committed to extending the advantages of a liberal education to all students, regardless of academic specialization or intended career. Founded in 1915,

A. Lowrie, *Understanding Branding in Higher Education,*
Marketing and Communication in Higher Education,
DOI 10.1057/978-1-137-56071-1_7

AAC&U now comprises nearly 1,400 member institutions—including accredited public and private colleges, community colleges, research universities, and comprehensive universities of every type and size. (Source: AAC&U website)

Typically, in such institutions committed to a liberal arts education, students are required to gather two years of credit hours studying general subjects that have little or nothing to do with their major. Proponents argue that this is a form of higher education that develops critical thinking.

There are two important points here. (a) Critical thinking is a floating signifier often used in ambiguous ways to avoid definition and specification and so accountability. Even the AAC&U's definition of critical thinking is open to critical analysis that leaves the definition confused and of little use as a methodological tool for framing the measurement of learning: 'Critical thinking is a habit of mind characterized by the comprehensive exploration of issues, ideas, artifacts, and events before accepting or formulating an opinion or conclusion' (AAC&U 2017, p. 11). It is unclear as to what is meant by critical. Indeed, the term could be dropped. There is no *a priori* basis for thinking, critical or otherwise, to be 'comprehensive' and furthermore how comprehensive is comprehensive? Who gets to make that judgment? One can imagine an infinite array of comprehensive thoughts on any topic where comprehension becomes impossible. Habits of mind are neither necessarily good, nor bad, nor indifferent. Medieval scholastic thought is based on habits of mind cultivated for hundreds of years but did not necessarily produce thoughtful and intelligent work. The definition fails to take into consideration that thinking is not devoid of power, self-interest, and human desire. (b) Unfortunately, liberal arts education as it is currently structured and delivered in the classroom does not develop (critical) thinking. The lack of critical thinking skills (Arum and Roksa 2011, 2014) or cognitive advantage *a la* Pinker (2010) and Tooby and DeVore (1987) is so much bemoaned and evidenced by surveys such as National Survey of Student Engagement (NSSE) and the Wabash National Study of Liberal Arts Education that it is difficult to refute the evidence that students are not developing their cognitive ability as much as they might. I have sat in numerous meetings discussing NSSE and Wabash surveys and wondered along with many other faculty members how no intellectual progress appears evident at least according to these self-reported surveys completed by students.

There is a case to answer on this cognitive development failure. Over many years, I have listened to students often complain that much of what they are studying is like high school and given the choice they would rather concentrate on their major. However, administrators refuse to listen to this student message yet listen to students when it comes to student evaluations of teaching (SET). Listening to students and being student centered appears selective; what gets listened to and changed is in accordance with administrative vested interests.

PROLIFERATING SUBJECTS

The problem here for the liberal arts in higher education is not one of the subjects studied, but rather the number of subjects studied in the given time. There is no deep learning but rather skimming across subject after subject; however, we interpret the floating signifier 'deep'. Because of this skimming approach to learning inherent in liberal arts, students do not gain a 'comprehensive', 'deep', or 'critical' understanding of the subject as a specialism, or a concrete grounding in the theories and concepts that form the foundations of that subject. Students do not learn how specialists think in and about that subject and form theories, concepts, and constructs through the lens of that subject and so see the world from that perspective. Students do not learn how those working in subject areas weight up arguments, deliberate, and discuss the knowledge in that subject. In other words, students never learn to think and use the cognitive tools specific to thinking in that subject and how knowledge may be formed and contested in that subject.

It is rather like the cliché, 'everybody's friend is no one's friend.' If you want to get to know people, then get to know a few well and not many on a superficial basis. Spend time with people. If you want to learn to think, specialize in a subject over time. Spend time in subjects. People need to make choices about what they want to spend their time doing. They need to learn to focus on a subject of study. A liberal arts higher education encourages indecision by presenting a superficial array of pick and mix classes often selected by students on the basis of easy grades. Given the circumstances and the importance we give to grades, who could possibly blame students for making the choices they do. In their situation, it is in their best interest to behave as they do. Being intelligent people, they have figured this out. There is no point in complaining about student behavior and lack of cognitive development from entry point as a fresher to exit point as a senior when the liberal arts system is structured to do exactly that.

You will learn to think critically, or put more simply learn to think, by focusing on one or a few subjects in detail rather than skimming across many. Often as much as 60% of a liberal arts degree is spent on subjects that are unrelated to the student's major based on a false claim that a liberal arts education develops critical thinking. Furthermore, even in the major students spend only about 50, sometimes less sometimes more, credit hours studying their major subject, not sufficient time for the serious learning of any subject. Furthermore, the learning is diluted by a myriad of loosely related, often not intellectually related, topics in the subject area. In part, this is because (a) classes are developed by individual faculty members with little and often no discussion with other faculty. (b) Without discussion and coherent curriculum design, learning content fails to build learning unit upon learning unit within modules and module upon module within the degree specified to achieve a higher level of cognitive development. A coherent curriculum design based on the cognitive development you would like to achieve for the student upon graduation should specify each learning unit within modules and assessment of learning in that learning unit. Each module and assessment of learning in that module should also be specified with regard to the cognitive development you would like to achieve for each learner upon graduation. In this way, you build a continuous development of the learner's cognitive capability and intellectual rigor in a degree structured by further and further focus in the knowledge produced by the specialists in that subject. Such a structure will teach students to think. Such a structure takes the student further and further into the study of the subject and in this way, they learn to think as well as become specialists. The specialist skills may or may not be transferable, but the thinking skills are always transferable.

Currently, we are teaching students to think that thinking is easy and is based on a casual skimming of the subject. Not only is this misleading it is mis-selling the purpose of higher educating someone with the inference that a higher education can be achieved without too much work (Arum and Roksa 2011). Between administrators and faculty, we re-name and re-brand higher education, in the mind of many students, as high school without discipline. Anyone who pays large amounts of money for such an education has something else in mind other than a higher education when purchasing. It is certainly not to be higher educated. More likely it is payment for securing the American Dream. The fantasy is not only hard to resist, you resist to your disadvantage and against your own self-interest. Despite all the concerns expressed about the lack of cognitive development and the costs, it still pays, for some at least, to have a degree. See Chart 3.3, for example. However, I am sure the question arises in the minds of many students and their parents: are all these liberal arts subjects that are required to graduate adding educational value? Or am I being oversold on educational services unnecessary for the next destination, whether work or graduate school?

Revised Curriculum

Consider a revised curriculum where students study a limited number of subjects in depth, meaning that they study a subject to a higher degree of education. Presently, in liberal arts education there is no named common denominator that unifies a student's field of study. There is just a mess of differences in a range of subjects. Students currently do not learn how human beings think a problem all the way through using the intellectual tools developed by those working in disciplines. The only way to learn to think in 'depth' is to do it and the only way to do it is to fixate on a subject of study and learn how those in that field of study think in terms of (a) positions on and arguments from different perspectives, that is, learning within subject breadth; (b) learn how to take up a specific position within the subject and defend this position against those trained in the discipline but who take a different perspective, that is, learning within subject depth; and (c) this necessitates learning in depth a plurality of perspectives within the specific subject; (d) what is subject breadth and depth is decided by faculty members academically qualified to know what is considered to be the knowledge in the discipline. Points (a), (b), (c), and (d) above are directly in conflict with the system of SET and the employment of those who are not sufficiently knowledgeable in the discipline. Those who are well-read in the discipline that they are teaching are proven to be so through blind peer-review.

To get to this depth of learning, decided upon by academically qualified faculty members, the number of subjects taught needs to be reduced. One hundred plus credit hours covering *circa* 25 to 30 tenuously-related taught courses runs counter to human cognitive development. People have always learned because they had an interest to do so. Why would anyone want to learn anything if you did not have an interest in what it did for you? To be clear, there is no such thing as art for art's sake or learning for the love of learning. The bracketing of self-interest from knowledge is difficult to justify post Schutz (1970), Habermas (1987), and Foucault

(1989a, b). Human interests give rise to knowledge (Habermas 1987). Cognitive development is social (Pinker 2010; Tooby and DeVore 1987). If we want to achieve depth in learning, given what we know about cognitive development, educators and learners should focus on fewer subjects of interest to them.

Instead of students trying to learn lots of subjects at a skimming level, as most liberal arts institutions now do, it would be worth considering having students concentrate on three or possibly four subjects in depth that lead to a final focus in a single subject. One of each of these three or four subjects should be selected from the humanities, the sciences, social sciences, and the arts. Each of these three or four subjects should be studied in depth over two years with the third and fourth years focused on a single subject. A student could study something like American literature, mathematics, psychology, and theater or Mandarin, statistics, business, and visual design. Subjects should be intellectually and academically related in a way that subjects studied in each of the discipline areas (humanities, sciences, social sciences, and the arts) would build upon one another so that a growing depth of knowledge in each subject is supported in a cross-discipline way. But the cross-discipline selection should make academic sense. Who gets to decide what makes cross-discipline academic sense? Academically qualified faculty members do.

As subjects across discipline areas are studied where this makes academic sense, such as social science and statistics, or literature and theater, then students would learn to think as people in the discipline think and so develop their cognitive ability to a degree worthy of the name higher education rather than high school. Approaching curriculum design and teaching and learning in this way retains the liberal arts ideal without spilling over into a vapid accumulation of course credits that have little or nothing in common and would differentiate learning outcomes through increasing levels of discipline knowledge. Over the period of the four-year degree, disciplines could be whittled down according to the interest of the student. In junior and senior years of the degree only the major selected from one of the disciplines would be studied. Such a curriculum design is in contradistinction to the current growth of proliferation of courses being made available to students at many liberal arts institutions. Over time, it may be possible to achieve the same level of critical thinking/cognitive development in three years and so cutting the costs of a college degree by 25%. This is assuming that we want to develop critical thinking/cognitive ability and not a proliferation of learning income generation.

WORLD-CLASS EXCELLENCE

The liberal arts requirements, it could be argued, are requirements for income and securing bonds by requiring students to take unnecessary courses thereby forming a desired income stream for colleges for more years than necessary to get a higher education that delivers the learning outcome of cognitive development. In other professions that might be sufficient for a law suit. However, if you surround your brand name with both (a) floating signifiers (ambiguous numerators in our model of naming) such as 'student centered', 'world class', and 'critical thinking', and (b) empty signifiers, that is, denominator names in our naming model such as 'excellence' and 'diversity', then it becomes difficult to challenge the selling of unnecessary services. Claims of being 'student centered' or claims to provide a world-class education float with ambiguity and are contingent upon the market-competitive performance of other colleges. Claims of excellence need to be at least verifiably better than the average performance; they are currently open to vastly different interpretations but remain difficult to challenge due to the naming process. Every Roulette College calls itself excellent, world class, student centered, and diverse. What, for instance, does it mean to provide an excellent, world-class, and student-centered education in a US college when 'the U.S. ranks 14th in the world in the percentage of 25-34 year-olds with higher education (42%) and the odds that a young person in the U.S. will be in higher education if his or her parents do not have an upper secondary education are just 29% -- one of the lowest levels among OECD countries.' Moreover, 'across all OECD countries, 30% of the expenditure on higher education comes from private sources, while in the U.S., 62% does.' (OECD, US Country Note 2012, p. 1). To my mind, this is not world-class higher education, this is not encouraging 'diversity' nor is it public minded to develop and define the cognitive ability of students in terms of ambiguous interpretations of those signifiers floating around college brochures and websites. These signifiers are slippery brand names designed to mislead, mis-sell, and oversell.

QUO BONO?

It becomes a question of who do you trust to keep the till. *Quo bono?* Who gets paid the most in not-for-profit liberal arts institutions? Senior administrators at our liberal arts colleges are in the top 5% income bracket.

Median household income in the USA was $53,657 (all households) in 2014: white ($56,866), white non-Hispanic ($60,256), black ($35,398), and Asian ($74,297). These total household incomes compare very poorly with senior college administrators who fall within the top 5% of the total household income bracket, that is, $206,568 or more[1]. I would suggest that there is little commonality between the interests of senior administrators paid $200,000 plus and the average, middle-class person. Those households with incomes (all races) of $200,000 and over represent 5.6% of the income distribution (DeNavas-Walt and Proctor 2015). The question the average middle-class person must ask is do they trust such administrators with the higher education of their college-bound children? Who and what gets the attention of such highly paid administrators?

Considerable controversy exists, for whatever reason, regarding self-acclaimed student-centered colleges not educating students to acceptable levels of cognitive development. In addition to high fees and room and board, administrators use students as security against bonds raised in the marketplace. However, Moody's credit rating sometimes goes Baa Baa Baa[2] which has consequences for college financial sustainability when (a) student income in the form of fees and room and board, often the only source of any significant income for the private not-for-profit, is considered at risk due to factors such as the declining demographics (Selingo 2016) of the younger population in many regions of the USA and so (b) the future cost of borrowing increases and (c) any surprises in the market will more severely affect college finances which are in this position. It is not in the interest of college administrators to educate students to degree level faster than they currently do, say in three years rather than four, because this destroys revenue streams and threatens their credit rating. Administrators also turn their interest to donations and fundraising and how to increase fees and room and board income. Building additional dorms is a favorite choice, along with building the brand name for excellence in order to appear a more attractive proposition in the market and so facilitate further fee increases. The difficulty is, of course, that every Roulette College is doing something similar. Budget projections are sometimes more optimistic than is prudent, for example, projected increases of 5% per annum in student fees. Considering the current political and economic environment and rising student debt, such fee increases compared with a consumer price index of *circa* 2% is likely to raise public and legislative eyebrows and should most certainly concern boards of trustees who are the legal guardians of not-for-profits with fiduciary responsibility. None of this helps the student develop cognitive skills and most certainly does not help reduce the cost of higher education.

As well as a cheap selling tool, it costs little to nothing to make a claim of excellence; excellence is one of those slippery names of higher education brand architecture used *inter alia* as the slings and arrows against faculty. Moreover, it could be considered that naming excellence is more of an effort in brand misdirection than it is an effort to improve the quality of educating students to a higher level. Faculty members often do not discuss the excellence, or otherwise, of their teaching and for good reason. Not only is it thought embarrassing not to be considered excellent, but excellence is the ideology of administration used in a struggle with faculty. A claim of excellence is also a form of marketing promotion. Excellence is the deliberate and planned use of student power/ignorance, a twist on Foucault's power/knowledge, in the *form*ation of fantasy excellence in a student-centered working environment. Not to be excellent is a road to perdition in the liberal arts model of a student-centered institution.

Through internal communication and instruments such as SET, students are encouraged to place themselves at the center of this educational universe (student centered) and masters of the faculty. In this way, students become the pawns of unscrupulous administrators who place students between themselves and faculty as a form of power to manipulate faculty into doing what administrators want rather than doing what students may need or what is best for students and their learning outcomes. However, this administrative strategy of divide and rule is open to resistance and reform from both faculty members and students. Faculty, I believe, must prevail on their masters to learn their letters[3] and ensure students become conversant with the politics of their own education. Their education matters not just to themselves, although this is most important, but it also matters to their communities. Any instrument, and those promoting such an instrument, that interferes with their education should be questioned and students should learn to ask *quo bono* and to get independent and reliable answers to their questions. As young adults, students should learn what is and is not in their interest and then where and with whom those interests align. Students and faculty have more interests in common than any other groups working in higher education. Each would benefit from a closer alliance. Excellence should be named by faculty and students working together not by administrators working for their own interests.

MEASURING EXCELLENCE?

Maybe a little more humility with an emphasis on the ordinariness and contingency of life may be a worthy quality that administrators could communicate to students along with making them aware of their own biases when evaluating faculty who are committed to the educational welfare of students and their future. No talk of microaggression here. The word 'no' or the words 'you are wrong' get airbrushed from higher education teaching and learning. It is as if there is something wrong with saying no and with being wrong. We do students a grave disservice by encouraging them to a fantasy perception of their cognitive abilities; this puts students in harm's way. Do administrators believe that students make good judgments about how they have been taught? I suspect not, but SET is a convenient stick to herd faculty into submitting to the administrative will that destroys the students' education because faculty cannot be rigorous or honest, cannot challenge students as part of the process of learning in fear of bruising egos that results in poor student evaluations of teaching. Last semester, I provided a student with feedback on a paper and suggested they re-write it and improve their grade. The student's reply was, 'I don't have time for this'. There was an element of stress in the student's response. Eventually they re-wrote the paper in the light of the feedback and they did improve their grade. But how much easier it would have been to give the student a good grade in the first place and for me to get rewarded with a better SET score. Concepts such as SET form part of the numerators of excellence. SET is a mechanism of administrative power in the battle of control over students. One group wants money from students, the other group wants to educate them, but you can't educate students without the ringing till of the foul rag-and-bone shop. Money is a necessity, but it is not the generator of excellence or diversity in higher education. On the contrary, it seems to get in the way of achieving excellence and diversity.

SET is an educational and administrative fantasy built on top of the empty signifier excellence. However, SET is moving toward becoming an empty signifier, that is, a denominator name that organizes discourse, and so it becomes difficult to challenge and resist despite the name being intellectually and academically bankrupt. SET is not sustainable as an intellectual and academic argument but it is eminently playable with students, parents, administrators, and accreditation agencies. Evidence of lack of validity for SET is ignored because to accept the evidence would be administratively too difficult. It is convenient to pretend that it works as an instrument for measuring teaching quality. But students lack knowledge concerning (a) the subject being taught until it is learned and sometimes students are insufficiently motivated to learn, (b) pedagogy, and (c) their own inherent biases in their responses to teaching evaluation and this makes the instrument invalid. SET is a case of the administrator's new clothes majestically dressed by the ignorance and prejudice of the unqualified, namely the students. The farce of this performance is played out by Chairs and Deans who either do not have the time or will not take the time or do not have the skills and capabilities to innovate the process of teacher evaluation. Imagine, a simple to read number is all that is required to make administrative judgment. And yet, despite the shame of the situation and the disservice to students, their parents, and faculty, the system limps onwards toward academic and intellectual disgrace. SET is a major contributor to grade inflation because many faculty members find the easiest path to job security is pandering to student fantasies of excellent academic ability, achievement, and future success. I have witnessed clinical faculty, *a la* Carrell and West (2010) and Braga et al. (2011) (see below for account of this literature), tell students that they can show them how to be successful in three lessons and I have witness accounts of clinical faculty members telling students that what s/he is teaching will get them a job. The question administrators should ask themselves is why any faculty member would engage in such controversial behavior. Maybe such faculty members are a little too eager to please students, even if unconsciously, because they need good evaluations from students in order to secure their jobs. In other words, SET acts as a behavior modification tool and not in a good way if you want to improve the quality of teaching. Indeed, the reverse case would be expected, that is, SET is likely to drive down the quality of teaching and learning. And yet SET persists. *Quo bono?* Not the student, not the faculty member.

This tail of named excellence is wagging the claim of quality improvement in teaching and learning with fabricated and false evidence. The evidence is fabricated by the production of data collection instruments known to collect invalid evidence in support of the purpose for which it is used. The validity of any methodology cannot be determined outside what is the object of study. And what is an object? 'An object gets investigated by a research tool, which … decides what the object is' (Adorno 2000, p. 376). Here the desire of administrators comes into play. The reason an invalid instrument has lasted so long in face of so much criticism (see below) is because administrators desire and want it. Motivated perhaps by unconscious desire, perhaps connected to issues of control and self-esteem, and the conscious self-interest around the pursuit of career and income generation, their own and their colleges. This form of desire is both conscious and unconscious. In the realpolitik of higher education administration, evidence is not just conveniently ignored to strengthen the powerbase of the individual and/or group, but is manufactured and re-named to seem incontestable when in fact everybody with any statistical knowledge knows it to be controversial and so insupportable as a universal tool to evaluate teaching quality and learning. The baptism of excellence goes further as administrators say, it is not me it is what the students say. Administrators negate their own responsibility and slide it across to the students in a fantasy form of excellence named SET. The abdication of authority by citing a spurious holder of such authority in order to do what you want is a particularly intellectually weak argument. It is an argument devoid of reason. It is a form of argument used by ill-trained managers to retain the status quo when it suits them or simply avoid having to make a reasoned case for the proposed action and/or behavior.

BLIND PEER-REVIEW OF TEACHING AND LEARNING

All the curriculum designs and SET instruments in the world do not amount to a small tin of beans when it comes to learning outcomes and teaching quality. What happens in a classroom is not what a professor has in her or his syllabus and SET does not measure teaching quality. While more time-consuming and perhaps more expensive, it would be much better for faculty members to judge the teaching of another faculty and for faculty to develop portfolios of teaching in consultation with other faculty members. Even better if that consultation was conducted by another unrelated institution, which would be unbiased. Better again if independent auditors came in and evaluated the teaching: a blind peer-review procedure. This peer-review could be blind to the extent that the evaluator would not know the instructor and the instructor would not know the evaluator and notice of the evaluation would not be given. I have previously proposed such a process and it was not the faculty but administrators who appeared terrified of it. In my entire career as an academic, I have only ever met two instructors who appeared to be somewhat dubious characters in terms of their teaching and treatment of students. While it would be expected that there is a normal distribution for teaching ability, academically qualified faculty members tend to be good at teaching. They tend to be engaged with the subject they teach and committed to the students. Academically qualified faculty members have everything to gain from an independent audit where judgment and feedback would be based on knowledge, would be free from bias and the pressure of pandering to students wanting grades further up the alphabet without putting in the effort that we see reported by academics such as Arum and Roksa (2011, 2014), the Wabash Studies and the larger OECD planned study on Assessment of Higher Education Learning Outcomes (AHELO).

If independent evaluation of teaching was conducted then accreditation agencies, federal government, state government, parents and students could have faith in the results. Faculty should take control of this and keep administrators, who appear only to want to use invalid instruments such as SET for their own unconscious and conscious desires, away from it. The results of any individual evaluation could be limited to the faculty member being evaluated and the evaluator(s) with the 'rules of engagement' set out in faculty handbooks perhaps agreed nationally through organizations such as the American Association of University Professors (AAUP) with faculty representation on the board of a national center for the evaluation of university and college teaching. Aggregate college data could be reported to a body such as the National Centre for Education Statistics/ Integrated Postsecondary Education Data System (NCES/IPEDS/ College Scorecard) and so aid transparency. The focus would, in all likelihood, shift over time from the quality of academically qualified faculty teaching to what is taught and learned. The quality of learning and teaching would fall within normal parameters of good teaching as deemed by those knowledgeable in the discipline. Good teaching would become standard, the norm, the ordinary. Remember, excellence cannot be ordinary/ normal as by definition excellence must fall beyond the average in the normal distribution curve. By definition, most of us cannot be there, by necessity we must be within or around the average. Any denial of that necessity is a denial of the human condition. Excellence is a fantasy form of denial of the ordinary, normal human being. The claim of excellence is an impediment to transparency and a restriction on continuous professional development for teaching and learning because those who propose and promote the concept pretend that it is a derivation of SET.

As confidence and trust in an independent system of evaluation of teaching grows, the independent system could be extended. Within departments, individual and/or departmental aggregate reports could be shared with tenure and promotion committees on a consensual basis. After testing, an independent evaluation of teaching could be conducted on a national-census basis (across all colleges in the USA and all faculty members). Later, a random sample could be conducted thereby cutting the costs of independent teaching evaluation after an initial heavy investment. If a national random audit of teaching evaluation was running smoothly and proved to be robust, we could dispense with regional accreditation based on self-reports with all their in-built administrative biases, unreliability, and lack of transparency. College departments could be audited by an independent body on a random basis. Such a commitment to an independent evaluation of teaching would remove administrative vested interests, and remove a burden and growing area of conflict administrators have inadvertently created for themselves. Administrators are often keen not to be transparent with the public who fund them and for good reason. Such transparency could result in poor reports, but only initially. Colleges and their departments would be quick to ensure that academically qualified faculty are teaching and teaching to high standards.

An independent system of teaching evaluation would be a benefit to academically qualified faculty members who tend to be professionally responsible, know their discipline, and have proof of that knowledge through publications, hold themselves to high ethical standards and tend to have an unconscious and conscious desire to engage with students and help students master the discipline that faculty are so demonstrably committed. Such an independent system of evaluation would also help faculty members improve their teaching and raise the national average and so the overall standard of teaching. A national independent center for the evaluation of college and university teaching could be used to create a national database and a national center for the improvement of university and college teaching through the development of best practice across the country rather than taking a mystery tour of student biases and administrative manipulation. An independent national center could also train students working toward their PhDs and a career that involves teaching, tenure-track faculty as well as developing continuous professional development programs for tenured faculty. Data for individual departments and by degree within institutions could be reported and compared to other departments and degrees across all higher education institutions and by type of institution, region, and even by demographic categories attending institutions and the readiness of students to attend higher education. Teaching those who lack economic and cultural capital requires different teaching skills. With training in the skills of evaluation of teaching, evaluators working in a national independent center could easily take into account the degree of preparedness of the student for higher education in the evaluation process. Something SET could never achieve.

Crucially, such an independent system with trained evaluators is more likely to improve teaching across all colleges and universities compared to the current insular silos created by administrators who refuse to be transparent on teaching quality by promoting SET. SET could be stood down and internal institutional funds currently allocated to it could be paid into the public national center for teaching and learning evaluation. Funds currently allocated to regional accreditation agencies based on institution self-assessment, and so unreliable, could also be reallocated to an independent national center for the evaluation of teaching. Federal and state funding should also be made available. This or something similar is the only way to both improve teaching nationally and restore public confidence in our colleges and universities whose administrators continually game the system.

Moreover, because of the way SET is used by administrators in the naming of excellence, especially with regard to tenure and promotion, SET has become a taboo subject and shuts down honest conversations about teaching. Although very much promoted by administrators, it is becoming more and more a named topic of conflict which administrators may be very happy to see removed from their remit and so facilitate consensus across faculty and administrators in a joint effort to improve teaching and learning as this becomes a vested interest for both of these parties across all universities and colleges. Claims of excellence by every Roulette College is an impossibility given that there must be a distribution around some sort of average with excellence by logical necessity being above average. Self-reported claims of excellence by Roulette Colleges are somewhat like conversations about driving; everyone thinks they are better than average drivers. As it is impossible for everyone to be a better than average driver, so too is it impossible for all colleges to be better than average.

In conjunction with a revised curriculum that has more focus and structure to build learning upon learning, an independent audit of teaching will help students learn with more rigor and with a progressive understanding of how to think in any given academic subject because faculty will be free from SET coercion. Cognitive development is more likely to be enhanced by the following two policies: an independent national evaluation of college and university teaching and learning, and a revised curriculum with an academic subject focus with learning outcomes assessed independently. Such learning is applicable to any context and area because thinking is a transferable skill. An undergraduate student may learn to think like a critic of literature, a social scientist, artist, or mathematician but later with additional training become a lawyer, an accountant, a teacher, a plumber, or a gardener. If you learn to develop cognitive skills by studying a subject to the degree that you can think like a specialist in the subject then you have learned the ability to think, regardless as to whether or not you name this critical thinking or otherwise.

AN ETHNOGRAPHY OF EXCELLENCE: 'DEEPER' INTO THE NARRATIVE OF SET

Having sat on many tenure and promotion committees and having had access to much documentation and read through many cases, it was tempting to use such data. However, it would be entirely unacceptable to use other people's data. After much reflection, considering the personal downside, I have decided to use my own data for the analysis of SET. Some readers may think this a little self-indulgent, some may think it foolhardy, but if we are trying to encourage a more open and honest conversation about the evaluation of teaching then self-disclosure has some merit. It is my contention that we need to shine transparency onto the denial of evidence by academic administrators when it comes to SET. Most administrators in higher education, who are often academics, sing the praises of evidence and call for an evidence-based approach to all areas of managing higher education. Yet when it comes to teaching and learning they are in denial. An ethnographical application has considerable merit (Hackley 2016) in opening up the conversation to analysis. Although outside the scientific paradigm, ethnography can include quantitative methods as part of the rhetorical account. Validity and reliability are derived from the credibility of the narrative, the persuasiveness of the argument, and how the account resonates with the experience of the reader. In this way, statistical elements may be squared with an ontology (what is) and an epistemology (how we know what is) associated with Critical Discourse Analysis (CDA) as a way of exploring text and meaning (Lowrie 2016) and in this case the brand naming process in higher education associated with the architecture of excellence.

In order to illustrate this fusion of analytics within a CDA of excellence, I have set out SET in tables and charts, see below, along with commentary and interpretation of the analysis. I argue the case for why a number on a scale should not count as the definition of excellent teaching. First, I explore the general case through the literature on SET then relate this to the ethnographical case.

SET: The General Case

SET scales do not measure the effectiveness of teaching, they measure a rather different thing, they measure what students say and then administrators pretend that this is a measure of teaching effectiveness. It has been argued by Stark and Freishtat (2014) that SET is misleading, and the authors argue for spending more time observing teaching and reviewing of portfolios of teaching.

There is a considerable amount of literature on SET; however, there are very few controlled experiments. Two of the most important controlled experiments on SET are Carrell and West (2010), and Braga et al. (2011). One was conducted in Europe and the other at the US Air Force Academy. Studies on SET are usually observational and causality cannot be inferred. Controlled experiments can infer causality.

Controlled, randomized experiments find that SET ratings are negatively associated with direct measures of effectiveness (Stark and Freishtat 2014; Carrell and West 2010; Braga et al. 2011). In other words, 'professors who excel at promoting contemporaneous student achievement teach in ways that improve their student evaluations but harm the follow-on achievement of their students in more advanced classes' (Carrell and West 2010, p. 409). In short, cognitive development is impeded where student evaluations are high. The higher the evaluations, the more likely the teaching is conducted in a way that restricts learning. This finding comes from the two independently conducted and controlled experimental-based research projects that offer reasonable proof of causality (Carrell and West 2010; Braga et al. 2011). High evaluations scores on SET do not indicate excellent teaching. Students punish good teachers, that is, those who encourage hard work and learning and who grade according to student achievement rather than grading for student evaluations. As Braga et al. (2011) state, 'the model is capable of predicting our empirical finding that good teachers receive bad evaluations'. While difficult for some administrators to accept, the conclusion of these researchers has intuitive logic.

The question arises, if SET does not measure teaching effectiveness, what does it measure?

In brief, according to the literature on SET, student teaching evaluations measure something other than effective teaching, for example:

- Student teaching evaluations scores are highly correlated with students' grade expectations (Marsh and Cooper 1980).
- Effectiveness scores and enjoyment scores are related (see Stark and Freishtat 2014)

- First impressions may dictate end-of-course evaluations scores, and physical attractiveness matters (Ambady and Rosenthal 1993).
- The gender and ethnicity of the instructor and student matter, as does the age of the instructor (Anderson and Miller 1997).
- The questions in SET concerning curriculum design, subject aims and objectives, and overall teaching performance appear most influenced by variables that are unrelated to effective teaching (Worthington 2002, p. 13).

Given the review of this literature, at the very least it would seem that SET needs to be used and interpreted with great care. SET is not a measure of teaching quality, yet administrators, and even some ill-informed tenure and promotion committee members, insist on excellence of teaching equating to a number. Often student comments are searched for and used in evidence as if distinct from the number, when in fact such comments like the number on the SET scale are only reflections of the same biases. You would not expect the numbers and comments to be different. One bias is used to support another bias. At best, there is far too much controversy concerning results and far too much inconsistency in the findings of research on SET for SET to be acceptable as a measure of teaching quality in any institution that prides itself on taking an evidence-based approach to managing higher education. Having established from the research and literature on the subject of SET that any reading of such evaluations must be treated with great care, I now turn to the ethnographic case study. Please note that ethnographic research is subjective. It cannot be generalized to a population of interest, but it can be generalized to theory and used in evidence to promote the case for the abandonment of such prejudicial instruments. These instruments are not only intellectually and academically dubious, they also lead to wrong decisions with harmful consequences for the cognitive development of students. Given such a conclusion, those who insist on using them are most likely using them for their own vested interest (unconscious and conscious) despite the harm caused to the student population who pay for and reasonably expect a level of professional service free from bias and manipulation from whatever source.

SET: The Case of Naming Excellence

To contextualize, this is a case where the professor was refused promotion to full professor because the teaching was not considered excellent. The insights offered in this case illustrate the naming of excellence in the specific institution, and how excellence is also the naming of a more rigorous form of teaching as non-excellence. Naming excellence is a rhetorical political process that has nothing to do with what most people would think of as teaching excellence, that is, achieving beyond the average learning outcomes. Furthermore, in naming excellence it is illustrated how naming has nothing to do with quality measurement and management but rather providing what students want as opposed to what they may need and what may be their desire to get a rigorous higher education in return for fees paid. The case study also provides guidance for tenure-track professors. The professor of the case study, of course, is the author of this book. From a contextual perspective, it is worth noting that the professor was considered excellent in terms of research and service and was recommended for promotion on these two elements. The professor was also considered an excellent teacher at other institutions. However, having failed to achieve excellence in teaching in the case institution, the promotion to full professor was not given. Excellence in all three, research, service, and teaching, must be achieved. In this case, the professor will only have to resubmit the teaching part of his application for full professor. As only the teaching element was considered not excellent, I concentrate on teaching in connection to the naming of excellence.

To further help the reader with context, previous samples of teaching evaluations have been provided (Tables 7.1 and 7.2). Like most people, the more historic my notes and files, the less comprehensive the data is. This is also my journey to becoming what I consider an excellent teacher and I provide an interpretation of the meaning of these evaluations through

Table 7.1   Illustrative student evaluations of teaching (SET) scores for site 1

Questions	Scores	Questions	Scores
1. Well organized	4.11	9. Overhead projector, boards, etc., ok	3.36
2. Material challenging	4.21	10. IT facilities ok	3.00
3. Right place	3.93	11. Well prepared	4.54
4. Business related	4.21	12. Enthusiastic	4.82
5. Coursework helped	4.18	13. Explained clearly	4.50
6. Books in library	3.31	14. Participation	4.54
7. Library help	3.70	15. Overall effective	4.54
8. Room ok	2.07		

Source: Author

Table 7.2   Student evaluations of teaching (SET) scores for site 2

Fall 2007			Spring 2008				
Mktg. 310 Mean	Mktg. 310 Mean	Mktg. 421 ITV Mean	Mktg. 421 ITV Mean	Mktg. 422 Mean	Mktg. 422 Mean	Mktg. 310 Mean
Q1	4.3	4.3	3.9	3.5	4.6	3.6	4.2
Q2	4.8	4.8	4.4	4.8	5.0	4.3	4.7
Q3	4.6	4.8	4.4	3.9	4.8	3.9	4.7

Fall 2008				Spring 2009			
Mktg. 310 Mean	Mktg. 310 Mean	Mktg. 421 Mean	Mktg. 421 Mean	Mktg.421 ITV Mean	Mktg.421 ITV Mean	Mktg.422 Mean	Mktg.422 Mean
Q1	4.0	3.8	4.4	4.3	4.4	4.5	4.2	4.4
Q2	4.4	4.7	4.8	4.7	4.8	4.8	4.6	4.7
Q3	4.1	4.4	4.6	4.6	4.9	4.3	4.5	4.1

Fall 2009			Spring 2010		
Mktg. 310 Mean	Mktg. 421 Mean	Mktg. 421 Mean	Mktg.421 Mean	Mktg.422 Mean
Q1	4.1	4.3	4.2	3.9	3.7
Q2	4.7	4.7	4.7	4.5	4.4
Q3	4.2	4.7	4.1	3.7	3.5

Fall 2011 (missing data)				Spring 2012		
Mktg.	Mktg.	Mktg.	Mktg.	Mktg.310 Mean	Mktg.310 Mean	Mktg.422 Mean
Q1					3.7	3.9	4.0
Q2					4.3	4.6	4.5
Q3					4.1	4.1	4.6

Source: Author
310 = principles of marketing, 421 = consumer behavior, 422 = marketing research, ITV = Television broadcast to remote site.
Q1 = How would you rate the instructor's overall teaching performance?
Q2 = How would you rate the instructor's knowledge of the subject matter?
Q3 = How would you rate the instructor's respect and concern for students?

the lens of the literature discussed earlier and Critical Discourse Analysis. Academics like to conceptualize, analyze, and interpret data. In other words, academics evaluate evidence and base their case on that evidence, showing the reader how they get to and use theories and concepts to help them analyze data and interpret results.

Linking back to Carrell and West (2010, p. 412), these authors found that:

> Academic rank, teaching experience, and terminal degree status of professors are negatively correlated with contemporaneous value-added but positively correlated with follow-on course value-added. Hence, students of less experienced instructors who do not possess a doctorate perform significantly better in the contemporaneous course but perform worse in the follow-on related curriculum.
>
> Students evaluations are positively correlated with contemporaneous professor value-added and negatively correlated with follow-on student achievement. That is, students appear to reward higher grades in the introductory course but punish professors who increase deep learning.

What does this mean? It means that less experienced professors, adjuncts, and clinical/practitioner faculty members get better student evaluations but do not teach as well in terms of superior or rigorous learning outputs. Relating this to the ethnographic case and explaining prior student evaluations, the story goes like this.

For the UK student evaluations (Table 7.1) I was a clinical, practitioner-teaching fellow without a PhD at the time. These evaluations relate to my early career and indeed my inexperience as a teacher. The argument that high evaluations is not evidence of excellent learning outcomes and therefore teaching has a degree of veracity based on this study here. I recall as a teaching fellow (clinical professor) that I was extremely proud of my 4s and so was somewhat distraught to be told at one institution in the UK that these scores were too good and I was probably not rigorous enough in my teaching and sufficiently demanding in my assignments and exams. It was at this point that I started to reflect on the rigor of my teaching.

The evaluations (Table 7.2) are also explicable in terms of Carrell and West (2010) and Braga et al. (2011). There, I was at first untenured and so we have a similar line of student evaluations. Even after tenure these scores remain high. Why? Because in part I continued with the same approach. Forming and developing a seasoned style of teaching and evaluative methods that helps students develop their cognitive ability takes time and experience. Furthermore, a confident critique of students' work is likely to have a downward pressure on student evaluations and is not undertaken lightly. But there is a further explanation. My Irishness fitted the community I was teaching rather well. As pointed out by Ambady and Rosenthal (1993), first impressions, and as pointed out by Anderson and Miller (1997), gender, ethnicity, and age all count. Students often commented that they liked my accent; a form of prejudice that happened to work in my favor. Does this mean that because I retained my high evaluations I was not improving as a teacher and achieving more rigorous learning outcomes? The answer to that question is no. What it does mean is that I was able to use inherent student prejudices, albeit unconsciously, as leverage. Due to my Irish origin, I was able to increase academic rigor without negatively affecting my teaching evaluations.

As a full professor, I mentored junior faculty members whose teaching was rated poorly. I evaluated their classes and teaching portfolios and found their teaching as good as my own, but these faculty members happened to be from cultures not as appreciated by students as other cultures were (these 'things' matter) and this factored into their ratings. I also taught a lot of students in the lower level courses. I prepared them well for the advanced courses I taught, which they later took, and so students did not struggle as much with the advanced work in my higher-level courses. In a sense, I was lucky because the structure of the major facilitated follow-up teaching with the same students. In this sense, SET scores are contingent and not necessary factors that follow on from how a professor teaches. Being named a good or bad teacher may depend upon a score but actually *being* a good or bad teacher rather depends on something quite different.

Site 1

In 1966, U obtained its royal charter and became the first university of technology in the country. In the mid-1990s, U carried the words 'university of technology' across its letterhead. Toward the end of the 1990s, the 'of technology' was dropped, and emphasis was placed on 'university'. In the mid-1990s to late 1990s, a major capital investment was made in the form of a new building for the business school in contrast to the closure of the history department. Later, efforts were made to woo Ford to invest in further capital investment and the new Ford Retail College was built. Early in the 2000s, a new chair was created: the Ford Professor of Automotive Retailing.

U is situated in the Midlands in the UK and sits on a campus of just over 400 acres. At the time of my working there, U employed around 3,000 staff and had about 12,000 students within 24 academic departments and 30 research institutes and centers. Teaching Quality Assessment (TQA) scores averaged 22.5 (out of 24) across three faculties: engineering, sciences, and social science and humanities. In May 2002, it was ranked within the top 16 by the *Financial Times* University League Table.

Site 2

I worked here for five years. This is a regional public university in the midwest of the USA. When I started teaching here it was not Association to Advance Collegiate Schools of Business (AACSB) accredited. By the time I left, it had been accredited for three years. This institution has a strong liberal arts aspect and undergraduates spend two years studying liberal arts subjects before concentrating on their major. It is in many respects a typical public regional university and liberal arts institution. The area is rural with the state capital over three hours' drive away. The university had *circa* 10,000 students. My SET scores here are in Table 7.2.

Site 3

This is a liberal arts college in the north-eastern part of the USA. It is in a large city. It is a private not-for-profit, tuition-dependent college with *circa* 4,000 students. My SET scores here are in the table below (Table 7.6). Since joining this college, I have taken a confident, seasoned, and ethical approach to teaching. Often my grading reflected 20% fewer 'As' at the undergraduate level and less than half the number of 'As' given at the graduate level compared to the grade distribution of other faculty in the department. The department was staffed by *circa* 50% clinical/practitioner faculty, all full-time faculty, not including adjuncts. Even these 'As' tended to be 'A−' (minus) and not straight 'As'. See Table 7.3 for my typical undergraduate distribution of grades. I taught not with an eye to pleasing students, but with an eye to helping them, challenging them, and putting them under sufficient (beneficial) stress following advice given in various teacher training courses I had taken over the years and the literature on teaching and learning.

Table 7.3   Row 1 = grades April, 20xx. Row 2 = final grades, May 20xx

B+	D–	A	B+	D+	B	A	A	F	F	F	B–	A	B+	B–	B+	A	A
B+	A–	A–	A–	A–	A–	A–	A–	B	A–	C–	B+	A–	B+	B	A–	A–	A–

Source: Author

SET: The Challenge

Considering how pedagogic literature suggests content may be 'deepened', the metaphor often used in contrast to surface learning and intellectual rigor strengthened, it is not at all clear what 'deep learning' may mean without the negatively constituted case. The importance of these dual aspects of learning is important not simply in terms of the content learned (deep not surface) but how people learn. Learning is difficult and can challenge self-esteem and long-held beliefs. The Socratics knew this. Current research on the subject of learning also places emphasis on the need for optimum challenge and stress. The 'sweet spot' for learning is 'Eustress' (beneficial stress) based on the Yerkes-Dobson (1908) curve (see below) and much has been written on the relationship between learning and stress. Of course, acute and chronic stress are never good. See, for example, Rock (2009), Jensen (2009, 2013), Medina (2014). The unstated assumption here is that students in a group are reasonably homogenous in terms of capability of learning the content of the subject. Sometimes this is true and sometimes it is not true. For example, students may well be reasonably capable of learning humanity subjects but then the same group may be quite diverse in terms of learning mathematics.

The theory behind the curve (see Chart 7.1) is that if people are too relaxed then performance will be lower than the maximum, and likewise if too much stress is introduced then performance is again lower than the maximum. However, it is difficult to know where the maxima may be for any given group or groups of people. Would the absolute maximum point be the same for all groups? For instance, would the maximum for excellent learning outcomes be the same for a group of students in different countries such as the UK compared to the USA? Would the maximum learning outcomes be different for a group of students from a regional public university in the mid-west compared to a private not-for-profit college on the east coast? If the same maximum applies for achieving excellent learning outcomes for all groups then this implies that in terms of learning outcomes there is no difference between student groups. This seems unlikely.

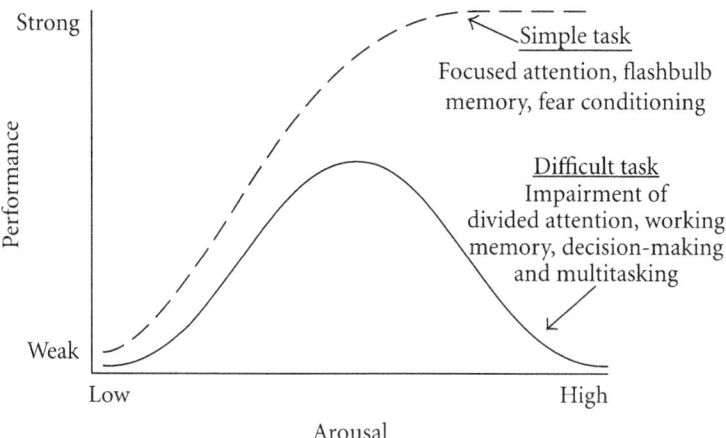

Chart 7.1 The Yerkes-Dobson cure
Source: Diamond et al. (2007)

But even here there is an assumption that learners in the same class experience the same stress levels. In this case, there would be an absolute maximum of stress for excellent learning outcomes in that class of students. Introducing that maximum would then produce the same levels of stress for everyone in the class and achieve the same level of learning outcomes for every student. This also seems highly unlikely. For all people in any class there is more likely a diverse group in that different learners are going to feel different levels of challenge and stress in the same learning environment with the same level of learning content.

As it is impossible to teach each student separately given budget restrictions and class sizes, then each student in the class is going to experience the same learning content but react differently to it in terms of challenge and stress and so individual excellence of learning outcomes is an impossibility. In the latter case, you would expect different learning outcomes for different students, different stress levels, different grades and so a greater range of SET evaluations across the class. A uniformity of high SET scores would then be informative in terms of the level of intellectual rigor and challenge in the class, assuming diversity in terms of student capability. If all students in the group were of the same intellectual capability and motivated by the same desires, which seems unlikely, then a homogenous range of grades and SET scores with less standard deviation is more likely. In such a case, you would expect to see the same SET scores.

As it seems highly unlikely that all students are the same in terms of ability and motivation, seeing a consistent high range of grades should ring alarm bells. More importantly, given diversity in ability and motivation you would expect students to experience different levels of challenge and stress. Therefore, a consistent high range of SET scores should also ring alarm bells. Even more alarming is the seeking for, by administrators and tenure and promotion committees, consistently high SET scores as a measure of excellent teaching. High SET scores are likely to be consistent with the opposite meaning that most administrators and tenure and promotion committees tend to interpret, that is, high SET scores are more likely to be consistent with poor teaching and learning outcomes given the diversity of cognitive ability, rigorous teaching, and level of difficulty. Note, this does not mean that low SET scores equal good teaching, but it does mean that experienced and rigorous teachers are likely to get poorer scores compared to less experienced and rigorous teachers. Given the diversity of cognitive ability, why would anyone expect to see consistent SET scores across the higher range of the scale unless it is not the degree of rigorous teaching and learning that is driving the SET score.

Where you have consistently high SET scores across a student group something else is going on in the classroom that may be connected to the level of work required to meet the challenge and the expected grade? It is reasonable to assume that if the level of difficulty is pitched to the top end of cognitive ability then those not in that range are likely to feel dissatisfaction and give low SET scores. But does this mean that if the level of difficulty is pitched low then those not in that range would give low SET scores? If the level of difficulty is pitched right in the middle range of the group then would those at the top end of the range and those at the bottom end of the range give low SET scores?

SET: Setting Up the Quasi-experiment

In the pre-experiment period, I taught in my usual way, that is, in terms of my approach to subject knowledge derived from my work on my PhD and research as well as using what I had learned about teaching and learning from (a) the literature on the subject, (b) conferences such as the Marketing Management Association, (c) in-house training, (d) external face-to-face training, (e) external on-line training, and (f) having experienced professors make class-visits and provide feedback along with class-visits to the classes of other professors. This is probably not far from how most professors develop their teaching and learning skills. However, I was not getting my usual student feedback and so I was beginning to wonder what was going on. I, of course, talked to colleagues. Often, I was told that it takes time in site 3; that site 3 students are different. Well this did not ring true to me. I don't believe that these learners were any different from other students I had taught in the past. This seemed to me like another form of prejudice. I decided to run a quasi-experiment.

I monitored my teaching, made notes on my teaching and controlled the level of difficulty in the content. I increased the challenge and stress in my class to the level I judged to be within optimal/maximum range parameters on the curve. I ensured that control was given to the students by 'flipping' the class and encouraging democratic pedagogy. Students were asked to take control of deadlines and set these based on a class discussion of the work involved after they had studied the learning unit and felt that they could undertake the work. Any issues or concerns were discussed and cleared up before the deadline was set. Once set, the deadline was not negotiable. I also made sure that all my grades were posted on the teaching platform, thereby ensuring visibility of grades to students. Students saw their grades and developed expectations for their final grade. This put a downward pressure on my evaluations (see Marsh and Cooper 1980). For example, given that we know from the literature that students evaluate professors based on how challenging the work is and the grade they then expect, you would expect my SET evaluations to fall. Table 7.3, row 1, sets out the grades that the students would have seen in their grade book in April, 20xx (year withheld). Final grades that the students received and submitted by me to the registrar in May are in row 2. Students would not have seen these grades in row 2 until they had submitted their SET.

SET and Assessment

For the experiment, the learning content and assessment changed over time. In the parlance of contemporary pedagogy, the amount of content was reduced, that is, made easier in terms of (a) quantity and (b) level of rigor. In the case of (b), the inference is that as the level of difficulty is reduced so is the level of work required to master the taught subject. You would therefore expect the level of challenge and stress to reduce. I wanted to know at what point would content reduction make a significant difference, if any, to SET scores and so improve both the student perception of my teaching and my SET scores. Table 7.4 is the number of initial pre-test

Table 7.4   Initial pre-test assignments and grade points

Activity	Points
Reading presentations	100
Quizzes (10 × 20 pts)	200
Mid-term exam (written)	200
Mini project I	100
Mini project II	100
Mini project III	100
Mini project IV	100
Mini project V	100
Mini project VI (may be removed*)	100
Group project	100
Final exam	200
Total	1400/1300*

Source: Author

Table 7.5   Final post-test assignments and grade points

Activity	Points
Mini projects (2 × 150)	300
Group assignment (case study)	200
Performance Contribution	200
Computer based simulation game	50
Total	750

Source: Author

assignments used to evaluate student learning and points allocated to each assignment. Table 7.5 is the final number of post-test assignments used to evaluate student learning and points allocated to each assignment at the time SET is statistically significantly different from the previous SET. These assignments also reflect the level of work covered, the challenge and the stress. A basic description of the initial pre-test assignments is set out in Box 7.1. A basic description of the final post-test assignments is set out in Box 7.2. To put this another way, my professional judgment on teaching quality and rigor was suspended in favor of the students' judgment in post-test assignments.

Box 7.1 Initial pre-test assignments for evaluation of student learning

Team reading presentation of the set textbook

Teams will present to the class on a chapter of the textbook. Marks will be awarded for the relevancy of the chapter, understanding of the content, how this may connect to other literature and branding theories and demonstrating a critical analysis of the content. It is expected that the basic, mainstream literature such as Aaker/Keller and basics of brand architectures are covered in these reading presentations and discussion sessions while the more complex and difficult theories are covered in the direct teaching sessions. Presentations should be limited to 15 minutes (maximum) with an additional 5 minutes for questions. Guidelines will be discussed in class.

Quizzes

For selected aspects of your reading, quizzes will be given and must be completed in class. There is no make up for these quizzes. The rationale behind these quizzes is (a) to ensure you attend class, (b) participate, and (c) learn and understand the material in an ongoing and timely manner. Quizzes will be assigned on a random basis, that is, you will not be given notice on what day the quiz will be given but you will be told what content area is likely to have a quiz. Note, quizzes are based on what has been covered in class and designed to test a basic understanding of content.

Mid-term examination

There is one mid-term, written examination consisting of open-ended questions. Questions are based on what was covered in the course prior to the examination.

Mini project I (individual)

Using the Zmet method, students will develop a short strategy paper by exploring brand meaning, drawing conclusions from the exploration and making recommendations for the brand you selected to explore. This tends to work best for brands that are in the news or have some controversial issues connected with them as this tends to give rise to strong opinions about the brand. Guidelines will be discussed in class and posted on the teaching platform.

Mini project II (individual)

Using Fishbein's Theory of Reasoned Action (TRA), students will develop a basic model for evaluating brand attributes desired by

(continued)

Box 7.1 (continued)

customers and estimate the propensity for customers to act and thereby provide organizations and companies with brand strategy direction. Students are expected to design their own basic TRA study in an area of interest to them. Guidelines will be discussed in class and posted on the teaching platform.

Mini project III (individual)

Students conduct a market segmentation project using SPSS. Students will develop scales, collect and analyze data, and produce an individual report which directs strategy and allocation of resources in order to deliver value to the targeted customer brand segments. Students are expected to design their own segmentation study on an area of interest to them. Guidelines will be discussed in class and posted on the teaching platform.

Mini project IV (individual)

Students will develop a Kano study of an area of interest to them: students develop a set of questions, collect and analyze the data, present the results and draw conclusions from the results. Guidelines will be discussed in class and posted on the teaching platform.

Group project: Developing a brand strategy

Working in teams, students develop a brand strategy for a domestic brand with another country image and brand attributes. Research information will be provided, but students are encouraged to explore further secondary research data. Each group submits a report. Guidelines will be discussed in class and posted on the teaching platform.

Final Comprehensive Examination

As implied, this exam covers all the material covered in class and the recommended textbook.

SET: Quasi-experiment

You would expect the considerable number of Fs and lower grades in Table 7.3 to lower my SET scores because students would typically expect their grade to be worse than they often turn out to be after the final exam. But the teaching strategy is designed to focus the mind of the student and get them engaged with the topic. Nor is this simply a ploy—the grade is fair and based on my assessment of student work at the time. Students realize

Box 7.2 Final post-test assignments for the evaluation of student learning

Mini projects x 2

There are two individual, mini projects during the semester. Each will focus on an advanced marketing technique, namely segmentation and conjoint analysis.

Group assignment

This is a large case study and team based. The case study is posted on the teaching platform.

Computer based simulation game

You will receive the full 50 points when you complete this game.

Contribution performance

1. Grade yourself.
2. Write a one-page report on why you deserve the grade you gave yourself. Word document only. Double spaced. One inch margins. Upload to the teaching platform.

I am looking for a convincing argument backed by evidence.

The *approximate* timing of deliverables is indicated for you in the syllabus (*flexibility required!*).

Details regarding the assignments will be discussed in class as each gets underway.

along their academic journey that they cannot get away with minimum work and see that they need to improve based on my feedback. Assignments are re-graded based on resubmitted work that they have been allowed to improve after feedback. As students have the option to resubmit or not, often those students happy with their standing grade do not resubmit. Resubmitted work tends to come in on the deadline agreed through consensus in the class, which is often the last week or few days of the semester. Many, but not all students take up the challenge and submit improved work, hence some final grades improve considerably and some fall after the exam. This process gets students to learn 'deeply' and engage with the topic, but such a teaching strategy hurts teacher evaluations. As you would expect (a) inexperienced and (b) those professors experienced in the art of SET grading take a very different approach to grading. My teaching strategy is the reverse of what many inexperienced professors or those 'experienced' in the art of SET do: give students great grades upfront, which encourages great student evaluations, then give much lower grades in the final exam or course assignment. Students do not then get feedback on that last exam/assignment. Such a teaching strategy lowers student grades and improves SET because students do not see their final grades until after they submit their evaluation of the instructor. By this time, it is too late for the student to give a bad evaluation of teaching. In this way, some professors, rather like their student counterpart, game the situation. Simple but somewhat unethical. Ethics aside, the gaming does nothing to improve learning outcomes. Administrators tend not to want to open that box and so encourage such gaming by default in their use of SET.

In a situation where professors are forced by administration to depend on students for their tenure and promotion, gaming the situation is not without a sense of reason arising from an unconscious desire to appear excellent and so 'loved', Lacan's root of all desire, and a conscious desire to survive, to feel safe, secure and rewarded. Gaming behavior is a result of SET behavioral modification and is no more instrumental than the administrators' or indeed the student's use of SET. Some professors do not 'hit' students with lower grades in the final exam grade but allow the high grade to stand. The latter often happens where administrators do not particularly care about grades or grade inflation. Indeed, some administrators prefer such an outcome as it plays into the naming of excellence, that is, excellent teaching, excellent students, and so the excellent grades are all interpreted as excellent learning outcomes and excellent Roulette College which is far from an accurate representation of what is happening. Where administrators are now looking at and asking for grade distributions as well as SET scores, faculty members may well indulge in more gaming of 'lower' grades to sustain administratively-named excellence. It would seem a perfect storm for the worse possible learning outcomes that goes by the name 'excellence'. However, those faculty members who refuse to game the learning environment, consider themselves not to be in the name of excellence game, and resist grading to SET, but do encourage rigorous learning are punished for their ethical behavior and good teaching, as Carrell and West (2010) and Braga et al. (2011) maintain.

In the pre-test period, I knew deep learning was taking place because my final exams were tough but fair and encouraged study and rigorous learning. Students were given the opportunity to re-write assignments after feedback. Students only got exam questions on material I knew they had learned and they also had the opportunity to write their own questions for part C of the exam. This is important because being able to write good exam questions told me that they knew the topic well. It is not always easy to write good exam questions. Note, not all submitted exam questions ended up in part C of the exam. Submitted questions were vetted by me and students got feedback on their questions and the opportunity to re-write them as many times as they wished up until an agreed cut-off point. But as the good Dr. Johnson says, 'Depend upon it, Sir, when a man knows he is to be hanged in a fortnight, it concentrates his mind wonderfully' (Boswell 1901, p. 344); there is a cut-off point, a deadline, and an exam to focus the students' learning (beneficial stress). On the importance of tests/exams that claim to measure critical learning see Arum and Roksa (2011, 2014) and the OECD's AHELO project. See also Benjamin (2012).

The following Table 7.6 sets out SET scores pre-test and post-test. The intervention at six pre-test courses is like a breaking point. It is the point at which the reduction of content, assignment difficulty, and challenge show a significant difference to SET scores. A description of the initial pre-test assignments is set out in Box 7.1. A description of the final post-test assignments is set out in Box 7.2. The initial pre-test assignment activities and points allocated to them are set out in Table 7.4. The final post-test assignment activities and points allocated to them are set out in Table 7.5.

Results

A paired-samples t-test was conducted to evaluate the impact of the intervention (reduced level of difficulty) on average student evaluation of teaching scores. There is a statistically significant increase in post-test evaluations (M = 4.27, SD = 0.27) over pre-test evaluations (M = 3.72, SD = 0.44), t = 4.97, p < 0.002 (two-tailed). The mean increase in SET is 0.55 with a 95% confidence interval ranging from 0.29 to 0.81. The eta squared statistic (0.78) indicates a large effect size. In other words, the magnitude of the intervention is large according to Cohen (1988, pp. 284–7). The guidelines for interpreting this effect size value are 0.01 = small effect, 0.06 = moderate effect, 0.14 = large effect. Given our eta squared value of 0.78, we can conclude that there is a large effect with a substantial difference

Table 7.6 Student evaluations of teaching (SET) scores for site 3 and quasi-experiment data (six pre-test and six post-test taught courses)

| PRE | | | | | | | Exp.[a] POST | | | | | | |
Fall 12	Spring 13	Fall 13	Spring 14	Fall 14	Spring 15	Avg.	Spring 16	Fall 16	Spring 17	Spring 16	Fall 16	Spring 17	Avg.
2.96	3.58	3.38	3.11	2.87	3.23	3.19	3.92	4.04	3.95	3.93	4.09	3.70	3.94
3.26	3.53	3.19	3.05	3.13	3.38	3.26	4.31	4.58	4.50	4.38	4.69	4.07	4.42
4.39	4.63	4.69	4.37	4.31	4.31	4.45	4.46	4.54	4.65	4.69	4.75	4.50	4.60
3.83	4.05	4.25	3.89	3.94	4.46	4.07	4.08	4.33	4.61	4.38	4.47	4.17	4.34
4.39	4.47	4.53	4.06	2.88	3.85	4.03	4.15	4.79	4.74	4.72	4.75	4.67	4.64
3.17	3.37	2.81	3.21	4.19	4.69	3.57	4.00	3.88	4.22	4.10	4.00	3.60	3.97
3.48	3.68	3.80	4.05	3.25	4.08	3.72	3.85	4.13	4.30	4.39	4.41	4.10	4.20
3.22	3.32	3.63	3.63	3.75	3.31	3.48	4.00	4.13	4.14	4.18	4.03	3.80	4.05

Source: Author

Note: During the quasi-experiment questions in the SET instrument changed. Comparability was retained by matching like for like questions

[a]Point at which the lowering of rigor makes a significant difference to student evaluations of teaching

between before and after interventions in student evaluations of teaching. In other words, reducing the level of difficulty in teaching content significantly increases the SET scores.

While I cannot say with absolute certainly, I imagine that the post-test scores would have been sufficient to gain my promotion to full professor. The question that may arise in the mind of the reader is which part of this dataset supports the better teaching? I will leave it to the reader to draw their own conclusions. I further explore the pre-test SET data to see if there is a relationship between SET and level of difficulty. In terms of the student-perceived level of difficulty and the student-perceived level of clarity of material presented, I wanted to know if there was a relationship between these variables. Looking at the following charts suggests a possible relationship. As clarity declines in the mind of the student, difficulty appears to increase.

Given the experiments conducted by Carrell and West (2010) and Braga et al. (2011) you would expect to see a correlation between the perceived level of difficulty and presented material clearly. When initially viewing Charts 7.2 and 7.3, there is a suggestion of a correlation. As the level of difficulty appears to increase, the level of clarity appears to fall. These appear to be negatively correlated, in other words as one variable increases the other decreases. To the eye, when you increase the level difficulty you can expect your SET scores to drop. A correlation analysis and univariate regression analysis is set out below to explore the relationship between these two variables further. A univariate regression was chosen because the

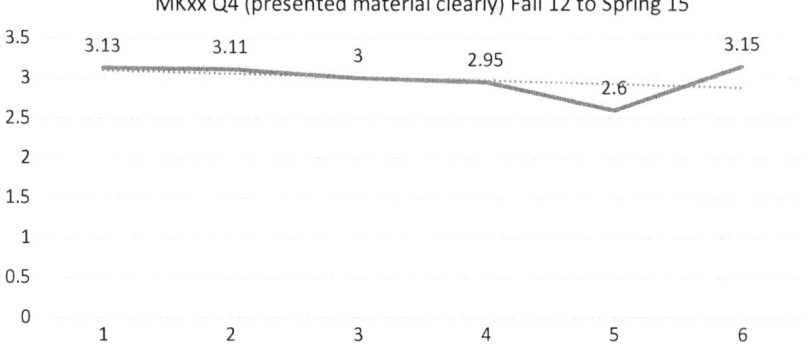

Chart 7.2   Presented material clearly
Source: Author

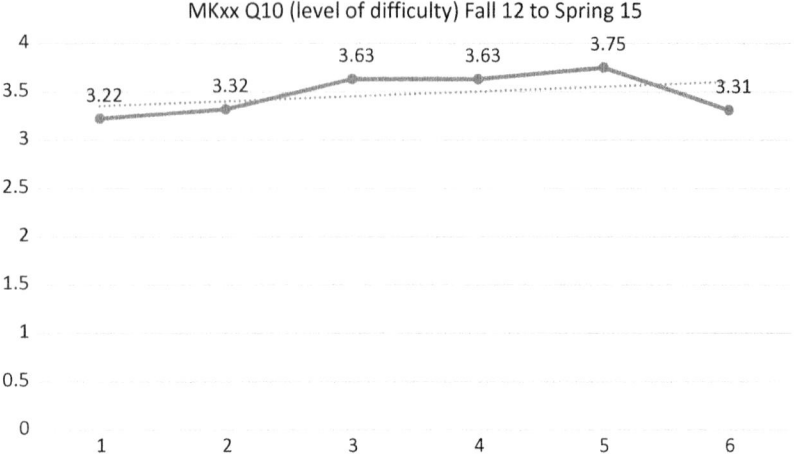

Chart 7.3   Perceived level of difficulty
Source: Author

dataset is small and a multivariate regression would be meaningless. There is support for a univariate regression to be reliable with a small dataset (Austin and Steyerberg 2015).

Correlation Analysis

The relationship between question 4 ('Anthony Lowrie presented material clearly') and question 10 ('Anthony Lowrie presented material at an appropriate level of difficulty for you') was investigated using the Pearson product-moment correlation coefficient. There is a strong, negative correlation between the two variables, $r = -0.85$, $n = 6$, $p < 0.05$. The more students believe the material to be difficult the lower the score on clarity of presentation of material. Introducing difficult material into the class is likely to result in low scores for clarity of presentation of material. This strongly suggests that students are not evaluating clarity but how they feel about the difficulty of the material. Gaining high scores in question 4 may indicate that the class is too easy. Cohen (1988, pp. 79–81) suggests the following guidelines for interpreting the strength of the relationship: small $r = 0.10$ to 0.29, medium $r = 0.30$ to 0.49, and large/strong $r = 0.50$ to 1.0.

To contextualize the strength of −0.85, a correlation of 0 means that there is no relationship, a correlation of 1 means that there is a perfect positive relationship, a correlation of −1 means that there is a perfect negative relationship. This finding shows that there is a very strong, negative relationship between question 4 and question 10.

Univariate Regression Analysis

To explain this relationship further, I conducted a simple regression analysis. As in the correlation analysis above, r = 0.85, which shows us the strength of the relationship. Because there is only one predictor variable (Q 10) this value represents the simple correlation between perceived difficulty (Q10) and perceived clarity (Q4). The value of R^2 (R Squared) 0.724 tells us that perceived difficulty (Q10) accounts for 72% in the variation of perceived clarity (Q4). In other words, if we are trying to explain what it might be that encourages students to answer Q4 (see the material as presented clearly) in the way they do, the perceived level of difficulty (Q10) is likely to form a large part of that explanation. With small datasets, however, adjusted R^2 (66%) is likely a more accurate account of that variation (Austin and Steyerberg 2015). These authors reported that 'linear regression models require only two SPV [subjects per variable] for adequate estimation of regression coefficients' (p. 624).That something like 66–72% of the variation in clarity of presented material is explained by the perceived level of difficulty resonates with much of the literature on SET. While such a large percentage of variation is explained this is not quite the same thing as explaining why students answer Q4 as they do, but it is likely to be a large part of the explanation.

If students are struggling with difficult material they will shift responsibility for their difficulty to the professor. The question arises, is the material genuinely too difficult? If so it may be the professor's misjudgment. The answer to that question is maybe. However, as (a) not all students find the content too difficult and (b) in my experience as a seasoned professor of marketing, junior and senior level students in their major should be able to learn this material. This is based on experience, and resonates with the previous SET evaluations set out above (Tables 7.1 and 7.2). Nevertheless, the fact that some students do find it too difficult suggests (a) the class is of mixed ability and (b) the level of difficulty in material content may need to be reduced if the professor wants tenure and/or promoted, that is, good SET scores.

The F-ratio is 10.5 and significant at $p < 0.04$ (p = 0.032). There is less than a 4% chance that this F-ration would happen by chance alone.

The regression model results in a significantly better prediction of perceived clarity than if we used the mean value of perceived clarity. In short, level of difficulty predicts (lack of) clarity significantly well. The b value is -0.803, and this is the slope of the regression line. The value represents the change in the outcome associated with a unit change in the predictor (i.e., Q10—level of perceived difficulty). For every unit change in perceived difficulty, perceived clarity of presentation decreases by 0.803. Therefore, if our predictor variable (Q10) is increased by one unit (difficulty goes up by 1) then the model predicts that clarity will decrease by 0.803.

While a cautionary note must be sounded given the small numbers used in this analysis, it is strongly indicative of SET scales to not measure teaching quality. The notion seems intuitive and reasonable and resonates not only with the literature on the subject discussed above but with my experience as a teacher and mentor to many other faculty members who relate similar experiences.

Professional Subjective, Independent Assessment, or Something a Bit More Radical?

There will always remain an element of subjectivity within every professional judgment, including judging whether learning is occurring or whether assessments are fair. The learning situation in the USA is both good and bad and is beginning to look like an oddity compared to the rest of the world. The learning situation in the USA depends on faculty judgment derived from training for a PhD and working with supervisors and mentors and then grabbing whatever training can be had while on the job. On the job training usually consists of working with colleagues and usually a mentor of one's own choice. Some colleges and universities have official mentoring systems in place, but often young faculty members don't like being allotted to a senior faculty member, and see this as an extension of administrative manipulation. Often younger, and sometimes not so young, faculty members seek out faculty they have learned to trust.

As a form of training and self-development this may be fine and perhaps the academy should re-learn to trust faculty members to deliver what they have been trained to do. Unfortunately, fewer academically qualified faculty members are teaching in colleges. Perhaps trust in faculty ability needs to be more formal, and not only be impartial but be shown to be impartial. How do we know that a professor's exams and assessments are fair, and reflect high and rigorous standards that are equitable for all students across all department faculty? One professor may be 'easier' than another. One professor may cover this set of learning material in a subject and another professor cover entirely different topics for the same course. Duplication of content can often occur across classes so students end up taking different courses with the same content. Students see little intellectual development as they progress through the courses that make up their major and we see this in National Survey of Student Engagement (NSSE) reports.

Perhaps it is time for faculty in the USA to adopt and/or adapt; other countries have independent audits/assessments. Perhaps faculty could develop their own policy of independent assessments of teaching and learning and how professors assess students. For example, if a professor sets an exam, mid-term and/or final, that professor could be required to have that exam blind peer-reviewed by colleagues in the department. It would be a simple task for a junior administrator to take in faculty exams then place them with another faculty member for review. Feedback could be given to the professor setting the exam via the same mechanism. External examiners could be put in place. After initial review from colleagues in the department, the revised exam could go to the external examiner who can make judgments about its fairness and rigor and make final recommendations on the exam. This would ensure that learning outcomes were being tested. Furthermore, post-exams, a random sample of student exam scripts could be second-marked internally and then by the external examiner to help ensure (a) that learning is taking place and (b) that grades are fair, consistent, and not overinflated. Such a system relies on tenured faculty members taking the lead in ensuring teaching, assessment, and learning standards based on a system they are well used to, namely, blind peer-review. In conjunction with a national center for the evaluation of teaching and learning, this also has the advantage of removing the gaming that currently goes on in the system through administrative reliance and insistence on SET as a means of naming teaching and learning excellence.

In addition to a pre-blind and post-blind review of student assessment/exams, department faculty members could consider exam boards where all the faculty would review student exam results. Individual student grades across all classes could be discussed as could grades for each class and any apparent aberrations explained. If the faculty saw, for example, all students were getting As across a class then something is likely to be amiss. Each class should show something like a normal distribution curve. Each student should show a reasonable degree of consistency across subjects. Any inconsistencies could be explained. All this could happen before students get to see their final grade.

An independent blind review of teaching and learning by a national center and blind review of student assignments/exams may be healthier and provide a more honest option given the current state of teaching and learning in the USA as is set out in the review of the literature: Ambady, and Rosenthal (1993) on 'predicting teacher evaluations from thin slices of nonverbal behavior and physical attractiveness'; Anderson and Miller (1997) on 'gender and student evaluations of teaching'; Arum and Roksa (2011 and 2014) on the poor quality of learning with the implication of poor teaching; Braga et al. (2011) whose evaluation of students' evaluations of professors shows SET not to be indicative of good teaching; Carrell, and West (2010) who again show that good teaching is not captured by student evaluations of teaching; Marsh, and Cooper (1980) that prior subject interest matters in how student evaluate teaching; Stark, and Freishtat (2014) on evaluating course evaluations; and Worthington (2002) on the impact of student perceptions and characteristics on teaching evaluations. An independent audit of teaching and learning as set out above in the section on blind peer-review of teaching along with a blind peer-review of student assessment/exams in conjunction with an appointed external examiner and exam boards would stop the gaming behind SET, stop grade inflation and restore confidence in college education. Such a system would be an ally to academically qualified faculty members who are rigorous teachers impeded by the false and invalid claims of SET which names those faculty quite differently.

Current internal institutional funding for SET should be redirected to a national center for college and university teaching and learning and independent audits, the state and federal government should also fund this. Funding for regional accreditation agencies could also be redirected to a national center. Faculty members should work with such a center to help develop the audits, perhaps through organizations like the AAUP. Although in the initial stage these audits should cover all colleges; as improvement in learning outcomes are demonstrated the audits would become much less frequent but randomized and thereby maintain teaching and learning standards. Such a move would empower faculty members and remove the gaming that favors administrators who desire to name excellence in teaching and learning differently for the purposes of (a) marketing without having to substantiate their claims and (b) disempowering rigorously minded faculty and their role in joint governance. What ought to be the denominating name factor, learning outcomes, is being replaced by the name learning income in many liberal arts institutions. Above the denominator line of teaching and learning are numerator signifiers such as student centered (dependent), SET, and student satisfaction rather than student need, and so rigorous teaching practice is eroded by a process of renaming. Teaching and learning are becoming vague and ambiguous, governed by the epithets of excellence and SET signaling the epitaph of not only rigorous learning but the communitarian values between students and their professors.

A Radical Alternative

There is a radical alternative to examination and assessment. With a national center for the evaluation of teaching and learning, the whole exam and assessment of students could be scrapped. If we as a community (faculty members, parents, employers, students, administrators) are assured that learning is taking place, there would be no need to examine students. After all, what is the point of exams and grading if not to test for learning taking place? If there was a guarantee that learning is taking place then the scrapping of exams/grading would free up more time for teaching and learning. It may even prove to be more conducive to developing cognitive skills and improve rigorous learning, which is the desired outcome for all. Or are deeper desires lurking in the dark backward of our unconscious minds?

If we as a community (students, professors, parents, administrators and employers) wanted reassurance or further assurance that learning was taking place and cognitive development was occurring then a national test could be devised that tested for pre-college and post-college cognitive ability administered by the independent national center for college teaching and learning. This test would not name and brand the student with any level of cognitive ability. The test would show, however, which institutions of higher education were performing better while taking into account the level of student college-readiness. The focus of interest would be on intellectual/cognitive development for the benefit of the community not on grading the individual student.

Notes

1. Those interested in who gets paid what and how much can Google 990 (i.e., the IRS tax form) to find the financial details of charities including not-for-profit colleges and universities. There are organizations providing free information on the filings of charities.

2. Moody's credit rating ranges from triple A (Aaa), that is, the best rating to C where an obligor has failed to pay. Baa means that adverse economic conditions or changing circumstances are more likely to lead to a weakened capacity of the obligor to meet its financial commitments.

3. Paraphrase of Robert Lowe's (1st Viscount Sherbrooke) comment in the British Parliament after the passing of the Reform Act of 1867 that extended the franchise to some urban working-class males.

BIBLIOGRAPHY

AAC&U. (2017). *On Solid Ground: Value Report*. Retrieved from http://www. aacu.org/sites/default/files/files/VALUE/CriticalThinking.pdf. Accessed 10 June 2017.

Adorno, T. W. (2000). *The Essential Frankfurt School Reader* (A. Arato & E. Gebhardt, Eds.). New York: Continuum.

Ambady, N., & Rosenthal, R. (1993). Half a Minute: Predicting Teacher Evaluations from Thin Slices of Nonverbal Behavior and Physical Attractiveness. *Journal of Personality and Social Psychology, 64*(3), 431.

Anderson, K., & Miller, E. D. (1997). Gender and Student Evaluations of Teaching. *PS: Political Science and Politics, 30*(2), 216–219.

Arum, R., & Roksa, J. (2011). *Academically Adrift: Limited Learning on College Campuses*. Chicago: The University of Chicago Press.

Arum, R., & Roksa, J. (2014). *Aspiring Adults Adrift: Tentative Transitions of College Graduates*. Chicago: The University of Chicago Press.

Austin, P. C., & Steyerberg, E. W. (2015). The Number of Subjects Per Variable Required in Linear Regression Analyses. *Journal of Clinical Epidemiology, 68*, 627–636.

Benjamin, R. (2012). *The Seven Red Herrings About Standardized Assessments in Higher Education* (Occasional Paper 15). Champaign: National Institute for Learning Outcomes Assessment.

Boswell, J. (1901). (ed.) Arnold Glover. *The Life of Samuel Johnson*. (Vol. 2). London: J.M. Dent.

Braga, M., Paccagnella, M., & Pellizzari, M. (2011). *Evaluating Students' Evaluations of Professors*. www.econstor.eu

Carrell, S. E., & West, J. E. (2010). Does Professor Quality Matter? Evidence from Random Assignment of Students to Professors. *Journal of Political Economy, 118*(3), 409–432.

Cohen, J. W. (1988). *Statistical Power Analysis for the Behavioral Sciences* (2nd ed.). Hillsdale: Lawrence Erlbaum Associates.

DeNavas-Walt, C., & Proctor, B. D. (2015). *Current Population Reports*. Income and Poverty in the United States: 2014. Retrieved from https://www.census. gov/content/dam/Census/library/publications/2015/demo/p60-252.pdf. Accessed 20 May 2017.

Diamond, D. M., Campbell, A. M., Park, C. R., Halonen, J., & Zoladz, P. R. (2007). The Temporal Dynamics Model of Emotional Memory Processing: A Synthesis on the Neurobiological Basis of Stress-Induced Amnesia, Flashbulb and Traumatic Memories, and the Yerkes-Dodson Law. *Neural Plasticity*, 1–33. Retrieved from http://dx.doi.org/10.1155/2007/60803. Accessed 30 September 2017.

Foucault, M. (1989a). *The Archaeology of Knowledge*. London: Routledge.

Foucault, M. (1989b). *The Order of Things*. London: Routledge.

Habermas, J. (1987). *Knowledge and Human Interests*. Cambridge: Polity Press.

Hackley, C. (2016). Autoethnography in Consumer Research. In P. Hackett (Ed.), *Qualitative Research Methods in Consumer Psychology: Ethnography and Culture*. London: Routledge.

Jensen, E. (2009). *Teaching with Poverty in Mind*. Alexandria: ASCD.

Jensen, E. (2013). *Engaging Students with Poverty in Mind*. Alexandria: ASCD.

Lowrie, A. (2016). Ethnography: Textual Methodology. In P. Hacket (Ed.), *Consumer Ethnography: Qualitative and Cultural Approaches to Consumer Research (Chap. 17)*. New York: Routledge.

Marsh, H. W., & Cooper, T. (1980). *Prior Subject Interest, Students Evaluations, and Instructional Effectiveness*. Paper presented at the Annual Meeting of the American Educational Research Association.

Medina, J. (2014). *Brain Rules*. Seattle: Pear Press.

OECD. (2012). *United States Country Note, Education at a Glance 2012*. Retrieved from https://www.oecd.org/unitedstates/CN%20-%20United%20States.pdf. Accessed 10 June 2017.

Pinker, S. (2010). The Cognitive Niche: Coevolution of Intelligence, Sociality, and Language. *PNAS, 107*(Supp. 2), 8993–8999.

Rock, D. (2009). *Your Brain at Work*. New York: HarperCollins.

Schutz, A. (1970). *Reflections on the Problem of Relevance*. New Haven: Yale University Press.

Selingo, J. J. (2016). *2026 The Decade Ahead: The Seismic Shifts Transforming the Future of Higher Education*. Washington, DC: *The Chronicle of Higher Education*.

Stark, R., & Freishtat, P. B. (2014). An Evaluation of Course Evaluations. *ScienceOpen Research*. https://www.scienceopen.com/document/id/ad8a9ac9-8c60-432a-ba20-4402a2a38df4?3

Tooby, J., & DeVore, I. (1987). The Reconstruction of Hominid Evolution Through Strategic Modeling. In W. G. Kinzey (Ed.), *The Evolution of Human Behavior: Primate Models*. Albany: SUNY Press.

Worthington, A. C. (2002). The Impact of Student Perceptions and Characteristics on Teaching Evaluations: A Case Study in Finance Education. *Assessment and Evaluation in Higher Education, 27*(1), 49–64.

Yerkes, R. M., & Dodson, J. D. (1908). The Relation of Strength of Stimulus to Rapidity of Habit-Formation. *Journal of Comparative, Neurology and Psychology, 18*(5), 459–482.

CHAPTER 8

Concluding Remarks

Faculty members tend to learn for the first time about a branding project in their college when it is announced that a discussion or consultation will take place about how we see or would like to see ourselves as an institution. While it is rare for a college or university to replace one name with another, this does occasionally happen. Regardless of the form the name change takes, the meaning of the name will always change, which is rather the point of the exercise. Someone, somewhere, is unhappy with the current situation and wants to change it. Thus, before consultation takes place, the decision has been made to change. Indeed, the consultation process signifies that the decision has been made. If you are having the conversation or required to have the conversation, the process of naming is in progress, which sets the remit for any and all conversations. Someone, somewhere, has already named the terms and remit of the conversation. In this sense, branding is a unilateral determination to (re)name. While the signifying word may remain, the same x college, the rationale is to change what is meant by that signifier. The case has been previously made for words and the meaning of words to be quite different entities and units of analyses with meaning and not the word being the priority in this book. As language is public and not private, there is more than a small degree of arrogance in making the claim that x means what I want it to mean. That someone initiated, usually a college president, the (re)branding process, there is clearly intention (conscious desire), albeit that the intention may

© The Author(s) 2018
A. Lowrie, *Understanding Branding in Higher Education*,
Marketing and Communication in Higher Education,
DOI 10.1057/978-1-137-56071-1_8

be unclear to others, and an unconscious desire to name in the image of the initiator what is or ought to be.

Given my argument in this book, the attempt to control the meaning of a name is futility to the power of absurdity. This is not to say that you cannot change people, processes, and outputs, for example, all of which will give meaning, but it is to say that you cannot control the meaning of those people, processes, and outputs. It is not within the remit of a single person or even group to change brand names and control their meaning. It would be better to control what it is that you are supposed to do, that is, develop the cognitive ability of students to the highest possible level and be transparent about how you go about doing that and what it is you have achieved regarding that purpose. The meaning of your institution will follow from those achievements as people are allowed transparent access to your achievements. People will retroactively invest meaning into your institutional name as they read and judge your achievements in a comparative process in a way that suits their own desires (unconscious and conscious). False and unsubstantiated claims will be revealed for what they are in a transparent and independent system of assessment along the lines set out in Chaps. 6 and 7. If colleges and universities refuse to be transparent then it is reasonable to assume they have something to hide and as such should not make the short list for a student's choice of college.

In defense of the (re)branding president, it is difficulty not to engage in marketing. Of course, because it is difficult does not make the case for it being ethically the right thing to do. In the current competitive system, bums on seats are required if you are to keep the lights on. This is especially true in the student-centered college where the name student-centered equates to dependent on student fees. From this premise stems a lot of bad practice, often named as best practice, for the recruitment and retention of (student) income. Presidents and their management teams are locked into a continuous and rather vicious circle of competing for students, which often translates to fees and tax dollars spent on marketing. It is hardly visionary and innovative to stay locked in this circle. Far-fetched as it may sound, consider funding arrangements based on cognitive development and transformational gains in students. Of importance is not the bums on the seats but the minds that walk out of the college door at the end of a given period. Indeed, why bother measuring that period of years or credit hours, as neither are reliable proxies for cognitive development. Once students reach a level of cognitive development in their chosen subject or subjects they should be allowed to graduate. This would motivate students to focus on studying and graduating with time and money saved. This would not only save money for students and their families but save on *per capita* spending in higher education, which would facilitate throughput rates and so allow more students to go to college. To be clear, increasing the number of people who attend higher education is important, but it is pointless if the quality of that higher education is dubious.

The downside of a graduating system based on cognitive development would be that the college administrators, especially at the private not-for-profit colleges, would get even more selective and so increase their throughput at the expense of other institutions. Essentially, we would have a more virulent form of the current selectivity. The way to end selection would be to have students go through a national clearing house that would allocate students randomly to colleges that teach the subjects of interest to the student. I can imagine that many readers would see this as an outrageous infringement of the right to choose. But consider further how much more outrageous and undemocratic it is to deny the majority of potential first-time students the right to be educated to their full potential. Is it not more egregious to deny a higher education as good as the best that can be had on the basis of affordability (price) and an ability (merit/selection) that has been consistently and systematically denied because of your economic and social status. This is rather like Plato saying to women that they can be leaders if they are like men. You can't get access to an 'excellent' higher education unless you are exceptional, and you are not afforded the opportunity to be exceptional. Those with economic and cultural capital do not have to be exceptional, they just have to have the ability to pay and fall within the fairly ordinary distribution of human ability. The game is rigged. In effect, we have justifiable discrimination based on the *exceptionals*, a derivation of named excellence conjured by higher education administrators to try and substantiate claims for being diverse without having to accept too many undesirables. The greater utilitarian value and social good lies with an equal higher education for all. All communities will benefit. We need a form of busing for higher education.

If we are to have an equal higher education for all then more stringent reviews of colleges would make sense. Self-completed assessment reports are not reliable vehicles for evaluating quality. Colleges that fail to develop and transform students should face formal investigation which sets an action plan detailing how they will reform and improve student cognitive development. Colleges and universities and those who teach in them should be required to hold a license that allows them to practice similar to the way doctors and lawyers are required to be licensed. If colleges continually fail to improve the cognitive ability of their students their license to practice as an institution of education should be withdrawn. You would not hire a lawyer or consult a doctor who was not professionally qualified and licensed by the state so why would you want to be taught by someone who was not academically and professionally qualified. Is not your well-being as intrinsically linked to your education as it is to your physical health?

Despite the importance of higher education to community and individual well-being, students are willing to sit in a classroom and accept what instructors say as gospel without a shred of evidence that the instructor is academically qualified through professional examination and blind peer-review of their work. This may not be surprising; why would students have any reason to doubt the professional capabilities of any professor put in front of them. Like many services it can be difficulty for consumers to evaluate the quality of the service. As set out in Chap. 7, students use other criteria to evaluate the quality of teaching and this is encouraged by administrators who gain the advantage from the system they promote. In the absence of an easy mechanism to evaluate the service, the brand name becomes more important as a means to make judgments about quality and hence the importance of branding. The name is the thing. In most commercial enterprises, this is a reasonable position to take but in higher education it ought to be the cognitive development of the student that is important.

IN THE NAME, WE TRUST

We give names to important things, and we trust the names we give them. The object is elevated to the dignity of the thing and the thing is nothing other than the retrospective naming. While our desires, Lacan's *objet peti a*, are without object and cannot be satisfied, we mis-recognize our desires by making an investment in objects, Freud's *form* attached to the desire, and that investment drives us toward them. Some things are more important to us than other things, such as our higher education which I have explored in the previous chapters, based on the investment in the name. The investment is the meaning, the meaning is the name and some names are so important that they become nodes of organization, Lacan's *point de capiton*, such as diversity and excellence in higher education discourse. These names *form* the frontiers and battle lines that give identity to the particular forces invested in those names. In these names we trust, and in these names parents fight for the education that suits their interests. Those with economic and cultural capital are unlikely to give up these privileged positions without a fight. Few politicians will take on the fight for equality of higher education. Some politicians even proclaim their love of the uneducated.

Unit of Analyses

The unit of analyses is meaning that carries the desire which goes unrecognized except in its named *form*, that is our conscious desire or self-interest which we demand. The desire can never be satisfied but its named demand can on a temporary basis, for once we have what we demand we can no longer want or desire the named *form*, which ultimately leads to unsatisfied desires, and so desire seeks new forms for the *objet peti a*. More often than not our demands are not met and a unity between our demands and the community is formed in the articulation and pursuit of that demand, such as in the case for the pursuit of diversity and excellence in higher education. The adult cries of demand can be heard by others with similar named demands and so others will join in and form multiple calls of demand across a unifying denominating name (empty signifier) such as diversity.

Often the quickest way to kill a demand is to give, meet, or appear to meet that demand. The art of diplomacy for the would-be college president becomes very important. The dodge-duck-dive and dodge of rhetorical management becomes paramount in managing distributed organizations such as colleges and universities. Perhaps a more important presidential skill is the capacity to shut down or limit the unification of demands across multiple numerators that connect to *point de capiton* that organize the discourse of numerating names. The job of those who want to resist presidential initiatives is to reach out and connect those numerating names (floating signifiers) across the unifying node or denominator (empty signifier) of discourse which Lacan and Laclau refer to as the *point de capiton*. Innovators of resistance do not have to wait on the emergence of numerators. They can start to develop these and stitch them together to form a unity of resistance to divisive policies such as the continual enlargement of unqualified academic faculty and the abuse of diversity, that is, using diversity for the furtherance of partisan objectives such as control over faculty, the dismantling of shared governance, the use of diversity as an internal and external marketing tool, and the placing of limits on diversity by requirements governed by named investments such as *exceptionals.*

Counter intuitive as it may seem, qualified academic faculty members should embrace their non-academically qualified faculty colleagues and ensure they have the same benefits and rights as those instructors who are academically qualified. There is only one good reason for non-academically qualified faculty members to be employed in universities and colleges and it is not because they are cheaper to employ. The only reason for non-academically qualified faculty members to be employed as an instructor is because they deliver important aspects of cognitive development for the student. Qualified and non-qualified faculty members should stitch together their interests across a range of named numerators that includes students and their learning and cognitive development. In this way, the faculty will resist mere cost cutting exercises that impairs student learning dressed as practitioner experience. While practitioners can add to the cognitive development of students, determination of the proportion and contribution to learning is important. For example, the Association to Advance Collegiate Schools of Business (AACSB) puts limits on the number of practitioners/non-academically qualified faculty members and insist on academic qualified faculty members publishing in order to maintain their academically qualified status. Non-academically qualified faculty members are required to show continuous development and/or contributions to their profession. Many business schools maintain levels of academically qualified faculty members in the 90-percentile range. For those college administrators who hold practitioners in high esteem, it would be interesting to see what proportions of non-academically qualified faculty instructors they maintained if these instructors were paid the same level of salaries as academically qualified instructors. The same logic applies to the employment of adjuncts. What is named as practical experience is cost reduction and this cannot easily square with the name of excellence. Students can learn to ask who benefits from such administrative practices.

Traction

The notion of satisfaction of need has gained much traction over many decades. Much of the literature, especially by those interested in consumer culture theory, has been generated in and around the themes of the tyranny of the object and the irrational exuberance of consumers in the pursuit of their desires. There is no tyranny of objects or folly of our desires for most ordinary people. Nor is there a digging down into the psyche to find a universal need that someone can innovate into a miraculous product that will provide a solution to that universal need. There is a normal switching from one object of desire to another in the search for the satisfaction of the desire that can never be met. In the process, particular needs and wants are satisfied. More often than not, needs and wants are co-terminus and aligned such as in the satisfaction of hunger by eating beans, if that happens to be your taste preference. But some needs and wants are not aligned, such as in the case of higher education. Satisfying the wants of students may be harmful to their needs and the needs of communities.

NOT ALL DESIRES ARE EQUAL

While there is only one object of desire, *objet peti a*, our desires take many forms in the pursuit of satisfaction. Desires do not have moral standing; they are neither good, nor bad, nor indifferent. Desires connect with what is important to us, and whatever is important to us connects with biology in the *form*ation of satisfying survival needs which are locked into communitarian necessities that are never contingent but the temporary satisfaction of which is always contingent. It is at the edge of where unconscious desire connects with conscious desires (self-interests) that ethical judgment takes place. We must consume or die, but what we consume is environmental and communitarian dependent. The latter becomes more of a contributory factor the more control we need over the former. Control of the environment requires greater cooperation and community involvement. As the meaning of control over the environment is communitarian, communitarian values are of the utmost importance and probably why we obsess about them. This is the case over the education of our children, which is community based regardless of how much we try and buy individual control over it. Self-serving interests can extend to buying so much individual control over higher education that we do harm to others. We obsess about the balance between communitarian values and personal control not because our communitarian values are diminishing, rather on the contrary; communitarian values are so strong and interwoven that they do not take up much of our mental time in worrying about their demise. We do not think about the harm we do to the community when we pursue our own conscious interest. There is a presumption of the importance of community and its continued existence. In the final analysis, we not only depend upon our community but we know we can depend upon it because without it no one survives. The basis of our health, the basis of our well-being and the basis of our education is communitarian, and in the end all are political as we negotiate the levels of differences between how we make demands for these and want them delivered to satisfy our desire. One thing is for sure, we can have none of these demands without a community. There is always a split between (a) an egalitarian commitment to community, the ontology of how we can be, and (b) individual cries for more cake because the epistemology of cake is always contingent (whether the environmental mOther will turn up to meet your cries) within the parallax of reflective comparators, that is, others. Our higher education system is split between (a) and (b). Our survival depends upon our learning, our learning depends upon others and whether we get it or not, to what degree and the quality of that learning is contingent on the organization of that learning. In all of this the need for communitarian values and our desire for survival ensure the pre-eminence of community.

ONTOLOGICAL INVESTMENT

Expansion across the numerator (more named floating signifiers) driven by a named denominator (empty signifier) such as diversity does not conceal the partisanship of the naming and the capacity of those doing the naming to exclude those they unconsciously and consciously desire to exclude. Diversity by necessity must be exclusionary. The enemy is named. As emancipation cannot exist in any form without something that represses it and so gives birth to the identity of emancipation and the identity of that which opposes it, so too it is with diversity. The promotion of diversity in higher education identifies and brands that which is selective and exclusionary. Diversity is always someone's *form* of diversity.

To claim excellence and diversity simultaneously is the devil's trick that is unstitched in the detail. The empty signifier excellence is numerated by different floating signifiers such as selectivity that block off diversity and its sequitur non-excellence. Diversity cannot act as a denominator for excellence because diversity acts for numerators such as open and non-selective, and to be open to everyone regardless of cultural and economic capital negates excellence because everyone cannot be excellent. Both diversity and excellence are empty signifiers that form part of the brand architecture of most if not all liberal arts institutions. But these empty signifiers or brand nodes are mutually exclusive with named investments from different rhetorical poles: one communitarian the other individual.

Malleability of (Self) Identity

The idea of a college identity and belonging to it is a concept that shifts constantly and indefinitely. Pluses and minuses of invoking particular identities such as excellence can be substituted by other empty signifiers or brand nodes such as heritage, privilege, or elitism, and the meaning of these brand nodes will vary depending on the chain of equivalence articulated with the empty signifier (brand node). The multiplicity of social demands for higher education, the heterogeneity of which can be brought into unity through equivalential naming, are curtailed and articulated by unimaginative forms of desires and demands of administrators who are often pleased just to be able to keep the place running and to collect their self-determined and generous salaries justified by named excellence that suits their own purpose rather too well. To stretch the articulated chain of meaning beyond what the name can sustain, such as the oxymoron Trump University, will only induce incredulity if not farce. The brand node cracks and allows insight into the discourse of the self-interest of (un)affordability (price) and the merit (selection) of exclusion. The social demand for diversity cannot be met with excellence. You cannot be diverse if *exceptionals* are your only basis for the claim. You may as well hang a big sign on your college door saying, 'ordinary people not welcome'. The question remains, how do we want to name our higher education? From that name, from the retroactivity of affective investment in the name, all else follows. If there is a refusal to name higher education as 'open to all', to be diverse without exception, then we have no claim to democratic society, and that is the stuff of revolutions. It is time to brand higher education 'as open to all' by the actions of equality.

A Note on Costs and Transparency

The more conservative will still cut back to costs (the affordability argument) as a *form* of realism named in the case against an egalitarian higher education. The argument is often accompanied by the claim of the innate unfairness of having people pay taxes to cover the cost of higher education when they will not financially benefit from attending college. 'Those who benefit' should pay is the argument. The question is who benefits? The answer is that we all benefit. Society is improved for us all when more people are educated to a higher level. Nevertheless, the case for extending higher education does not end with social benefits. All should benefit from an extended higher education by attending higher education. Every ordinary person can benefit by studying for and attaining a college degree. While there will be a current residual of people who did not have the opportunity to go to college, their sons and daughters or family members will, and over time this residual will reduce. Eventually, it will be the norm for everyone to have a degree. If everyone in the population is educated K through 16 then the most efficient way to pay for it is through the tax system. And the most effective way of running the system is to ensure that it is entirely transparent and accountable to the public through our democratically elected bodies at the state and federal level. This includes all information for all institutions of higher education being made public and easily accessible through platforms such as the Integrated Postsecondary Education Data System (IPEDS) and the College Scorecard. There should be no place to hide for colleges and those who work in them and that includes salaries and the professional standing of instructors and researchers.

In Chap. 7, I said three things were important to academics. The first was publication, the second was publication and the third was publication. We 'live and die' by them and the blind peer-review that adjudicates the process. I stand by that claim. In the course of normal academic events, this claim usually refers to research publications only. In Chap. 7 I suggested that this should be extended to teaching outputs, and I have published in this book my own teaching outputs in the form of student evaluations of teaching (SET), which I have argued are biased forms of teaching evaluation and that these should be replaced by a national and independent audit of teaching. I believe in academic freedom and this extends to the public having the opportunity to see and question what academics do. This is especially true, I think, if we are to be fully funded by the public. What we do in our professional lives should be entirely transparent and this transparency should be extended to all aspects of inputs and outputs of administration. Not to be entirely transparent gives the right to the public to ask why are you not transparent and what do you have to hide? A demand for transparency seems a reasonable public demand of our colleges and universities on which our higher education, our democracy, our communities and our very desires to survive and live well depend. Education stitches together the very fabric of our society and higher education's role makes those stitches critical by providing the cognitive ability to question, challenge, and educate our masters, whoever they think they may be.

BIBLIOGRAPHY

AAC&U. (2017). *On Solid Ground: Value Report*. Retrieved from http://www.aacu.org/sites/default/files/files/VALUE/CriticalThinking.pdf. Accessed 10 June 2017.

AAC&U Website. Retrieved from http://www.aacu.org/about. Accessed 10 June 2017.

Aaker, D. A. (1996). *Building Strong Brands*. New York: The Free Press.

Adorno, T. W. (2000). *The Essential Frankfurt School Reader* (A. Arato & E. Gebhardt, Eds.). New York: Continuum.

Althusser, L. (2005). *For Marx*. London: Verso.

Ambady, N., & Rosenthal, R. (1993). Half a Minute: Predicting Teacher Evaluations from Thin Slices of Nonverbal Behavior and Physical Attractiveness. *Journal of Personality and Social Psychology, 64*(3), 431.

Anderson, K., & Miller, E. D. (1997). Gender and Student Evaluations of Teaching. *PS: Political Science and Politics, 30*(2), 216–219.

Arnould, E. J., & Price, L. L. (2006). Market-Oriented Ethnography Revisited. *Journal of Advertising Research, 46*(3), 251–262.

Arum, R., & Roksa, J. (2011). *Academically Adrift: Limited Learning on College Campuses*. Chicago: The University of Chicago Press.

Arum, R., & Roksa, J. (2014). *Aspiring Adults Adrift: Tentative Transitions of College Graduates*. Chicago: The University of Chicago Press.

Arum, R., Roksa, J., & Cook, A. (Eds.). (2016). *Improving Quality in American Higher Education: Learning Outcomes and Assessments for the 21st Century*. San Francisco: Jossey-Bass.

© The Author(s) 2018

A. Lowrie, *Understanding Branding in Higher Education*,
Marketing and Communication in Higher Education,
DOI 10.1057/978-1-137-56071-1

Austin, P. C., & Steyerberg, E. W. (2015). The Number of Subjects Per Variable Required in Linear Regression Analyses. *Journal of Clinical Epidemiology, 68,* 627–636.

Barnett, R. (2000). *Realizing the University in an Age of Supercomplexity.* Buckingham: The Society for Research into Higher Education.

Bauman, D. (2016a). Bonuses Push More Public-Colleges Leaders Past $1 Million. *The Chronicle of Higher Education.* Retrieved from http://www.chronicle.com/article/Bonuses-Push-More/237152. Accessed 7 Mar 2017.

Bauman, D. (2016b). 39 Private-College Leaders Earn More Than $1 Million. *The Chronicle of Higher Education.* Retrieved from http://www.chronicle.com/article/39-Private-College-Leaders/238561. Accessed 7 Mar 2017.

Belk, R. W., & Xin, Z. (2007). Live from Shopping Malls: Blogs and Chinese Consumer Desire. *Advances in Consumer Research, 34,* 131–137.

Belk, R. W., Ger, G., & Lascu, D.-N. (1993). The Development of Consumer Desire in Marketizing and Developing Economies. *Advances in Consumer Research, 20,* 102–107.

Belk, R. W., Ger, G., & Askegaard, S. (1996). Metaphors of Consumer Desire. *Advances in Consumer Research, 23,* 368–373.

Belk, R. W., Ger, G., & Askegaard, S. (2000). The Missing Streetcar Named Desire. In S. Ratneshwar, D. G. Mick, & C. Huffman (Eds.), *The Why of Consumption: Contemporary Perspectives on Consumer Motives, Goals, and Desires* (pp. 98–119). New York: Routledge.

Belk, R. W., Ger, G., & Askegaard, S. (2003). The Fire of Desire: A Multisited Inquiry into Consumer Passion. *Journal of Consumer Research, 45*(December), 326–351.

Benjamin, R. (2012). *The Seven Red Herrings About Standardized Assessments in Higher Education* (Occasional Paper 15). Champaign: National Institute for Learning Outcomes Assessment.

Bernstein, L., Hull, A., & Kindy, K. (2016, April 10). A New Divide in American death. *The Washington Post.* Retrieved from http://www.washingtonpost.com/sf/national/2016/04/10/a-new-divide-in-american-death/

Best, B. (2000). Necessarily Contingent, Equally Different and Relatively Universal: The Antinomies of Ernesto Laclau's Social Logic of Hegemony. *Rethinking Marxism, 12*(3), 38–57.

Bok, D. (2015). *Higher Education in America.* Princeton: Princeton University Press.

Bonvillian, G., & Murphy, R. (2013). *The Liberal Arts College Adapting to Change: The Survival of Small Schools.* New York: Routledge.

Boswell, J. (1901). (ed.) Arnold Glover. *The Life of Samuel Johnson.* (Vol. 2). London: J.M. Dent.

Bourdieu, P., & Wacquant, L. (2001). NewLiberalSpeak: Notes on the New Planetary Vulgate. *Radical Philosophy, 105,* 2–5.

Braga, M., Paccagnella, M., & Pellizzari, M. (2011). *Evaluating Students' Evaluations of Professors.* www.econstor.eu

Campbell, C., & Rozsnyai, C. (2002). *Quality Assurance and the Development of Course Programmes.* Papers on Higher Education Regional University Network on Governance and Management of Higher Education in South East Europe Bucharest, UNESCO, Bucharest.

Carey, K. (2015). *The End of College: Creating the Future of Learning and the University of Everywhere.* New York: Riverhead Books.

Carlson, S., & Supiano, B. (2016, July 27). How Clinton's Free College Could Cause a Cascade of Problems. *The Chronicle of Higher Education.* Retrieved from http://chronicle.com/article/how-clintons-free-college/237266. Accessed 3 Aug 2016.

Carrell, S. E., & West, J. E. (2010). Does Professor Quality Matter? Evidence from Random Assignment of Students to Professors. *Journal of Political Economy, 118*(3), 409–432.

Carson, E. A. (2014). *Prisoners in 2013.* Washington, DC: The U.S. Department of Justice, Office of Justice Programs, Bureau of Justice Statistics.

Case, A., & Deaton, A. (2015). Rising Morbidity and Mortality in Midlife Among White Non-Hispanic Americans in the 21st Century. *PNAS, 12*(49), 15078–15083.

Chapleo, C. (2015). Brands in Higher Education. *International Studies of Management & Organization, 45*(2), 150–163.

Cohen, J. W. (1988). *Statistical Power Analysis for the Behavioral Sciences* (2nd ed.). Hillsdale: Lawrence Erlbaum Associates.

College Board. (2016). *Trends in Student Aid 2016.* Retrieved from https://trends.collegeboard.org/sites/default/files/2016-trends-student-aid.pdf. Accessed 5 June 2017.

College Board. (2017). *Trends in Higher Education. Tuition and Fees and Room and Board Over Time.* Retrieved from https://trends.collegeboard.org/college-pricing/figures-tables/tuition-fees-room-and-board-over-time. Accessed 8 June 2017.

Cooley, C. H. (1922). *Human Nature and the Social Order.* New York: Charles Scribner's Sons.

Coulter, R. H., & Zaltman, G. (2000). The Power of Metaphor. In S. Ratneshwar, D. G. Mick, & C. Huffman (Eds.), *The Why of Consumption: Contemporary Perspectives on Consumer Motives, Goals, and Desires* (pp. 259–281). New York: Routledge.

de Saussure, F. (1983). *Course in General Linguistics.* London: Duckworth.

de Weert, E. (2011, December). *Perspectives on Higher Education and the Labour Market: Review of International Policy Developments.* The Netherlands: Center for Higher Education Policy Studies, C11EW153.

Delanty, G. (1998). The Idea of the University in the Global Era: From Knowledge as an End to the End of Knowledge? *Social Epistemology, 12*(1), 3–25.

Delanty, G. (2002). The University and Modernity: A History of the Present. In K. Robins & F. Webster (Eds.), *The Virtual University: Knowledge, Markets and Management.* Oxford: Oxford University Press.

DeNavas-Walt, C., & Proctor, B. D. (2015). *Current Population Reports.* Income and Poverty in the United States: 2014. Retrieved from https://www.census. gov/content/dam/Census/library/publications/2015/demo/p60-252.pdf. Accessed 20 May 2017.

Department for Business Innovation and Skills, UK. (2013). *The Benefits of Higher Education Participation for Individuals and Society.* Retrieved from https:// www.gov.uk/government/uploads/system/uploads/attachment_data/ file/254101/bis-13-1268-benefits-of-higher-education-participation-the-quadrants.pdf. Accessed 10 Jan 2017.

Derrida, J. (1976). *Of Grammatology.* Baltimore: John Hopkins University Press.

Derrida, J. (1978/2001). *Writing and Difference.* London: Routledge.

Dewey, J. (1916/1997). *Democracy and Education: An Introduction to the Philosophy of Education.* New York: The Free Press.

Diamond, D. M., Campbell, A. M., Park, C. R., Halonen, J., & Zoladz, P. R. (2007). The Temporal Dynamics Model of Emotional Memory Processing: A Synthesis on the Neurobiological Basis of Stress-Induced Amnesia, Flashbulb and Traumatic Memories, and the Yerkes-Dodson Law. *Neural Plasticity,* 1–33. Retrieved from https://www.hindawi.com/journals/np/2007/060803/abs/. Accessed 30 September, 2017.

Dichter, E. (1964). *Handbook of Consumer Motivations: They Psychology of the World of Objects.* New York: McGraw-Hill Book Company.

Dichter, E. (2008). *The Strategy of Desire.* New Brunswick: Transaction Publishers.

Digest of Education Statistics. Table 302.60, 1970 to 2014. http://nces.ed.gov/ programs/digest/d15/tables/dt15_302.60.asp?current=yes. Accessed 27 July 2016.

Dufresne, T. (2003). *Killing Freud: Twentieth Century Culture and the Death of Psychoanalysis.* London: Continuum.

Dummett, M. (1973). *Frege: Philosophy of Language.* London: Duckworth.

Eagleton, T. (1983). *Literary Theory: An Introduction.* Oxford: Basil Blackwell.

Eckhardt, G. M., Belk, R. W., & Wilson, J. A. J. (2015). The Rise of Inconspicuous Consumption. *Journal of Marketing Management, 31*(7–8), 807–826.

Elliott, A. (1999). *Social Theory and Psychoanalysis in Transition: Self and Society from Freud to Kristeva.* London: Free Association Books.

Engel, J. F., Kollat, D. T., & Blackwell, R. D. (1968). *Consumer Behavior.* New York: Holt, Rhinehart, and Winston.

Fairclough, N. (2003). *Analysing Discourse: Textual Analysis for Social Research.* London: Routledge.

Fonagy, P., Rost, F., Carlyle, J.-A., McPherson, S., & Thomas, R. (2015). Pragmatic Randomized Controlled Trial of Long-Term Psychoanalytic Psychotherapy for Treatment-Resistant Depression: The Tavistock Adult Depression Study (TADS). *World Psychiatry, 14*(3), 312–321.

Foucault, M. (1989a). *The Archaeology of Knowledge.* London: Routledge.

Foucault, M. (1989b). *The Order of Things.* London: Routledge.

Foucault, M. (1991a). *Discipline and Punish: The Birth of the Prison.* London: Penguin.

Foucault, M. (1991b). What Is Enlightenment. In P. Rabinow (Ed.), *The Foucault Reader: An Introduction to Foucault's Thought* (pp. 3–50). London: Penguin.

Frege, G. (1949). On Sense and Nominatum. Translated by Herbert Feigl in *Readings in Philosophical Analysis*, edited by Herbert Feigl and Wilfrid Sellars. London: Appleton Century Crofts.

Freud, S. (1997). *Dora: An Analysis of a Case of Hysteria.* New York: Touchstone.

Freud, S. (2006). *Interpreting Dreams.* London: Penguin Books.

Gibbons, M., Limoges, C., Nowotny, H., Schwartzman, S., Scott, P., & Trow, M. (1994). *The New Production of Knowledge.* London: Sage.

Girard, R. (1977). *Violence and the Sacred.* Baltimore: Johns Hopkins University Press.

Graham, P. (2002). Predication and Propagation: A Method for Analysing Evaluative Meanings in Technology Policy. *TEXT, 22*(2), 227–268.

Green, K. (2007). *Bertrand Russell, Language and Linguistic Theory.* London: Continuum.

Greenaway, D., & Haynes, M. (2000). *Funding Universities to Meet National and International Challenges.* Nottingham: University of Nottingham.

Grey, C. (2001). Re-imagining Relevance: A Response to Starkey and Madan. *British Journal of Management, 12*(Special Issue), S27–S32.

Gruber, T., Lowrie, A., Brodowsky, G., Reppel, A., & Voss, R. (2012). Investigating the Influence of Professor Characteristics on Learner Satisfaction and Dissatisfaction. *Journal of Marketing Education, 34*(8), 165–178.

Habermas, J. (1970). *Towards a Rational Society.* London: Heinemann.

Habermas, J. (1987). *Knowledge and Human Interests.* Cambridge: Polity Press.

Hackley, C. (2016). Autoethnography in Consumer Research. In P. Hackett (Ed.), *Qualitative Research Methods in Consumer Psychology: Ethnography and Culture.* London: Routledge.

Harriman, P. (1935). Antecedents of the Liberal Arts College. *The Journal of Higher Education, 6*(2), 63–71.

Harvey, L. (undated). *Analytic Quality Glossary.* Quality Research International. Retrieved from http://www.qualityresearchinternational.com/glossary/. Accessed 6 Jan 2017.

Harvey, L., & Green, D. (1993). Defining Quality. *Assessment and Evaluation in Higher Education, 18*(1), 9–34. Retrieved from pre-publication draft available here. Accessed 6 Jan 2017.

Hendrickson, R. M., Lane, J. E., Harris, J. T., & Dorman, R. H. (2013). *Academic Leadership and Governance of Higher Education.* Sterling: Stylus.

Hoover, E. (2017, June 23). Where the Journey to College Is No Fairy Tale. *The Chronicle of Higher Education*, pp. A14–A18.

Howarth, D. (2000). *Discourse.* Buckingham: Open University Press.

Husserl, E. (1964/2010). *The Idea of Phenomenology.* Netherlands: Kluwer Academic Publishers.

Jensen, E. (2009). *Teaching with Poverty in Mind.* Alexandria: ASCD.

Jensen, E. (2013). *Engaging Students with Poverty in Mind.* Alexandria: ASCD.

Kano, N., Seraku, N., Takahashi, F., & Tsuji, S. (1984, April). Attractive Quality and Must-Be Quality. *Journal of the Japanese Society for Quality Control, 14*(2), 39–48 (in Japanese).

Keller, K. L. (2003). *Strategic Brand Management: Building, Measuring and Managing Brand Equity.* Upper Saddle River: Prentice Hall.

Keller, K. L., & Lehmann, D. R. (2006). Brands and Branding: Research Findings and Future Priorities. *Marketing Science, 25*(6), 740–759.

Kerr, C. (1963/2001). *The Uses of the University.* Cambridge, MA: Harvard University Press.

Kirpke, S. (1981). *Naming and Necessity.* Oxford: Blackwell Publishing.

Kövecses, Z. (2000). *Metaphor and Emotion: Language, Culture, and Body in Human Feeling.* Cambridge: Cambridge University Press.

Lacan, J. (1998). *The Seminar of Jacques Lacan: Book XI the Four Fundamental Concepts of Psychoanalysis.* New York: W.W. Norton.

Lacan, J. (2006). *Écrits* (B. Fink, Trans.). New York: W.W. Norton.

Laclau, E. (1990). *New Reflections on the Revolution of Our Time.* London: Verso.

Laclau, E. (1996). *Emancipation(s).* London: Verso.

Laclau, E. (2004). Glimpsing the Future. In S. Critchley & O. Marchart (Eds.), *Laclau: A Critical Reader.* London: Routledge.

Laclau, E. (2005). *On Populist Reason.* London: Verso.

Laclau, E., & Mouffe, C. (1985). *Hegemony and Socialist Strategy: Towards a Radical Democratic Politics.* London: Verso.

Lee, G. C. (Ed.). (1961). *Crusade Against Ignorance: Thomas Jefferson on Education.* New York: Teachers College, Columbia University.

Leichsenring, F., & Rabung, S. (2008). Effectiveness of Long-Term Psychodynamic Psychotherapy: A Meta-analysis. *Journal of the American Medical Association, 300*(13), 1551–1565.

Lindblom, C. E. (1959). The Science of "Muddling Through". *Public Administration Review, 19*(2), 79–88.

Lowrie, A. (2007). Branding Higher Education: Equivalence and Difference in Developing University Identity. *Journal of Business Research, 60*(9), 990–999.

Lowrie, A. (2008). The Relevance of Aggression and the Aggression of Relevance: The Rise of the Accreditation Marketing Machine. *International Journal of Educational Management, 22*(4), 352–364.

Lowrie, A. (2016). Ethnography: Textual Methodology. In P. Hacket (Ed.), *Consumer Ethnography: Qualitative and Cultural Approaches to Consumer Research (Chap. 17).* New York: Routledge.

Lowrie, A., & Willmott, H. (2009). Accreditation Sickness in the Consumption of Business School Education: The Vacuum in AACSB Standard Setting. *Management Learning, 40*(4), 411–420.

Lury, C. (1996). *Consumer Culture.* Cambridge: Polity.

Marginson, S. (1997). Competition and Contestability in Australian Higher Education. *Australian Universities Review, 40*(1), 5–14.

Marginson, S. (2012). The Problem of Public Good(s) in Higher Education. In *41st Australian Conference of Economists, Melbourne, 2–12 July.* Retrieved from http://www.ses.unam.mx/curso2014/pdf/Marginson.pdf. Accessed 9 Jan 2017.

Marsh, H. W., & Cooper, T. (1980). *Prior Subject Interest, Students Evaluations, and Instructional Effectiveness.* Paper presented at the Annual Meeting of the American Educational Research Association.

Marx, K. (1990). *Capital I.* London: Penguin Classics.

McCarthy, E. J. (1964). *Basic Marketing: A Managerial Approach.* Homewood: Richard D. Irwin.

McLeod, A. (2009). "Pseudo-Scientific Hokus Pokus": Motivational Research's Australian Application. *Journal of Historical Research in Marketing, 1*(2), 224–245.

Mead, G. H. (1934). *Mind, Self, and Society: From the Standpoint of a Social Behaviorist.* Chicago: University of Chicago Press.

Medina, J. (2014). *Brain Rules.* Seattle: Pear Press.

Mill, J. S. (2012[1843]). *A System of Logic, Ratiocinative and Inductive: Being a Connective View of the Principles of Evidence, and the Methods of Scientific Investigation.* New York: Cambridge University Press.

Milrod, B., Leon, A. C., Busch, F., Rudden, M., Schwalberg, M., Clarkin, J., Aronson, A., Singer, M., Turchin, W., Klass, E. T., Graf, E., Teres, J. J., & Shear, M. K. (2007). A Randomized Controlled Clinical Trial of Psychanalytic Psychotherapy for Panic Disorder. *American Journal of Psychiatry, 164*(2), 265–272.

Mishra, P. (2017). *Age of Anger.* New York: Farrar, Straus and Giroux.

Mitchell, J. (1974). *Psychoanalysis and Feminism.* London: Penguin.

NCES. Table 235.10. Revenues for Public Elementary and Secondary Schools, by Source of Funds: Selected Years, 1919–20 Through 2012–13. Source: https://nces.ed.gov/programs/digest/d15/tables/dt15_235.10.asp. Accessed 5/6/2017.

NCES. re. Chart 3.3. (National Center for Educational Statistics). Earnings. Table 502.20 (2015). Integrated Postsecondary Education Data System (IPEDS), U.S. Department of Education, Institute of Education Sciences.

NCES. re. Chart 4.1. Nation's Report Card, NAEP (National Assessment of Education Progress). Early Educational Disparities in Mathematics. Retrieved from https://www.nationsreportcard.gov/reading_math_2015/#mathematics?grade=4. Accessed 10 Jan 2017.

NCES. re. Chart 3.2. (National Center for Educational Statistics). Four-Year College Costs. Integrated Postsecondary Education Data System (IPEDS), U.S. Department of Education, Institute of Education Sciences.

NCES. re. Chart 6.1. (National Center for Educational Statistics). Levels of Diversity. Integrated Postsecondary Education Data System (IPEDS). The College Navigator. U.S. Department of Education, Institute of Education Sciences.

Newman, J. H. (1905/2012). *The Idea of a University*. New York: Forgotten Books.

O'Leary, B., & Hatch, J. (2015). *Executive Compensation at Private and Public Colleges*. Retrieved from http://chronicle.com/interactives/executive-compensation?cid=FEATUREDNAV#id=table_public_2015. Accessed 9 Jan 2017.

OECD (2012a). *Education at a Glance 2012: OECD Indicators*. OECD Publishing. http://dx.doi.org/10.1787/eag-2012-en. p. 26. Retrieved from https://www.oecd.org/edu/EAG%202012_e-book_EN_200912.pdf. Accessed 10 June 2017.

OECD. (2012b). *United States Country Note, Education at a Glance 2012*. Retrieved from https://www.oecd.org/unitedstates/CN%20-%20United%20States.pdf. Accessed 10 June 2017.

OECD. (2015a). Re. Chart 3.1. Population with Tertiary Education (Indicator). doi: 10.1787/0b8f90e9-en. Retrieved from https://data.oecd.org/eduatt/population-with-tertiary-education.htm. Accessed 06 June 2017.

OECD. (2015b). *Education Indicators in Focus*. Retrieved from https://www.oecd.org/education/EDIF%2031%20(2015)--ENG--Final.pdf. Accessed 10 June 2017.

Olssen, M., Codd, J., & O'Neill, A.-M. (2004). *Education Policy: Globalization, Citizenship and Democracy*. London: Sage.

OU Facts and Figures. (2014/15). Retrieved from http://www.open.ac.uk/about/main/sites/www.open.ac.uk.about.main/files/files/fact_figures_1415_uk.pdf. Accessed 6 Jan 2017.

Park, C. W., Jaworski, B. J., & MacInnis, D. J. (1986). Strategic Brand Concept-Image Management. *Journal of Marketing, 50*, 135–145.

Peters, T., & Waterman, R. H. (1982). *In Search of Excellence: Lessons from American's Best-Run Companies*. New York: Warner Books.

Pinker, S. (2007). *The Stuff of Thought: Language as a Widow into Human Nature*. New York: Viking.

Pinker, S. (2010). The Cognitive Niche: Coevolution of Intelligence, Sociality, and Language. *PNAS, 107*(Supp. 2), 8993–8999.

Plato. (2007). *The Republic*. New York: Penguin Classics.

Prichard, C. (2000). *Making Managers in Universities and Colleges*. Buckingham: SRHE / Open University.

Prichard, C., & Trowler, P. R. (2003). *Realizing Qualitative Research in Higher Education*. Aldershot: Ashgate.

Quality Assurance Agency for Higher Education (QAA). (undated). *Glossary*. Retrieved from http://www.qaa.ac.uk/about-us/glossary?Category=F. Accessed 3 Jan 2017.

Rappert, B. (1999). The Uses of Relevance: Thoughts on a Reflexive Sociology. *Sociology, 33*(4), 705–723.

Redden, E. (2009). A Global Liberal Arts Alliance. *Inside Higher Education*. Retrieved from https://www.insidehighered.com/news/2009/04/06/liberal-arts. Accessed 10 June 2017.

Rock, D. (2009). *Your Brain at Work*. New York: HarperCollins.

Roth, M. S. (2015). *Beyond the University: Why Liberal Education Matters*. New Haven: Yale University Press.

Russell, B. (1992 [1903]). *The Principles of Mathematics*. London: Routledge.

Schutz, A. (1970). *Reflections on the Problem of Relevance*. New Haven: Yale University Press.

Schutz, A. (1973). On Multiple Realities. In M. Natanson (Ed.), *Collected Papers I: The Problem of Social Reality* (pp. 207–259). The Hague: Martinus Nighiff.

Searle, J. (1971). *Philosophy of Language*. Oxford: Oxford University Press.

Selingo, J. J. (2016). *2026 The Decade Ahead: The Seismic Shifts Transforming the Future of Higher Education*. Washington, DC: *The Chronicle of Higher Education*.

Slaughter, S., & Leslie, L. L. (1997). *Academic Capitalism: Politics, Policies and the Entrepreneurial University*. Baltimore: The John Hopkins University Press.

Smith, R. (1996). Addressing the Delusion of Relevance. *Education Action Research, 4*, 73–91.

Sperber, D. (1996). *Explaining Culture: A Naturalistic Approach*. Oxford: Blackwell.

Sperber, D., & Wilson, D. (1986/1995). *Relevance: Communication and Cognition*. Oxford: Blackwell.

Stark, R., & Freishtat, P. B. (2014). An Evaluation of Course Evaluations. *ScienceOpen Research*. https://www.scienceopen.com/document/id/ad8a9ac9-8c60-432a-ba20-4402a2a38df4?3

Starkey, K., & Madan, P. (2001). Bridging the Relevance Gap: Aligning Stakeholders in the Future of Management Research. *British Journal of Management, 12*(Special Issue), S3–S26.

Sternberg, R. J. (2016). *What Universities Can Be: A New Model for Preparing Students for Active Concerned Citizenship and Ethical Leadership*. Ithaca: Cornell University.

Stigler, G. J. (1942). The Extent and Bases of Monopoly. *The American Economic Review, 32*(Supplement), 1–22.

Tadajewski, M. (2013). Promoting the Consumer Society: Ernest Dichter, the Cold War and FBI. *Journal of Historical Research in Marketing, 5*(2), 192–211.

Taleb, N. N. (2007). *Fooled by Randomness: The Hidden Role of Chance in Life and in the Markets*. London: Penguin Books.

The Chronicle Data. (2016). *The Chronicle of Higher Education*. Retrieved from http://data.chronicle.com/?cid=UCHESIDENAV2. Accessed 13 Jan 2017.

Tooby, J., & DeVore, I. (1987). The Reconstruction of Hominid Evolution Through Strategic Modeling. In W. G. Kinzey (Ed.), *The Evolution of Human Behavior: Primate Models*. Albany: SUNY Press.

Torfing, J. (1999). *New Theories of Discourse: Laclau, Mouffe and Žižek*. Oxford: Blackwell.

Trowler, P. R. (1998). *Academics Responding to Change: New Higher Education Frameworks and Academic Cultures*. Buckingham: The Society for Research into Higher Education and Open University.

Trowler, P. R. (Ed.). (2002). *Higher Education Policy and Institutional Change: Intentions and Outcomes in Turbulent Environments*. Buckingham: The Society for Research into Higher Education and Open University.

US Bureau of Labor Statistics re. Chart 4.2. Jobs Created by Establishments Less than One-Year Old, March 1994–March 2015. Retrieved from https://www.bls.gov/bdm/entrepreneurship/entrepreneurship.htm. Accessed 8 June 2017.

US Bureau of Labor Statistics re. Table 4.1. Survival Rates of Establishments, by Year Started and Number of Years Since Starting, 1994–2015, in Percent. Retrieved from https://www.bls.gov/bdm/entrepreneurship/bdm_chart3.htm. Accessed 8 June 2017.

Vargo, S. L., & Lusch, R. F. (2004). Evolving to a New Dominant Logic for Marketing. *Journal of Marketing, 68*(January), 1–17.

Vlăsceanu, L., Grünberg, L., & Pârlea, D. (2007). *Quality Assurance and Accreditation: A Glossary of Basic Terms and Definitions* (Revised and updated edition). ISBN 92-9069-186-7. (Bucharest: UNESCO-CEPES). Retrieved from http://unesdoc.unesco.org/images/0013/001346/134621e.pdf. Accessed 6 Jan 2017.

Wernick, A. (1991). *Promotional Culture: Advertising, Ideology and Symbolic Expression*. London: Sage.

Williams, R., & Maktoba, O. (2014). Applying Brand Management to Higher Education Through the Use of Brand Flux Model – The Case of Arcadia University. *Journal of Marketing for Higher Education, 24*(2), 224–242.

Willmott, H. (1995). Managing the Academics: Commodification and Control in the Development of University Education in the UK. *Human Relations, 48*(9), 993–1027.

Willmott, H. (2003). Commercialising Higher Education in the UK: The State, Industry and Peer Review. *Studies in Higher Education, 28*(2), 129–141.

Wimsatt, W. K., & Beardsley, M. C. (1958). The Intentional Fallacy. In *The Verbal Icon*. New York: Noonday Press.

Wittgenstein, L. (2000[1953]). *Philosophical Investigations* (3rd ed). Oxford: Blackwell.

Wollheim, R. (1973). *Freud*. London: Fontana Press.

Woodhouse, D. (1999). Quality and Quality Assurance. In Organisation for Economic Co-operation and Development (OECD) (Ed.), *Quality and Internationalisation in Higher Education* (pp. 29–44). Paris: OECD: Programme on Institutional Management in Higher Education (IMHE).

Worthington, A. C. (2002). The Impact of Student Perceptions and Characteristics on Teaching Evaluations: A Case Study in Finance Education. *Assessment and Evaluation in Higher Education, 27*(1), 49–64.

Yerkes, R. M., & Dodson, J. D. (1908). The Relation of Strength of Stimulus to Rapidity of Habit-Formation. *Journal of Comparative, Neurology and Psychology, 18*(5), 459–482.

Zaltman, G. (1997). Rethinking Market Research: Putting People Back In. *Journal of Marketing Research, 34*(November), 424–437.

Zaltman, G. (2003). *How Customers Think: Essential Insights into the Mind of the Market.* Boston: Harvard Business School Press.

Zaltman, G., & Coulter, R. H. (1994). Using the Zaltman Metaphor Elicitation Technique to Understand Brand Images. *Advances in Consumer Research, 21*, 501–507.

Zaltman, G., & Coulter, R. H. (1995). Seeing the Voice of the Customer: Metaphor-Based Advertising Research. *Journal of Advertising Research*, (July/August), *35*(4), 35–51.

Zaltman, G., & Zaltman, L. (2008). *Marketing Metaphoria: What Deep Metaphors Reveal About the Minds of Consumers.* Boston: Harvard Business Press.

Žižek, S. (1989). *The Sublime Object of Ideology.* London: Verso.

Žižek, S. (2006). *The Parallax View.* Cambridge, MA: Massachusetts Institute of Technology.

Index[1]

[1] Note: Page numbers followed by "n" refers to notes.

© The Author(s) 2018   185
A. Lowrie, *Understanding Branding in Higher Education*,
Marketing and Communication in Higher Education,
DOI 10.1057/978-1-137-56071-1

Printed by Printforce, the Netherlands